BECOME
ONE

DON & SALLY MEREDITH

CHRISTIAN
FAMILY LIFE
CHARLOTTE, NC

Becoming One
Published by
Christian Family Life, Inc.
9900 Twin Lakes Parkway
Charlotte, NC 28269

Copyright © 1979, revised 1997.
All rights reserved. No part of this book may be reproduced, stored in retrieval system, or transmitted in any form or by any means, except in the case of brief quotation printed in articles or reviews, without prior permission in writing from the publisher.

Unless otherwise indicated, all Scripture quotations are from the *New American Standard Bible* © 1960, 1962, 1963, 1968, 1971, 1972, 1975, 1977, by the Lockman Foundation, LaHabra, CA.

Scripture quotations designated NIV are from the *New International Version* © 1973, 1978, 1984 by the International Bible Society. Published by Zondervan Bible Publishers, Grand Rapids, Michigan.

Cover design by Journey Communications, Charlottesville, VA.
Printed by Colorhouse Graphics, Grand Rapids, MI.
Photo by Marchese Photographers, Charlotte, N.C.

Printed in the United States of America.
ISBN 0-9657965-0-7

(Previously published in Nashville, Tennessee, by Thomas Nelson, Inc.
ISBN 0-8407-5688-7)

Library of Congress Cataloging in Publication Data:
    Meredith, Don.
    Becoming One.
    1.   Marriage-United States. 2. Family-Religious life.
    I. Title.
    HQ734.M473   301.42   79-12691

For more information on the twelve-week marriage course,
Becoming One, write:

Christian Family Life
9900 Twin Lakes Parkway
Charlotte, NC 28269
704-875-3606
fax 704-875-3560
E-mail: Xnfamily@aol.com

---

*Dedicated to our children
who have blessed our lives incredibly
and have now become our best friends.*

*Todd and Sara Meredith
Scott and Carmen Gertz
Kathryn
Tiffany*

*May you continue to experience God's
gracious plan for your lives and
may you also reproduce a godly heritage.*

ACKNOWLEDGMENTS

When the book was first published twenty years ago, there were many who deserved acknowledgment. Dr. Howard Hendricks, of Dallas Theological Seminary, was greatly influential. During my years of study under him, I learned valuable lessons and received great encouragement. I cannot recount the infinite ways he has positively influenced me and this book.

Five other men I owe significant thanks and credit to are my original partners in Christian Family Life: Jody Dillow, Barry Leventhal, Tim Timmons, Waylon Ward, and Bill Wellons. I have a great love for them, and I deeply appreciate their contribution to my life and their direct responsibility for parts of this book.

During the late 1970's, tremendous support and wisdom were provided by several dear friends from Campus Crusade for Christ when we were asked to start the FamilyLife Ministry: Ney Bailey, Dennis Rainey, Dave Sunde, Enoch Williams, and Mick Yoder. A special thanks goes to Bill Bright and Swede Anderson for their commitment to marriages in general, and to me in particular.

My former secretary, Carol Weirman Sarian, has my gratitude for typing and retyping the original manuscript. During the last few months of the preparation of the original manuscript, when things really got tough, some faithful friends provided the impetus to help me finish. Next to my lovely wife, Sally, Steve and Shay Freeman were absolutely indispensable. Others who faithfully typed and edited were Skip and Michelle Coffman, Jo Atkins, Nancy Deas, Jim and Micky Grigsby, Gordon and Linda Beth MeNulty, Joanne Pryor, John and Merre Putnam, Shelby and Kay Woodall, Sam and Betty Primm.

I want to thank Peter Gillquist, of Thomas Nelson Publishers, whose patience, wise guidance, and literary ability helped bring about this book in the first place.

Current edition:
We've had fun updating the book after twenty years. When I first wrote it, our children's ages ranged from four to eight. Now they are all in their late twenties. In addition, Sally and I have had opportunity to apply these faith marriage principles through many more trials and phases of life. After many blessings, as well as bumps and bruises, we can joyfully thank God that His Word has exceeded our greatest expectations.

There are several people who have been indispensable to this current edition. Fifteen years ago God orchestrated our path to cross with Joe and Pat Gibbs. The union that resulted has been another confirmation of a faith relationship. Joe and Pat have greatly enhanced our lives and the lives of our children.

I want to especially thank my wife, Sally. Without her life, her input, her spirit, her editing and typing, (not only of this manuscript, but everything I have ever written), this book would not be in print today. Thanks for once again pushing me across the finish line! You have completed me in more ways than I could ever count.

In addition, I want to thank my assistant Christi Wilson for being a co-laborer in the time consuming process of revision. In addition, several irreplaceable people have had valuable input in the editing process: Chuck Merritt, Laurel Justice, and Brian Fitzpatrick. We also want to express our appreciation of Tim Howard for the layout of the book.

ABOUT THE AUTHORS

DON and SALLY MEREDITH are authors and marriage counselors who have taught relationship seminars for married couples, parents, and adult singles for the past twenty-five years. In 1971, they founded Christian Family Life, Inc. to further the training of professional counselors as well as lay people. In 1976, they helped start the Family Life Ministry of Campus Crusade for Christ. Together they have helped plant six churches in Texas, Arkansas, and Virginia. Their primary focus today is the distribution of a twelve-week small group series on marriage. Don is also actively involved in assisting Joe Gibbs and his family in building their NASCAR and NHRA racing teams.

Residents of Charlotte, NC, Don and Sally have four grown children: Todd, Carmen, Kathryn, and Tiffany. They have a daughter-in-law, Sara, and son-in-law, Scott Gertz.

ABOUT THE TWELVE-WEEK MARRIAGE COURSE

CHRISTIAN FAMILY LIFE offers a twelve-week small-group study on marriage. This discipleship course is designed for married and engaged couples. The group leader does not need specific expertise or training in marital or premarital counseling. However, Christian Family Life requires training in order to lead the study. The study was developed to help couples implement the principles from *Becoming One* into their lives. If you would like more information, please write or call: Christian Family Life Inc., 9900 Twin Lakes Parkway, Charlotte, N.C. 28269, (704)875-3606. Our E-Mail address is XnFamily@aol.com and our fax number is (704)875-3560.

CONTENTS

FOREWORD	11
1. MEANING WELL IS NOT ENOUGH	13
2. IT'S THIRD AND EIGHT, SALLY	17

|PART I|

3. FIVE REASONS MARRIAGES FAIL	27
4. THE PROGRESSION OF A DECLINING MARRIAGE	53

|PART II|

5. ONENESS: GOD'S PLAN, MAN'S HOPE	67
6. HOW ONENESS HAPPENS	77
7. POWER IN ONENESS	91
8. LOVING WHEN IT HURTS	103
9. LOVE AND SUBMISSION: FRIEND OR FOE	119
10. WISDOM OR DECEIT	135

|PART III|

11. A MAN OF COMMITMENT	149
12. A WOMAN OF WISDOM	165
13. NAKED AND UNASHAMED	187
14. FINANCIAL FREEDOM	211
15. LOVING THOSE IN-LAWS	229
16. GOD'S TESTING TIMES	241
17. WINNING, LOSING, AND OTHER STRANGE GAMES	253
SUMMARY	267
EPILOGUE	271
APPENDIX: SO YOU WANT TO GET MARRIED?	273

FOREWORD

Pat and I have been married for over thirty years now. We're both professing Christians, and we actively seek God's direction in our lives. But, I'll be the first to admit, I'm not always the world's best husband. Pat can readily attest to this. And she'd tell you that she's not always the perfect wife. We try, but though we deeply love each other, we sometimes fail.

I'll level with you, sometimes I used to put my career as a football coach above everything, occasionally even God! And the pressures of running our NASCAR team have made me difficult to be around at times. As for Pat, every now and then her frustration defining her role, now that our kids are grown up, surfaces. Or, there was the time when she faced a serious, life-threatening illness and her faith never wavered. I love her for the way she responded to God.

Yet, through it all, we believe that God made our marriage, and that He has a plan for it. That's why we strongly recommend, and practice, the marriage principles that Don and Sally lay out in *Becoming One*.

Becoming One provides a Biblical blueprint for marriage. Don and Sally show God's commitment to marriage, and our responsibilities to Him and each other. They call it the "faith" relationship, and it has revolutionized our marriage.

God does have a plan and practical solutions for your marriage. Whether you are happily married and think you'll have smooth sailing forever, or have hit some of the painful trials that most marriages face, or wonder if you're married to someone that perhaps isn't God's best for you, *Becoming One* will set you straight. It will give you Biblical hope and direction.

Don and Sally are dear friends and our families are very close. We've spent enough time together to know that they use these principles in their own marriage. So do our married children. Pat and I, our son J.D. and his wife Melissa, took the 12-week *Becoming One* course. We highly recommend that you take it after you have read this book.

For twenty-five years this material has blessed thousands of marriages. The material presented in *Becoming One* is the foundation for two fine ministries: Christian Family Life, which focuses on marital counseling and small groups, and the Family Life Ministry of Campus Crusade, which holds the tremendous weekend marriage conferences.

I believe your marriage will be blessed if you read, and apply, the faith concepts described in *Becoming One*. It has blessed our lives, and those of our children. We will be forever grateful to the Merediths for sharing the faith relationship concept with us.

Joe Gibbs
President, Joe Gibbs Racing
Former Head Coach, Three-time Superbowl Champion
of the Washington Redskins

CHAPTER ONE

MEANING WELL IS NOT ENOUGH

THE SENSITIVE young woman in my office was crying uncontrollably. Her face was flushed, her eyes blurred and red. She reached for another Kleenex and struggled as she said, "I didn't know it was possible to hurt so much."

Her husband had just finished revealing several desperately crushing personal experiences. The details were intimate and humiliating, causing his voice to break repeatedly. When his wife started to cry, the pressure became so stifling that he became quite agitated. He had to struggle for breath to speak.

> NO ONE HAS EVER MARRIED IN ORDER TO DESTROY THEIR MATE.

Their circumstances were painfully real and typical in our American culture today. I found myself emotionally involved before I knew it. The drama of the moment demanded a break, and as the couple left the room, my heart quickened. "How did these outstanding people allow themselves to inflict such pain on one another?"

We are not speaking here of a couple with inherent weaknesses in their background. In fact, they were so prominent in their community that they were driving more than a hundred miles weekly to see me, to keep local attention at a minimum.

Both had successful family and community histories. They had met during their second year in college. After three and a half years of dating, they were married. He attended one year of law school after college, while she taught school. Both families firmly endorsed their marriage.

What a contrast this was to our visit several years back during their engagement period. I had been genuinely impressed with her adoration of him. She viewed him as extremely talkative. In fact, the thing about him that attracted her most was his ability to communicate easily. They would talk for hours on any subject. He was so understanding. She had such confidence in his intellect and ability to make decisions. He had held several class offices in school, and she had been proud to be identified with him.

As Jim thought back over their dating period, his eyes were alive with pleasant memories. He talked a great deal about how proud he had been, and how good he had felt being with her. He had great respect and admiration for her opinions, so much, in fact, that he wouldn't think of attempting anything without seeking her counsel. He loved her sense of humor, and they laughed a lot. He was proud of her feminine appearance.

In countless ways I had sensed a wise and practical approach in the timing and planning of their marriage. In addition to this positive beginning, both enjoyed active Christian lives. Each had a personal relationship with Jesus Christ. He had considered attending seminary at one time; she loved her church.

Sadly, this picture-perfect beginning was followed by conflict and hurt. As the months and years passed, life grew very complex. In-laws, children, sexual stress, job changes, disappointments, personality differences, and broken communication seemed to overwhelm the promise of their beginning. Betty no longer found Jim to be sensitive and talkative. Instead, he had grown disappointingly distant. No matter how she tried, attempts at communication almost always ended in conflict.

"I find myself feeling such resentment and anger toward Jim now," she cried. "Last week after feeling guilty all day, I decided to fix his favorite dinner. Every effort to be creative seemed so labored and impossible. I shouted at the kids and blew up at every interruption while fixing the meal. I felt such inner conflict. On the one hand, I knew I desperately needed to be creative; yet on the other, I seemed to deeply resent every effort. After my two-hour drama in preparing the meal, I tried to compose myself for Jim's arrival. Just as I lit the candles, expecting Jim to appear at any moment, the phone rang. It was Jim, explaining that he would be home late. I resented his insensitivity at that moment. All I felt was hate and anger."

> HOW DO SO MANY PEOPLE WHO MEAN SO WELL END UP SO FRUSTRATED?

When Betty expressed her anger and hurt, Jim responded, "I never thought I would experience the day when working late in a lonely office would be more inviting than being with you!" Betty was paralyzed with frustration so deep that tears wouldn't even flow. The conflict had become so complex that hope was lost and only frustration remained.

Even more tragic, in many ways, was the change that had come over Jim. There was a spirit of sacrifice in his early commitment to Betty, a natural devotion. Betty's every need was an opportunity for Jim to exercise his genuine desire to serve her. This romantic drive on his part had resulted in security for Betty in the early days of their courtship and marriage.

How could a man's heart and attitude change so dramatically in just a few short years? A seemingly unlimited capacity for love had turned to the deepest form of resentment, almost to the point of repulsion. Where Jim had earlier sought Betty's opinion, now he met her opinion with fits of anger and rejection. The soft gentle touch that released Jim to satisfaction had turned to a methodical cold politeness that left both wanting.

My mind was searching for answers as Betty and Jim returned from our break. The tears had stopped, but the evidence of shock and deep uncertainty remained on their faces. Betty spoke first.

"How did this happen to us? What did we do wrong?"

Jim followed with, "Look, the thing that amazes me is that when I stop to evaluate things, I realize I still really love Betty. I am certain I couldn't find anyone better, but when I try to live with her nothing but frustration results. I don't know why."

The question that was born out of Jim and Betty's frustration is being asked by thousands of couples all over the world. How could this have happened to us?

The purpose of this book is to help couples avoid ever reaching this unfortunate and unnecessary point in marriage. Tragically, most couples naively feel this sort of situation will never happen to them. *"We are different: we love each other so much!"* they say.

In the last thirty plus years of counseling and speaking to Christian couples, I have observed that the one common reality in all marriages is this: *No one has ever married in order to destroy their mate.*

If that is the case, then the real pressing question is, *"How do so many people who mean so well end up so frustrated?"*

CHAPTER TWO
IT'S THIRD AND EIGHT, SALLY!

ALL THINGS CONSIDERED, marriage today is not a good proposition. In recent times, applications for divorce number about the same as applications for marriage licenses in most major U.S. cities. "In 1990, there were forty-eight divorces for each one-hundred marriages."[1] "The divorce rate has *risen 700 percent* in this century and continues to rise. There is now one divorce for every 1.8 marriages. Over a million children a year are involved in divorce cases and 13 million children under eighteen have one or both parents missing."[2] This simply means that of all couples marrying in America today, almost half will eventually divorce. As alarming as that figure is, additional research reveals that many other marriages are hurting but are attempting to "hang in there" for the sake of the children.

How many couples do you know whose marriages are of such quality that you would trade your marriage for theirs? Probably not many. Most counselors I have known agree that most marriages today are either hurting badly or are somewhere in the process of breaking up. Marriages are failing in tremendous numbers.

Is the situation hopeless? No. Not only is marriage as an institution not hopeless, it can succeed beyond one's expectations. However, couples planning to marry must beware: romantic feelings or good intentions give one a sense of false security. *Happy marriages are made, not found.* Begin now to earnestly seek the answers on how to succeed in marriage. *If God designed marriage, He can make it work!*

A PERSONAL NOTE

The love and satisfaction I feel for my wife, Sally, still amazes me today. Even though she is just another human being like me, with strengths and weaknesses, God many years ago showed me the key to loving her by faith. As my faith has grown, God has given me the ability to love Sally with a love that honors her and gives hope. In 1967, when I married her, such love was foreign to me. I tended to focus on other people's weaknesses, and this was especially true in regard to my wife. Today, I see Sally's weaknesses in a realistic way, yet I experience an exhilarating and complete love for her. That's a miracle. Think back with me for a moment. In the beginning my love was very different. *It was based on performance.*

One of our first dates was at Disneyland. I can still remember standing close to her in the lines, waiting for the rides. She had on a pretty silk blouse that was very soft to my touch. Emotional charges went through me! In the weeks that followed, I realized that here was a woman I loved to talk to, look at, and be with. I was impressed with her commitment to Christ. She was successful in her vocation, and I was proud of her. I can still remember our first private moments together. We were walking in the mountains overlooking San Bernardino, on the night I first kissed her. A few short weeks later I asked her to marry me.

After three months of seeing each other daily, our wedding day arrived. Sally and I had just turned twenty-seven. Because we were a little older than most newly marrieds, and we had been committed Christians longer than most, we thought marriage would be a little bit easier for us. Frankly, we were naïve and overconfident. While our age and spiritual maturity certainly helped, we were both shocked at the subtle ways our relationship struggled right from the beginning.

Reality came very quickly. It was on our *wedding day* that differences in our backgrounds began to surface. The ceremony was scheduled at 4:00 on a Saturday afternoon in the early fall. At about 3:00 I was a little ahead of schedule, so I turned on the television to catch the opening kickoff of the first football game of the season. I hadn't seen a football game in six months. I became so involved in the action that before I realized it, it was 3:45 and I wasn't ready. Honestly frustrated at having to leave the game, I rushed off to the wedding. Go ahead and chastise me, women. I realize now that I deserve it.

After the ceremony in Boulder, Colorado, we drove toward Vail, where we had reservations at a lovely hotel. We got away later than planned, and I turned on the radio just as soon as we drove out of the church parking lot, trying to catch the last series of plays of the first University of Texas football game. In 1967, it was supposed to be "the year of the Horns" (Texas Longhorns). I had to know the score!

Radio reception was limited by the mountains, so I could not find a network station. In a "sports panic," I decided to stop short of Vail and find another motel so I wouldn't miss the 10:00 news and the Texas score. To me, one hotel was just as good as another. When I suggested that we stop early, Sally thought I was anxious for the honeymoon night. I was, but the Texas score, now *that* was a really important issue. Mind you, I didn't intend to hurt Sally with my obsession. I was behaving exactly as twenty-seven years of living in my Texas home had conditioned me to behave. Unfortunately, my obsession with football reigned supreme on this particular occasion. (And I might confess, many more!)

Therefore, we stopped forty miles east of Vail, checked into a motel, and went to dinner. We got back to the room about 10:15, just about sports time. As my bride disappeared into the bathroom to prepare for our wedding night, I hurried over to turn on the television. Almost instantly, I discovered that Texas had been defeated. I was literally sick! I can still remember trying to clear my mind of disappointment as Sally came into the room. She had no idea how much a part of my life football was, and how affected I was by this loss! Of course, I had never communicated any of this to her.

The next day some new conflicts developed. That morning, our first full day of married life, we drove on to Vail. Sally had envisioned us spending time together, hiking in the mountains. She was dreaming of a romantic outdoors-type honeymoon in the countryside. I, on the other hand, was not too crazy about walking around gazing at trees! Besides, after two hours of mountains and trees, I found my mind drifting to thoughts of the NFL and all the activity on the football fields of our wonderful nation. Wouldn't you know, the Dallas Cowboys were to play the Green Bay Packers!

Thinking myself perfectly justified, I began to maneuver Sally toward Denver so we could find a Holiday Inn in time to see the game. I knew if we stopped for lunch we'd miss the start of the game. So we bought some cheese and crackers at a country store and headed east. By this time, Sally was a very disappointed bride. She was silent in the car. I just thought she didn't have anything to say.

When we arrived in Denver, I suggested we get some Kentucky Fried Chicken and take it to the room. She bought a magazine to read while I watched the game! From Sally's viewpoint, the honeymoon (perhaps even the marriage?) was a total disaster. The discussion we had that night was mild compared to the ones to come throughout the rest of football season! Every Saturday and Sunday I could be found sitting in front of the tube, watching football games.

Sally actually had nothing against football; she had just never thought much about it. Her idea of a pleasant autumn day was walking or riding through the woods, enjoying the changing colors of trees and smelling the brisk autumn air. Here, already, were seeds of conflict beginning to germinate in our marriage. We both meant well. Neither of us was right or wrong. But our differing backgrounds were beginning to collide and hurt our relationship.

Several things stood out. I was amazed at how my feelings of love for her could change so quickly when I was hurt. A jolted marriage relationship can be intensely painful. Rejection, insults, insecurities, and lost devotion can ravage one's emotions. I found that after being wounded emotionally, my strongest feelings of love could quickly change to bitterness.

Another discouraging force was *our tendency to focus on performance*. We began to notice every failure and weakness in each other. It became absurd! For example, Sally was a good housekeeper, but because she didn't do one particular thing the way my mother had, I became obsessed to the point that she might as well have been a poor housekeeper. I was mature enough to know better, but I couldn't seem to help my critical attitude. She, on the other hand, would criticize the fact that I read the sports page, rather than the Bible, in the morning. She wanted a "spiritual leader" and all I could think about was football!

> HAPPY MARRIAGES ARE MADE, NOT FOUND.

In spite of our good intentions, we were beginning to find it hard to live together. I can remember thinking to myself that I just couldn't let things continue in the direction they were going. But they did. In just two years, our very best intentions for a model Christian marriage had become, at best, a memory of the past. Things were just mediocre.

During our third year of marriage, while we were involved in student ministry with Campus Crusade at the University of Arkansas, I noticed that a number of students were getting involved in foolish dating relationships. There was a need to teach these students some guidelines for dating. So I began to page through the Bible for some practical thoughts that would apply to dating. It was during this study of dating and marriage, undertaken to help others, that we discovered our own need. *God changed our marriage.* Perhaps those students don't remember much of what we said, but for the Merediths, marriage has never been the same.

The rest of this book is an attempt to share with you the truths that have been so helpful, not only in the Meredith household, but in many other marriages as well. Believe me, our improvement has not been based on personal strengths. These discoveries stand on the certainty of the Scriptures and God's statement that He intends for marriage to be a blessing.

> *To sum up, let all be harmonious, sympathetic, brotherly, kindhearted, and humble in spirit; not returning evil for evil, or insult for insult, but giving a blessing instead; for you were called for the very purpose that you might inherit a blessing* (1 Pet. 3:8-9).

To begin, we will address the question, "*Why are so many marriages failing?*" The first step in solving problems is to be able to recognize what the problems are.

Part I of this book attempts to answer this question, exposing *five major reasons why marriages automatically disintegrate*. All five of these reasons will be examined, along with insights into what happens if they are not exposed and corrected. Couples who are aware of these factors will be far better prepared for marriage than couples who marry without understanding the obstacles they face.

The second and third parts of the book are directed toward a constructive solution.

Part II describes the *spiritual insight* necessary to make lasting commitments and changes in marriage. God's purpose for creating marriage will be readily seen as partners understand His creation plan. This plan can help empower couples to experience permanent and fulfilling love. Questions like the following will be answered: What is love and how does one experience it? What is God's blueprint for marriage? Did he design my mate for me? What part does the Holy Spirit play in marriage? What qualities in my life are necessary for me to be a loving spouse? How do the roles of the husband and wife work in harmony? These questions and others are discussed in Part II of the book.

> IF GOD DESIGNED MARRIAGE, CAN HE MAKE IT WORK?

Part III gives directions on *how to apply these biblical patterns* to everyday married life. Part III *integrates the spiritual and practical* sides of marriage. Questions like these are covered: What is the role of a woman and how is it different from that of a man? How can sexual expression grow? What should be our perspective on trials? What about in-law problems? Financial problems, personality differences, male/female differences, and many more issues are discussed. And last, if you are not yet married, how do you know God's will for marriage?

Couples who understand why marriages fail as well as how God intends marriage to work have a significant advantage. They are well on the road to a growing and thriving marriage. *God not only designed marriage, He can make it work!*

1. George Barna, *The Future of the American Family* (Chicago: Moody Press, 1993), pp. 67-68.
2. Armand Nicholi Jr., contributor to *Family Building* by George Rekers (Ventura, Ca: Gospel Light Publications, 1985), cited by Bill Bright, *The Coming Revival*, New Life Publishers, 1994, p. 54

PART I

CHAPTER THREE

FIVE REASONS MARRIAGES FAIL

WHAT WILL KEEP you and your spouse from joining the ranks of couples who are discouraged because they cannot live happily together and decide to "call it quits?"

You may say, "Our love is more mature than most other couples," or "We are wiser," or "We are better educated," or "We have been Christians longer." Even though all of these things are vitally important, they are not sufficient to insure marital success. Why do marriages fail? Fortunately, I began to ask that question early in our marriage. *No one gets married expecting their marriage to self-destruct.* Yet, nearly half of all marriages begin to deteriorate almost immediately, while many others are surprised when their marriage gradually slips into mediocrity.

The purpose of Part I of the book is to alert couples to basic forces that cause marriages to fail. Few newly marrieds have prepared themselves for the natural forces working against their union. Just knowing and anticipating these forces will help tremendously. We will discuss five major reasons why marriages naturally deteriorate. Certainly, these are not the only five issues that work against marriage, but these five encompass a natural progression that I have observed over many years.

The more confident couples are concerning their love and

commitment, the more naïve they tend to be concerning their future. The better the intentions, the more easily they might be hurt by anyone who questions or rejects them. Jesus exhorted His followers to count the cost before undertaking a significant commitment. He said, *"Estimate the cost . . . for if he lays the foundation and is not able to finish it, everyone who sees it will ridicule him, saying, 'This fellow began to build and was not able to finish'"* (Luke 14:28-30). Anticipating what is ahead is a significant part of being successful. Have you realistically counted the cost? Do you know why so many marriages fail in spite of "good intentions?"

REASON 1:
THE NEGATIVE RESULTS OF THE SOCIAL AND CULTURAL CHANGES IN OUR SOCIETY

Our Society

The first reason we will look at is an obvious one. It focuses on the tremendous social and cultural changes that have occurred in our nation over the last century. While we are a blessed nation that has many reasons to be thankful, we should also be realistic concerning the negatives. The simple fact is that many of these changes have been detrimental to families, marriages, and relationships in general.

A number of years ago I had the good fortune to attend a course taught by Dr. Howard Hendricks at Dallas Theological Seminary. During the course, "*The Christian Home*," Dr. Hendricks displayed a simple chart comparing a home of the 1870s with a home of the 1970s. The comparison provided keen insights into how vastly our society and culture have changed and the inevitable impact on marriage.

Think back for a moment over our nation's history and you will quickly realize that the 20th century has seen more change than any other comparable period in history. The resulting changes have been both good and bad. Two examples of these changes have been the growth of *population* and the growth of *knowledge*.

It took from the beginning of time until the 1800s for population to reach one billion. Yet in just the last hundred plus years, that figure has jumped to six billion! Social scientists now project that in fewer than twenty years that number will reach as many as eight billion people. The economic and social impact of such growth on families is staggering! Population growth affects our social lives in many ways. Police and health services are struggling as never before. Individuals feel less in touch with political and social institutions. Our churches seem to have lost touch with the masses. Marriage as an institution has suffered because of this discontinuity.

> AS POPULATION INCREASES AND FAMILIES DETERIORATE, OUR NATION IS FORGETTING ITS SPIRITUAL ROOTS.

Yet, we have far more space for more people. Population growth in and of itself is not bad, if fact, it was part of God's purpose to fill the Earth. The real problem comes not from growing numbers, but from the associated moral decline of our nation. As population increases and families deteriorate, our nation seems to have forgotten its spiritual roots. Marriage does not work apart from a spiritual and moral base. With a third of our children growing up in single-parent homes, we are fostering a distorted view of marriage and family.

With population growth has come greater amounts of information. The growth of knowledge tends to overwhelm men's minds. With the advent of the computer, the quantity of stored information now doubles and redoubles within months. With the advent of the information highway, i.e. the Internet, ideas spread very rapidly to virtually the entire globe. The media (TV, radio, computer technology) are dominated by people with anti-God values. This enormous growth in technology has impacted today's society in ways we are only now beginning to understand.

Like population, the growth of the information highway has outstripped its moral underpinnings. Media, apart from God, tends to reproduce darkness rather than light. With all the scientific, medical, and financial benefits that have resulted from this growth, there have also been many negative effects on society. While the information highway is superb in its concepts and information, the pornography industry alone has come into our homes and businesses unwanted . This affects not only adults, but youth who have access to computer technology. Even Christians have been entrapped by its snare.

Both of these examples represent just two of the changes that make this century unique. All of this has had significant impact on marriages. In 1870, one marriage in thirty-three ended in divorce. As we noted earlier, that figure today is close to one in two! More than one child in three lives in a broken home. Statistics show that children who grow up without a father are eleven times more vulnerable to drugs and crimes than a child in a two-parent family. Social scientists are now attempting to rewrite the definition of marriage and family because of the changes in the last hundred years. To appreciate the impact this century has had on marriage and the family, we need to examine some of these social and cultural changes.

Rural—Urban Shift

Before the turn of the century, American society was seventy percent agricultural and rural. One hundred years later, seventy plus percent of American society is urban and non-agricultural. America has switched from a rural-agrarian economy to an urban-industrial society. To illustrate this change and its impact on marriage, let me take you back one hundred years.

A hundred years ago the Merediths would probably have lived on and farmed about ten acres of land. Because of this isolation, my wife and I would have been extremely dependent on one another. Daily I would have observed her faithful and physically draining work. She would have prepared the food the family had grown. The nurturing and education of the children would have fallen primarily on her. Her value and creativeness would have been clearly observed by her husband and family. There would have been no television or readily available transportation to distract them.

In the same situation, the family would have looked to the

father as the protector and primary provider. His authority and worth would have been naturally acknowledged if he was a sincere and loving father. His long hours and hard work would not have gone unnoticed. Each year just surviving would have been a real accomplishment for Dad. This isolation of the family would have insured Dad's ability to communicate with and encourage each member. He would have worked with and trained his children to carry on the family farm or business. His masculinity would have been valued.

In contrast, men today, for the most part, own materially very little. Instead they are in debt to many (banks, credit cards, etc.). They have real authority in few areas of their lives. Research tells us they are frustrated by their jobs on the one hand, and their democratic families on the other. The omnipresent media, through television, movies, and print, constantly bombard their lives and families with unattainable material comparisons that cause men to feel inadequate. Our government-sponsored welfare system has caused tremendous "father flight," and many men no longer feel needed in the home. The rise of single parent homes has fostered frustration on all sides. "In some of the major cities, children born without a father has risen forty-five percent! Studies of young criminals have found that more than 70 percent of all juveniles in state reform institutions come from fatherless homes."[1]

A hundred years ago women were vital to the success of any family. Their work was time-consuming and difficult, but they generally developed great versatility and skill. She was educator, counselor, minister, and home builder, and she usually developed several crafts.

In contrast today, many women are influenced by current fashionable ideas, and have abandoned the home to find personal satisfaction elsewhere. Many other women are economically forced to work. There has definitely been a movement to leave the home. Tragically, many women today feel the home is a "prison." The impact on America's children has been staggering. Without Mom's first devotion, America has seen its children move toward crime, drugs, failed academics, and insecurities that strain our social and medical resources. Is Mom happy? Apparently not, since eating disorders, plastic surgery, soap operas ratings, depression and other mood disorders, and divorce rates are at all-time highs. Today, the primary goal seems to be looking "young and thin." Fifty years ago and before, women desired to be known for their character and faithfulness.

The growth of population, knowledge, and media communication, combined with the shift from rural to urban economies, has greatly affected marriage and the family. Husbands and wives must seek wisdom to establish a lifestyle that takes the best of the past and combines it with the realities of the present.

New Mobility

Another significant change in the last hundred years has been the shift from an immobile to a mobile society. In 1870, a thirty-mile trip was an important, all day event. Today, we travel that far to shop! For many, a two to three-hour commute to and from work is the norm, not the exception.

One hundred years ago people tended to live in ethnic groups. A group of Irish people might settle in one place; twenty-five miles away would be a group of German descent. This resulted in "cultural islands" being formed all over America. If my wife and I had met in 1870, it would probably have been because we had the same ethnic, religious, vocational, and cultural backgrounds. We would probably have grown up less than ten miles apart and our parents would have known each other. Our lives and backgrounds would have been very similar.

Mobility ended the natural protection these "cultural islands" provided. In this century, our society has become a "melting pot." Because we travel with such ease today, we are likely to meet a future mate almost anywhere. Therefore, we probably will not really know our mate's cultural, social, and religious background. Unless we date that person for years, marriage will bring some real surprises, and these surprises significantly challenge marriage.

Certainly I am not saying that the marriage of people from different backgrounds is in and of itself bad. Rather I am saying that the mobility unique to this century opened the possibility of cultural shock to which some marriages have a hard time adjusting.

Home-Centered Vs. Community-Centered Living
In 1870, the home was the center of almost all activity. Recreation, education, religious study, vocational preparation, and emotional development were all based in the home. Creativity was a necessity. If there was work to do, everyone was required to help. When it was time to play, everyone took part. There was no such thing as an unwanted child. Each child was an asset. Girls worked alongside Mom. Boys worked with Dad. Spectator activities were generally not available; television and movies did not exist. In fact, there was not much leisure time available. Every person was vital to survival.

Today, a completely different circumstance prevails. Activities outside the home, or activities that require one to be just a spectator, seem to be the norm. Therefore, feelings of isolation and unimportance can result during the formative years. Many times each child in a family may forge a significantly different path. Parents often feel exhausted and confused because of the multiple influences each may encounter. Additionally, mom and dad are required to run a "taxi service" to all the athletic and social activities. Children focus on television and computer games at home. It is easy for a child to be lost or left out in all of this activity. Emotional, social, and academic suffering is not uncommon.

Most moms and dads suffer today because of their busy schedules. Commuting to and from work, hobbies, health needs, and even church activities quickly consume the time and energy of each. Often, television replaces communication in our homes. Far too many wives today rely on soap operas to fill their emotional needs. Meanwhile, husbands often tune out their families and rely on "channel surfing" to relieve the accumulated stress of the work day.

The Value Of Children
Very subtly, *the way our society values children has changed*. Children today are often seen as a liability. No longer do they help

produce food for the family, but instead they are another mouth to feed, another body to clothe, and another educational expense. Our society places more value on children who produce. The less gifted and less fortunate suffer. If parents are not discerning, they may retaliate against their own children before realizing why.

Most couples are able, with the advent of birth control, to choose smaller families, and some choose not to have children at all. Birth control allows family size control, but also makes premarital sex more likely. Abortion is used throughout the world as a method of birth control. Again, this philosophy is fostered in America by the media and Hollywood as a viable alternative for population control. All too often children are no longer wanted and needed, but have become a "throw away" item, instead of the blessing God intended.

The spiritual and psychological implications of these social and cultural changes on children and marriages are immense. It takes great discernment to recognize and creatively offset their effects.

Practical Vs. Social Marriage

Until recent times, the decision to marry necessitated one to look seriously at practical considerations. A man generally looked for a woman with physical strength and character. Bearing children and running a farm took real stamina. Certainly appearance and personality were important, but they were tempered by practical concerns.

For the same reasons, a woman would have thought a long time before marrying an unstable man. Survival, for an abandoned woman with children, was extremely difficult. A strong back and courage were important if a man was going to bear up to the rigors of farming and protecting the family. Again, sexual attraction and romance were important, but life's realities tended to balance these less practical considerations. Today, however, the decision to get married is often based almost entirely on social issues. The decision is driven by emotional feelings and the desire to have a companion.

Divorce

Another factor from the past that caused people to view marriages more practically was society's attitude concerning divorce. Divorce was not a satisfactory alternative. It was not at all attractive. For the woman on the farm, divorce could mean fear for survival. For the woman in the city, it meant social rejection. Divorce for the man, too, meant social rejection combined with the likelihood of spending the rest of his life alone. Certainly these realities caused couples to evaluate the decision to marry more seriously, and to work through problems after marriage, rather than to end relationships quickly.

For most today, survival is no longer the issue. Women can readily support themselves. Our culture is more accepting of bearing children outside of marriage. In our time, divorce is an accepted way of life, as is living together without the bonds and responsibilities of marriage. If one does not succeed at first, simply try again. No big deal. Our society no longer values marriage as an institution at the level that it once did. Therefore, couples tend to approach marriage with less practical wisdom.

The social and cultural changes of the last century have adversely affected marriage, as the change in the divorce rate demonstrates. Probably one of the most devastating ways these changes impact marriage is the way couples decide to get married. Today, couples are getting married with *differing backgrounds,* with *differing motivations*, and with *less God consciousness* than a century ago. Let's consider why these factors threaten marriages.

First, couples often marry without knowing or understanding their future mate's background and culture. If not properly prepared, getting married with differing backgrounds can frustrate couples. Not anticipating your mate's differences can lead to immediate conflict. Many who marry without proper preparation never recover from their initial shock.

Second, these changes have caused many to *marry for the wrong reasons*. Proper motivations are vital to building a successful marriage. Today, couples put too much emphasis on social standing and sexual passion, instead of looking at the practical realities.

Third, couples are getting married with *very little awareness of God's role* in their relationship. If God created marriage, not consulting Him can be a terminal mistake. *If God designed the family, He can best instruct us in how to succeed in marriage.* Let's consider each of these conclusions in more detail.

Differing Backgrounds

Our "melting pot" society results in many couples getting married with very different backgrounds. These differences can result in immediate disagreement. Disagreement leads to conflict and hurt. At first, it's fun making up. As the differences become more personal and numerous, couples begin to focus on the *performance* of their mate. This progression over time begins to undermine their commitment to each other. These differences may touch every activity or belief of the couple.

Let me illustrate in some detail some of the adjustments Sally and I had to face early in our marriage. After a short engagement, we married only to discover we really did not know each other very well. Remember, women, as you read this, please do not give up on me! I really didn't intend to hurt Sally.

I grew up in Texas, and my parents were outgoing people of modest means. Because Dad was in sales, we were often involved in social encounters. We did not have a great deal of money, but I was fairly free financially. Sally, on the other hand, grew up in the mountains of Colorado. Her family had close friends and relatives, but were less social. In addition, she was very different in the way she approached finances. I was considerably more free about letting go of money, while she was more conservative in her spending.

When my family took vacations, we usually got up early in the morning and drove all day. We would stop at new motels that we could be sure were clean and comfortable. We were the "no-surprises" people. Thirty years ago, Holiday Inn fit the bill perfectly. We seldom stopped to eat at more expensive restaurants. When we traveled, we were very goal-oriented. The vacation started *after* we arrived at our destination.

By contrast, Sally's family considered the drive part of the vacation. They enjoyed eating out, so they splurged on good meals. To afford that, they economized in other areas, mainly in their choice of motels. They "shopped" motels to find the best deal. (I've learned since that many people do that, but at the time it was a real jolt to my "country-club" pride.) Sally always seemed to head for those old, beige-colored stucco motels. You know, the kind with the creaky furniture, the 1926 chenille bedspreads, and the "everyday low prices."

The first two days of our honeymoon we stayed in what I considered nice motels. On the third day, we headed for Tulsa. To Sally's great disappointment, I had decided to cut the honeymoon short. (After all, there were no more football games, and who wants to look at the trees?!) Being a Holiday Inn man, I kept driving trying to find one. I didn't realize that in that sparsely populated area of the country there might not be a Holiday Inn. I wasn't about to lower those standards, but because we were still ignorant of each other's choices, Sally couldn't understand why I wouldn't stop. She fell asleep in the car. After driving through town after town with no Holiday Inn, we finally ran out of gas at two o'clock in the morning. Fortunately, we were close to a small New Mexico town, one hundred miles from nowhere.

There were only three motels in town. To me, they were all the old, unpredictable kind that didn't appeal to me at all. To Sally there was nothing unacceptable about them. In fact, she encouraged me to check each motel at 2:00 a.m. for rates! Much to my discomfort, we had to stay, since no gas stations were open at that time of the morning. I lay awake thinking "bugs" were going to eat me, while Sally slept like a baby.

Throughout our travels later that fall, there were many opportunities to stay in motels. Sally, wanting to be a "good steward of God's money," just didn't feel right about paying Holiday Inn prices. Here again, it was not so much an issue of right or wrong, but of two people with different perspectives. That first year, we experienced some real hurt and conflict over such differences. Because of my strong "logical reasoning," I usually maneuvered her toward my thinking, but unknowingly destroyed some of her respect for me.

Another example of a difference that caused almost immediate struggle involved our different intellectual pursuits. All my life I had been an outgoing person who was interested in people and sports activities more than in reading. Although I had been a decent student, I almost never read a book. I was a "Cliff Notes" man. I don't think I had read ten books in my entire life up to that point.

My bride, on the other hand, is the intellectual in our family. She was, and is, an excellent student and loves to read. She came from a family who read constantly. Sally had worked closely the previous four years with a Christian supervisor who was a dedicated student of the Scripture. She had learned to appreciate his intellectual challenges.

We have since learned the difference between academia and common sense. But in those early days our divergent intellectual pursuits were a real problem. We simply placed different values on different things. I've since learned that I enjoy reading and even writing, while she has learned to enjoy various sports activities with me.

When people get married, they are usually at the peak of emotional love. Their intentions are so good, they would do anything for the other. Yet, immediately after the wedding day, they confront their many differences. The two examples just mentioned, concerning motels and intellectual pursuits, may seem small by themselves, but if multiplied by ten, they can quickly become an overwhelming obstacle.

The changes in our country during the last one hundred years have greatly increased the likelihood of couples marrying mates who are very different. These differences, if not properly anticipated, can start the couple down the road to hurt and rejection. Add to that the number of couples getting married with emotional baggage from a previous marriage. Often children are involved who are not "biological" children. Hurt and rejection are compounded when more than the spouses are involved. The "blending" process many times can take years to work through. (That is another book in itself!)

Differing Motivational Factors

The changes America has experienced in the last century have also changed the way people decide to get married. Certainly, many of the reasons that lead couples to marry today existed a century ago, yet the percentage influenced by modern motivations has changed significantly.

Generally, I see *five basic motivations* that move couples toward marriage. The first involves our emphasis on physical **feelings** and **emotions**. If one listens closely to society's definition of love, one would discover its primary ingredient to be "feelings." The following comments are typical of this feeling-oriented love. "I can't live without you." "I'll die if you leave me." The tragedy is that feelings are so changeable. *Nothing is more deceptive than feelings.* Although it is true that feelings are vital to a marriage, they are **not** *a healthy basis* for a relationship. Why? Because they tend to disappear when you need them most. We will be covering what is a healthy basis for a relationship as the book unfolds.

The second motivating factor is our society's emphasis on **sexual attraction**. Our culture has encouraged the *abuse of one of God's greatest gifts* by encouraging people to prematurely become sexually involved. Few issues can obscure an important decision more than sex. Emotions, encouraged by physical intimacy, will flare instantly beyond normal proportions. Couples easily mistake lust for love. A relationship based solely on sex is bound for disaster. Today, eighty percent of troubled marriages list sexual problems as a factor. For many, these problems started long before their marriage began. Living together before marriage does not insure the adjustment or the relationship. Statistics prove just the opposite. "Cohabitation may seem a good 'trial run' for a solid marriage. But in practice, cohabiting couples who marry—many of whom already have children—are about 33 percent more likely to divorce than couples who don't live together before their nuptials. Virgin brides, on the other hand, are less likely to divorce than women who lost their virginity prior to marriage."[2] It is not uncommon for people today to have had six or more sexual partners before marriage. This emotional "scar tissue" is devastating and most need extensive premarital or marital counseling to overcome hurt, rejection and memories.

Social prestige is the third motivating factor in today's marriages. People concerned about their images or their social standings have a tendency to marry based on their would-be partners' success. This tendency can lead to unreal expectations, especially if one fails at business endeavors, or goes through normal trials in life.

A fourth factor that motivates couples is a ***false world view***. Subconsciously, young people still believe that marital success is a brick home, two new cars, and a continual sexual holiday. Instead, they may find that marriage is work, debt, problems, illness, and children. Many never recover from the shock. Living "happily ever after" isn't the fairy tale life they expected.

Last, too often people are motivated to get married just to ***escape being single***. With our vast society, it is not hard to feel lost and lonely. I can still remember the weekends and holidays when I was single. At the end of a carefree day, I would lounge around and dream of my perfect mate. The older one gets, the stronger that dream becomes. Too many of us use marriage as an escape from school, parents, work, or loneliness. Singles must be careful to keep their loneliness from influencing their decision to get married. Single parents too can confuse their desire to marry with the need of their children to have a father or a mother. All of these issues can cause a whole new set of adjustments and problems.

The motivations mentioned above are certainly not inherently bad. Yet, each must be implemented with wisdom. Each couple must immediately seek a more realistic basis for a relationship. Couples who do not discover *God's basis for relationships* can end up hurt and confused for months or years after the wedding.

Lack Of God-Consciousness

The most significant result of the vast cultural change in society is that Christ and His church are no longer considered the example for marriage today. There is often very little real God-consciousness involved in most decisions to marry. Even many so-called "Christian" marriages have been significantly affected by our changing culture. Couples may consider finances, social acceptance, vocational potential, or many other practical life goals, yet few actually evaluate their decision to get married from God's perspective. Should God play a personal role in your decision to marry? If so, what should it be? This book will deal extensively with this issue.

REASON 2:
THE DECEPTIVE "FIFTY-FIFTY" RELATIONSHIP

There is a common saying today that marriage is a "fifty-fifty" relationship. It sounds good and makes sense. There's just one problem—it doesn't work!

I firmly believe that this proposition is the second major reason marriages fail. The fifty-fifty relationship doesn't work in marriage in spite of its attractive sound: "I'll do my part, and you do yours." Consciously and subconsciously we have been taught this maxim since birth. Brother-sister relationships, sports, teamwork on the job, roommate situations, and almost every venture of life suggests that it will work in marriage. Certainly, in some ways, marriage does involve teamwork. But Scripture presents a basis for relationships that is totally different from the fifty-fifty plan. The couple who discerns God's marital plan is set free from the bondage of this system.

Why, when it seems to make so much sense, is the "meet-me-halfway" concept dangerous? This peril manifests itself as it subtly leads each mate to focus on the other's performance. Each mate, over time, will want to insure that the *other* did *their* part. Human nature demands it. Unfortunately, there is no way to know who met who halfway. It is impossible to really know if the other mate *cared* as much, *worked* as hard, or *felt* as strongly. Ultimately, couples are drawn into deeper levels of examination and criticism. Furthermore, the fifty-fifty concept actually promotes independence: "You do your part; I'll do mine."

Once couples start focusing on each other's performance, *disappointment follows* close behind. Disappointment ultimately leads to feelings of rejection and hurt. Sometimes mates react with anger, other times with deafening silence. The frustration that will eventually result, reveals the fallacy of this plan. *It is impossible to believe that the other person has actually met you halfway.* The minute one mate believes the other is not meeting them halfway, their good intentions are quickly replaced by condemnation. The following couple is a good example of what happens.

David and Ruth, a newly married couple, began to have some of these initial problems. They became so tense and uptight that they would regularly overstate things and then make critical remarks about each other. "Well, maybe we shouldn't have gotten married," or "Maybe I'm not the person you thought I was!"

> THE FIFTY-FIFTY RELATIONSHIP IS A GREAT THOUGHT, BUT IS IMPOSSIBLE TO PRACTICE.

As they argued, Ruth would subtly communicate cutting remarks, and David would retaliate. Eventually, she would start crying and go to their bedroom and slam the door. He would get in the car and drive around town, frustrated to the core. His fist would be clenched, his stomach in a knot, and he would grit his teeth while driving nowhere. After an hour or so, David would return home. Early in their marriage, they would actually enjoy making up after they settled down. In fact, they actually thought they were maturing, "Well, we're working through these problems."

But after those same problems occurred numerous times, "making up" seemed inadequate. Even though David didn't see it then, he later understood the impossibility of either of them really being able to understand the other's pain. If Ruth couldn't feel his pain, nor David hers, then there was no way they could believe each had met the other at the proverbial fifty-fifty point. David could never believe that it was as painful for Ruth as it was for him. Ruth could never believe that David cared as much as she.

So it wasn't long before David was sure Ruth was not meeting him halfway. Such suspicion begins the journey toward disaster. In each little issue of performance David became very conscious of how Ruth responded. He began to watch her every move. If she didn't respond just right, *according to David's standard of performance*, he would be troubled.

Maybe you are thinking, "Christians shouldn't have those kinds of problems." No, they shouldn't, but believe me, they do. Frankly, I often find very little difference between the bitterness level in Christian and non-Christian couples. What a tragic commentary on our understanding of God's plan for marriage!

Entering marriage naively, planning to meet your mate halfway, will certainly guarantee the same results as David and Ruth. Christians and non-Christians alike will end up in bitter frustration if they expect another human being to meet them at the proverbial pass. The fifty-fifty relationship is a great thought, but is impossible to practice. *God has an infinitely better plan!*

REASON 3:
SELF-CENTERED HUMAN NATURE

Many times, people are amazed at how they can feel love for their spouse one minute and hatred the next. Add to this that people tend to remember the negative more than the positive, and one will begin to realize why almost every couple experiences incredible emotional swings. Human feelings tend to follow human emotions.

Why is this true? How can one so quickly change from having pleasant romantic fantasies to harboring deep anger and resentment? The problem is rooted in our self-centered human nature.

When our mate rejects or embarrasses us, our love can quickly change to feelings of frustration or even hate. A friend explained it this way: "I can remember days when I was greatly attracted to my wife. But then she made a cutting remark, and my feelings of attraction quickly turned to resentment."

What's the cause? Why can't emotional swings be controlled? The Bible tells us that each person has a capacity for selfishness that is capable of incredible devastation. Strong destructive actions will be responded to with equally strong reactions by our mates. Most couples naively believe their mates to be incapable of such actions before they marry. Failure to anticipate this tendency, understand it, and know God's solution to it, is the third major cause of marriage failure today. Jeremiah 17:9 says, *"The heart is more deceitful than all else and is desperately sick; who can understand it?"*

Each of us is born with a capacity for explosive selfish actions. Scripture calls this capacity "flesh," "old man," and "old nature." The Bible also calls it sin. Knowing how to properly handle this capacity to hurt one another is vital in marriage. This failure of human nature is described best in Paul's letter to the Romans.

> *As it is written, There is none righteous, not even one; There is none who understands, There is none who seeks for God; All have turned aside, together they have become useless; There is none who does good, There is not even one. Their throat is an open grave, With their tongues they keep deceiving, The poison of asps is under their lips; Whose mouth is full of cursing and bitterness; Their feet are swift to shed blood, Destruction and misery are in their paths, And the path of peace have they not known. There is no fear of God before their eyes* (Rom. 3:10-18).

If you are not married yet, your response will probably be, "That doesn't describe my mate," or "That's too strong." Most married couples will simply say, "Amen" to those verses. You don't have to be married very long to experience the truth of those verses.

Couples who get married without knowing how to control this capacity to sin very likely will inflict emotional pain on one another before much time passes. Two people with sinful natures who come together don't make for greater peace, but greater destruction.

In fact, this passage is often a good description of the discussions I hear in the counseling room: "He doesn't understand me anymore." "I thought she was a Christian, but if so, how could she say and do what she does?" "The language and things he says to me are unrepeatable!" "He hit me last night and threatened to kill me!"

Most of the couples I see are Christians! They get married with great feelings and good intentions, and then discover that the other person is capable of inflicting great hurt, sometimes with very little remorse. After being shocked by their husband or wife, they will quickly lose their desire to be creative and do what is right. Feelings of love are replaced by fear. When feelings stop, creative actions usually stop. When creative actions stop, human love turns sour, and a negative environment results. Negative environments are like fertile ground for our self-centeredness.

Each of us has a tremendous capacity to criticize and hurt others. This impact is often discouragement or defensiveness. Eventually, if unchecked, our mate will respond in like kind. Redirecting couples who are caught in this type of insult cycle can be difficult. You might be saying to yourself, "My mate doesn't have that extreme capacity for evil."

Let me inject here that there are many ways to manifest this self-centered nature. Not everyone is explosive or outwardly aggressive. Many of us do not fight, we just "get even." Someone has said that we are either "hiders" or "hurlers." Some of us hurl insults, others just give the silent treatment and won't talk. Both can be just as devastating if motivated by self-centeredness.

We either are a mirror that reflects approval, appreciation, and encouragement to our mates, or we are a mirror that reflects failure and disappointment. What are you reflecting to your mate? If your reflection is negative, the result will be fear and retaliation. If continued over time, feelings will become frozen and attitudes critical, resulting in an environment that will breed the kind of results mentioned in the Romans passage. Go back and read it again. Turn on the nightly news tonight and listen to the description of marriages. How can one spouse get to the point of killing the one he once loved? *Every family tragedy mentioned above started with good intentions.* As Christians, we need not lose hope. God's plan for our marriages is the focus of this book.

REASON 4:
INABILITY TO COPE WITH TRIALS

I'll never forget the first time someone shared with me God's view of trials. I used to believe that the successful Christian was one who dodged trials, kind of like running through a field of land mines.

The one who missed the most mines was successful. Trials were for the unfortunate or the unfaithful. Therefore, when I got married, I certainly did not prepare to face trials. Trials were for others. I was mature enough to realize there would be tough times. Yet, I honestly felt that because I was successful (in my own mind), trials would be few and momentary. Most couples get married with similar perspectives. This perspective is especially common among young people. It is therefore no surprise when counselors hear couple after couple say years later, "If I had known then what I know now, I would have never gotten married."

> TWO PEOPLE WITH SINFUL NATURES WHO COME TOGETHER MAKE FOR GREATER DESTRUCTION.

So, the fourth reason that marriages fail today is that couples do not anticipate or respond properly to the normal trials of life and marriage. After encountering various trials in our marriage during the early years, I reviewed what God had to say concerning trials, this time out of my own desperate need. My first reality shock occurred from reviewing I Peter 2:21: *"For you have been called for this purpose, since Christ also suffered for you, leaving you an example for you to follow in His steps."* The passage clearly states that God's will allows Christians to suffer trials with Christ as our model.

As Christians, we gladly accept the blessing of salvation through Christ's suffering. Yet, we quickly reject any thought of "joining" in His suffering. If it was necessary for Christ to suffer trials, why would we not expect to experience trials? Christ makes it clear that if we want to be like Him, we must be willing to suffer tough times as well. Obviously, God knows something about trials that people do not understand, but need to know. Christ's perspective is revealed in James 1. It is a difficult passage to read, but Scripture says that Christians should consider it a "joy" when they go through trials. "Joy" does not mean "happiness." It means a deep abiding peace, in spite of the circumstances.

Time and again, couples seek counseling to alleviate their marital frustrations, only to discover that they do not have a marriage problem. Instead they have a trial problem. But because of their failure to recognize the fact that they are going through a tough trial, they attribute the stress of that trial to their mate or their marriage. *Instead of hanging together, they begin blaming their mate for the tough time they are going through.* Most trials couples encounter are natural to life or marriage and are therefore, experienced by every couple. Yet, generation after generation of couples are caught off guard by these recurring trials that they could have mentally prepared for in advance. Although we're never fully prepared for trials, our recognition of God's purpose in trials can affect the outcome.

> COUPLES SEEK COUNSELING, ONLY TO DISCOVER THAT THEY DO NOT HAVE A MARRIAGE PROBLEM BUT A TRIAL PROBLEM.

I believe we have "streamlined" our contemporary gospel, leaving out the passages on pain, perseverance, and suffering. Therefore, our current crop of Christians cannot handle trials when they come. Theologically, we have glossed over the fact that in Christ there will be trials. A couple must know how to recognize suffering and how to give thanks in the midst of it, before they can succeed in marriage. Let me illustrate what I mean.

When we got married, Sally had been a Christian for a number of years and was a very effective counselor. Her work allowed her to counsel and minister to young women on several college campuses. A few years after marriage, we had our first child. Twelve months later our second child was born. Because Sally stayed at the same campus during these years, it was natural for the college women to help her with the children. Therefore, she was blessed by being able to continue her ministry pace. This thirty-year-old experienced few problems as a mother at home or in her career.

A couple of months after the second child was born, however, we moved to another city. With both children in diapers and demanding significant time and care, life totally changed. We were geographically isolated from our close friends because we had moved to an older established neighborhood where it was difficult to get to know people. I was gone almost every day, supervising my staff in a large five-city area. Sally was experiencing the first full blast of a twenty-four-hour day raising children, without the challenge of counseling with college girls, or getting much needed help from them.

Sally went through nine months of tremendous stress which unfortunately I didn't understand. Often when I came home she would be so upset and frustrated that we frequently had blow-ups. Because of the tension, we experienced very little "feeling" for each other during this period. What did we conclude during that time? *We tended to blame the pain of life on each other, and generalized that all of the frustration was because of our marriage!*

I began to feel that Sally didn't really love me anymore. She certainly wasn't very much fun to be with. Here I was, growing in the Christian life, having success in my job, and seemingly having marriage problems at the same time! Now, because I didn't understand normal trials, it was as if I was blind to her suffering. To make matters worse, I actually developed spiritual pride and would say such things as, "Sally, you've been acting like this for months! When are you going to snap out of it? What's the matter with you? You used to be such a stable Christian."

Sally was a godly woman, and my attitude was destroying what self image she had left! The confidence she had in her relationship with Christ began to fade away. After much prayer and perseverance, she came out of it, but tragically, with little help from me. How much easier it would have been if we had God's perspective on trials. We were simply experiencing what millions before us had experienced as well.

Now, we were not out of God's will in moving to another city, or in having two children so close together, or by having different tasks to do. In fact, God greatly deepened Sally's spiritual life during this time. But we missed some blessings together because we did not recognize we were going through a common trial, and as a result, we did not lift one another up. Unfortunately, we concluded that we were having marital problems.

Because of trials, many people come into my office thinking that their mate has faltered instead of realizing their mate's need to be supported. Raising children carries with it tremendous burdens, as does moving to a new location or changing jobs. These realities represent typical trials that all couples face.

Trials and suffering are a regular part of married life. Is this not confessed in our marriage vows themselves "for better or for worse, in sickness and in health?" Every couple must anticipate and prepare for these times. How a couple handles these periods of trials determine to a great extent how happy they will be. Having studied successful marriages for years, I have observed that trials actually enhance a marriage over the long haul. Yet in less successful marriages, trials become a source of struggle, bitterness, and division.

> FANTASY LOVE IS BASED ON "FEELINGS"... WHILE FEELINGS ARE VITAL, THEY ARE A TERRIBLE BASIS FOR A RELATIONSHIP.

Expect your husband to experience many severe ups and downs in his vocation. Expect your wife to experience burdens in the home and in raising the children. Support each other instead of criticizing and judging one another, thereby causing needless stress and hurt. (Later, Part III will deal specifically with some of the major trials in marriage).

REASON 5: A FANTASY VIEW OF LOVE

With a troubled tone, the man in my office stammered, "After sixteen years of marriage, how could she fall in love with another man? She hasn't spent more than ten hours alone with him, and I've already lost her!"

Minutes later his wife was speaking. "It's his fault," she said. "For two years he said he didn't care. I thought I would go crazy. Finally, in desperation, I turned to Jim and he was so understanding. Without meaning to, we fell in love almost immediately."

The fifth major cause of marriage failure today is what I have come to call "fantasy love." Fantasy love is based on "feelings" more than anything else. "If I cannot have you, I'll die!" It is the kind of love we read about or see in movies and on television. It represents an emotional experience that causes us to daydream and fantasize, one that sends chills up our spines.

Let me say that I believe God created emotions, and I feel they are an important part of human love. *However, while feelings are vital, they are a terrible basis for a relationship.* The tragedy of fantasy love is that it is primarily based on feelings.

Therefore, if a person doesn't feel anymore, he or she concludes that love has disappeared. It's gone! Like the couple I just mentioned, the majority of people today define love in terms of how they feel. There can be no weaker foundation for a relationship.

Love based almost entirely on feelings is hard to maintain in a culture based on comparison and performance. Many times I have heard a mate say, "I'm sorry, but I just don't love you anymore," or "She has lost her love for me." How tragic it is to think that millions of people actually base their marriage and family life on a feeling that can disappear in just a matter of days.

Some time ago a single woman came to ask my advice about a man with whom she was "terribly in love." I talked with her for about thirty minutes, and it was apparent she believed the relationship was really serious. After listening, I suggested that she continue to communicate on several points with her friend. Much to my surprise, she answered back with "Oh, I haven't actually talked to him yet." Can you believe it? She had created a complete love relationship in her mind, without ever talking to the man. She was deeply in love with a myth!

America is terribly confused about its definition of love. Not long ago, I read in the newspaper that soap operas have become such an important part of American women's lives that when television news stories preempt soap opera programs, the networks are deluged with complaints. The article went on to say that women are so caught up in these stories that when a marriage or death occurred on the screen, TV stations across the nation actually received flowers or condolence cards. "Computer love affairs" are certainly on the rise today. People fall in love over e-mail, having never even met. That is the ultimate example of fantasy love!

Instead of risking the disappointment of rejection by a real person, some people create fantasies to bring them emotional pleasure. The end result is often personal mysticism and deep depression. America is so focused on fantasy that it desperately wants to be "in love."

A type of fantasy love is found in the Old Testament in the story of David and Bathsheba. In the story, David had decided to stay home rather than fulfill his military duty. Shortly afterward, while strolling on the palace roof one day, he noticed a woman bathing. He found out who she was, and who her husband was. David then began having an affair with her while her husband was away at war. He then had her husband conveniently killed while in battle. His affair with Bathsheba transformed this man of God into a liar, an adulterer and even a murderer. It is not over-dramatic to say that affairs lead to lies and denials of all sorts and may even lead to murder. They can change an honorable person into one of dishonor.

We all marry with some kind of fantasy about what marriage will be like. We think we won't have the same problems as others, and then we are surprised when we do. We may think we have so much love for our spouse that it will never falter, only to find it does. We are always looking for the "greener grass," only to find that it doesn't exist. If we can't find it with our present spouse, maybe there's someone else out there. Someone once said, "If it looks greener on the other side of the fence, it's probably artificial turf!"

All fantasy love relationships, whether real or imagined, are simply counterfeit ways of trying to meet our needs. God's definition of love, on the other hand, provides the only real basis for permanent feelings. The Bible teaches that permanent feelings are only possible when couples learn to love by faith. Part II of this book describes that kind of love.

1. "Bringing up Father," *Time*, June 28, 1993, p. 55
2. "The Trouble With Premarital Sex," *U.S. News & World Report*, May 19, 1997, p.60

CHAPTER FOUR
THE PROGRESSION OF A DECLINING MARRIAGE

I AM CONSTANTLY faced with couples whose dreams are being destroyed by one or more of the five factors discussed in the previous chapter. Many times I have heard a husband or wife say, after I have explained their predicament, "If only I had known these things before we got married."

Yet a person may understand all the pitfalls and still become ensnared in a problem marriage. It is important to recognize the subtle process of decay that destroys millions of marriages. Things don't go to pieces overnight; dreams die *gradually and subtly*. As I have worked closely, both with couples and with individuals, over many years, I have observed a progression toward bitterness and isolation in marriage. This progression of decay seems to develop through four stages. While these stages are not absolute, they can be seen in almost all problem marriages.

1. Days of Romanticism
2. Days of Reality
3. Days of Resentment
4. Days of Rebellion

STAGE 1:
THE DAYS OF ROMANTICISM

Today, as never before in history, our society is being bombarded by media. Our five senses are tempted with the ultimate fantasy: experience the most tantalizing things in life without taking responsibility. Great emphasis is being placed on having all our needs met through "experiences and things."

Years of this programming have resulted in a society that is looking for the *experience* or the *romance*. The advertising industry seems to have one purpose: *to make us dissatisfied with what we have*. Further, the experiences portrayed by this media barrage are many times misleading or false. The pictures portrayed of marriage are often negative. Love is confused with sex. Fantasy sex is portrayed as quick and positive. Sex and love are greatly distorted from God's creation purpose. Our world view conflicts with God's view. No wonder we have no idea what it is all about. Only God can give us a clear picture of marriage and family from His Word.

So we see that people from different backgrounds and cultural programming are coming together through "experiences." They naively plan their lives and futures as if it were a theatrical production. The secular person (one who lives without thought of God), would violently disagree with these statements. The programming is so complete that romanticism has become reality. When most marriages begin, each mate's mind is filled with expectations that few can fulfill. Their "world view" has set them up for disappointment and hurt. Sometimes the crash is swift and painful.

STAGE 2:
THE DAYS OF REALITY

The second stage usually occurs in the first three to five years of marriage, although it is not unusual to see this stage begin in less than a year. Before the honeymoon is over, many myths about sex and romance are usually destroyed. But certainly before the first year is past, reality begins to hit.

The Progression of a Declining Marriage 55

Today, many young wives work. This is her typical schedule: She is up at six, getting dressed, cooking, and hurrying off to work. She gets home after six, fixes dinner, eats, and finishes the dishes by eight. Washing clothes or house details may keep her busy until ten. By that time she is already thinking about getting up early the next morning, and she has had no real time for herself. Her husband, who is oblivious to her work load and has been watching television, is now ready for her personal attention. Emotionally, she is unable to respond. And he wonders what is wrong with "her"!

> IT IS NOT LONG AFTER MARRIAGE THAT THE ROMANCE ENDS AND THE REALITIES BEGIN. THEIR ROMANCE GIVES WAY TO MEDIOCRITY.

Perhaps she is "waiting for the day she can have children" so she can stay home. But when that day comes she will discover even greater pressure and responsibility. After several years, instead of viewing marriage as a sexy honeymoon, she finds herself fighting for enough strength and personal time just to hold herself together.

Her husband, likewise, was idealistic when they got married. He thought his job was great. Before long, however, he became frustrated and unsure about his future. He can't change jobs because he is not sure he can afford to go back to a starting salary. His wife, on the other hand, has become frustrated because she feels trapped by their financial circumstances. He doesn't want to upset her even more.

In short, it is not long after marriage that the romance ends and the realities begin. Fantasy love gives way to job pressures and money problems. Children demand an even greater commitment. Their romance gives way to mediocrity.

During this sobering period, feelings begin to oscillate. Extended painful adjustments and depression appear, and each mate may experience periods of lost feelings. If not checked, these unromantic periods will get even longer. This can be catastrophic, because fantasy feelings were the primary basis for the decision to marry in the first place. Since their creative actions were initially also based on feelings, it won't be long before their sacrificial acts begin to wane. This loss will open the door to the next stage.

STAGE 3:
THE DAYS OF RESENTMENT

When feelings begin to change and creative, sacrificial actions begin to cease, marriage partners begin to deeply resent each other or blame their mates for the circumstances: "You're not meeting me halfway," or "You never talk to me anymore," or "We never have sex anymore."

As a counselor, I can always tell when one or both individuals reach the conscious point at which they feel they got "stuck" with their particular mate. The one who feels stuck resents the other's inadequacies, and can even resent God for "allowing this to happen." The other mate feels judged, rejected, misunderstood. Obviously, the rejected mate feels anger and resentment and the cycle continues.

When couples reach this point of deep resentment, they begin to lose all hope. If the couple does not find a solution, they usually begin to move in one of two directions. First, they may tragically move toward *divorce*. Frankly, there is very little social stigma in divorce today, so couples just give up and get out! Most secular counselors would agree that this direction is probably the more realistic of the two. Sadly, apart from God's intervention, they are probably right. But divorce is rarely the answer. All it brings on is more frustration, depression and financial hardship.

The second direction is the *compromised* marriage. A large segment of marriages today fit into this category. A compromised marriage is one in which people do not really deal with their mistakes, attitudes, weaknesses, or differences. Instead each goes his own way, and purposely stays away from the volatile areas of their marriage. On the surface, they appear to be all right, but inside they harbor deep resentment. Every few months the pressure may build until they explode in anger. Several days of frustration will end with this kind of statement: "Well, I wish things were different.

But I am not going to end the relationship because of what it would do to the children. So, I'll just put up with the problems." Try as they will, compromised couples cannot prosper over the long haul.

A compromised marriage often results in sexual dysfunction. The wife may have been so hurt that she just has no sexual appetite. The husband tries to ignore her passivity at first, but one night after a social event, he observes his wife undressing and his attraction cannot be restrained. Tired, and resentful of his lack of attention earlier in the evening, she refuses him. He explodes. She is angry and guilty at the same time. They go to sleep on opposite sides of the bed and awaken the next morning to "no comment."

> MANY SUPPOSEDLY "SUCCESSFUL" MARRIAGES ARE REALLY JUST TWO PEOPLE GOING THEIR OWN INDEPENDENT WAYS, BEING CAREFUL NOT TO STEP ON EACH OTHER'S TOES.

Another example is the wife who is raising the children with a husband who is never home or is uninvolved. The wife daily sees personality problems or discipline problems developing, and she cannot bear these burdens alone. She knows her husband resents her saying anything about it, so she tries to ignore the problems. One night her husband, who has not had a creative day with their son in weeks, gets angry at the kids and yells at their son or spanks him. Unable to stand it, she explodes, and the gap in their relationship widens.

Many supposedly "successful" marriages are really just two people going their own independent ways, being careful not to step on each other's toes. The husband overemphasizes his job to compensate for lost intimacy. The wife overemphasizes her relationship with the children to compensate for the lack of relationship within the marriage.

One never knows about such relationships until the partners reach their late forties or fifties and the children leave home. The true measure of their relationship comes when all they have is each other.

Ultimately, most compromised relationships lead to deeper and deeper resentment. If not checked, resentment can destroy one's life.

STAGE 4:
THE DAYS OF REBELLION

Every counselor hurts for men and women who have been caught in this spiral of resentment for years. Resentment damages lives in so many ways. Women can become fearful; men can become hardened and uncaring.

Think for a minute: a wife enters marriage with romantic feelings. She views her mate with trust and sees mostly perfection in him. She dreams of a model home and children. Her body is young and her self image is at its peak.

Several years pass and she finds herself in an absurdly contrasted state. Her feelings for him have long since waned. She not only lacks trust in her husband, but she now finds herself extremely critical of him. The struggle and disappointment of these few years added to the pain of bearing children have taken a toll on her youthfulness and her physical appearance. Her days too often seem burdensome, long, and introspective. She is constantly rethinking her situation. Her lost feelings for her husband and her bitter struggle have caused her to fear her future.

Here is a woman at thirty with two children, ages seven and four. She knows the tremendous personal responsibility they demand, and it occurs to her that the responsibility will not end for at least fifteen more years. By then she will be forty-five and her youthful years will be long gone. All that will be left is a husband for whom she has lost her enthusiasm.

These realities result in the woman becoming subconsciously *fearful* and *uncertain* of herself. Wives come to me saying, "I'm just not as sharp as I used to be." "Life isn't much fun anymore." "I don't enjoy people like I used to." All of these things are a direct result of her lost hope for the future.

Men, on the other hand, handle these painful realities differently. Rather than becoming fearful, they tend to *harden* and become callous toward others. They become more *insensitive* and *self-centered* in their relationships. Here is a guy who, at one time, would have literally died for his wife. But as his wife becomes more aware of his weaknesses, *she becomes more critical*. Every failure or uncertainty is closely observed and communicated. After a while, he is covered with guilt and feelings of failure. Because she continually observes his weaknesses more than his strengths, *he retreats*. His respect for her is replaced by disgust and avoidance.

Some years ago, this was vividly illustrated by a man who came to see me. He and his wife had been married for nearly twenty years. As I listened to their history, I was amazed at how romantic the initial years of the marriage were. The wife,

> RELATIONSHIPS ARE WHAT LIFE IS ALL ABOUT.

though, had an opinionated personality and after several years of marriage she began to voice her critical observations of her husband. Over the next ten years, she had dominated him with her thoughts and opinions. They had separated but were coming for counseling to see if the marriage could be repaired.

Not long after our first few appointments, she called me from the hospital and told me she was going to need emergency surgery for what looked like cancer. She was terribly frightened, and asked if I would call her estranged husband and see if he would visit her.

When I called him, he was preparing to go deep-sea fishing. After I told him the purpose of my call, he said, "That woman has been controlling my life for twenty years. I don't care if she dies and goes to hell, she isn't going to ruin my fishing trip!" And he hung up. Here was a man who had worshipped his wife early in marriage and now was so hardened against her, that he broke her heart and spirit at a time when she most needed him.

But remember, this deterioration did not happen overnight. These patterns of fearfulness and hardening, if not corrected, continue until both begin to feel that the *best of life was missed because of their mate*. The cancer of bitterness becomes overwhelming.

Before long this rebellion affects other relationships. Soon each begins to criticize, not only each other, but may doubt and criticize their children or their boss or their friends. It is shocking how few old people really have "bitterness-free" relationships with anyone, including their families.

The culture Americans are born into breeds the destruction of relationships. Even though people mean well, apart from God's pattern, they will certainly find themselves alone and wondering where it all went wrong.

A man in his seventies came into my office one day in total frustration. He told me he had not been able to live with his wife successfully since his retirement a few years before. They had been married for fifty years! Both of them were extremely attractive and alert. In fact, this man was so sharp and set in his ways that I couldn't tell him anything.

He had traveled to another part of the world and had observed a culture where women were subservient. He had tried to similarly demand submission from his wife. The result was separation.

In our first few sessions, I tried to talk with him about what true submission was. He was headstrong, and I could not break through. He said to me, in effect, "Here I am, a millionaire, a man twice your age. How do you think you can tell me anything?"

The next time I met with him I said, "You and I are not getting anywhere. Let me ask you a question. How long do you think you have to live?"

He thought for a moment and answered, "Well, probably five or ten years."

"Mr. Beck, I know you have a lot more experience at living than I, but let me ask you another question. If you died tomorrow morning, who would miss you by, say, noontime?"

I could see an immediate change in his tough exterior. I continued, "I don't mean miss you at the funeral, because I know you have done some good things in your life. But I mean who is going to have a vacuum in their life in the middle of the day because you're gone?"

Tears filled his eyes and he said, "I see what you mean. Here I am with all of my experience and wealth, but I don't have a relationship with anyone in the world."

How tragic—a man with every human success but no relationships. I cannot tell that story without being frightened that this could even happen to me! *Relationships are what life is all about.*

THE ULTIMATE COMMITMENT

A man said to me, "Don, is it necessary for you to mention God when discussing my marriage problems?" We had just spent several hours interacting on the destructive process just addressed.

I answered his question with a question of my own. "Mike, as we have talked about you and Judy, your struggles, conflicts, and rejection of each other, you said you could not seem to control your actions. Why?"

He replied, "I don't know."

I said. "Two people who are egocentric and self-centered will naturally struggle. Therefore, when their feelings fade, they have no natural basis upon which to build a relationship. Frankly, only Jesus Christ can provide a lasting basis for a relationship. Mike, your struggle is not with Jesus Christ, but perhaps with a caricature of Christ that men have presented. Don't reject Christ's love and power because of some hypocrisy you might have seen in others. God keeps on loving us even when we reject Him! Christ died for your sins to provide you with an ability to have a lasting relationship with Him. If you and Judy establish a relationship with Him, He will also provide you with a basis for marital oneness. Lasting relationships occur best when couples become 'one' in Christ. If you turn to Christ in humility, He will allow you to become a child of God."

And so it is for all of us. Receiving Christ requires each of us to put away our self-centeredness and come under His reign. If you have never done so, let me encourage you to commit your life to Him. Agree with Him concerning your self-centeredness. In the quietness of your own heart say something like, "Lord Jesus, I need you. Would you come into my heart and life right now and forgive my sin. Thank you for dying on the cross for me. Teach me how to live the Christian life. Help me to become a godly husband/wife. Thank you for coming into my life. In Jesus name, Amen."

If you prayed that prayer, you are now a child of God. Jesus has come to live in your life for all time and eternity. God says: *"And the witness is this, that God has given us eternal life, and this life is in His Son. He who has the Son has the life; he who does not have the Son of God does not have the life"* (1 John 5:11-12).

Submitting to Christ's love will allow you to have dominion over your self-centeredness and sin. You and your mate can now find oneness in marriage and a new beginning in life through Christ.

SUMMARY

In this first part of the book, we have attempted to demonstrate that good intentions are not sufficient to insure a successful marriage. Good intentions quickly give way to self-centered natures. Initially, couples struggle over differences. As feelings subside, they turn to a faulty 50-50 plan of responsibilities. Unsure that their mate is doing their part, they begin to watch the performance of the other. A short list of observed failures begins to grow. Soon, they begin to think they got "stuck" with a loser. Their self-centered conclusion certainly offends their mate. New shocks occur because of critical attitudes. Finally, they accept the fact that they have a problem.

> TO *DESIRE* TO LOVE IS NATURAL. TO *REALLY* LOVE IS SUPERNATURAL.

When couples are experiencing the process just covered, they normally are also having to deal with a constant barrage of trials. Instead of standing together to face these trials, the trials become just another issue to point out failure in their mate. Finally, frustration reigns, and all feelings are lost. Now they cannot even remember why they got married in the first place. Fantasy love is no more, and they begin to think, "There's someone else out there who can better meet my needs."

In a matter of a few years, couples can move from awesome feelings to shocking reality. As realities hit, feelings fade, and they begin to struggle to find a compromised position. They soon observe that compromise does not really deal with their problem. Finally, resentment prevails. Bitterness has replaced good intentions. Case tragically closed!

To *desire* to love is natural. To *really* love is supernatural. If God designed marriage . . . can He make it work? Parts II and III of this book will demonstrate that *God can and does make marriage work!*

PART II

CHAPTER FIVE

ONENESS: GOD'S PLAN, MAN'S HOPE

A PERSON RECENTLY SAID to me, "Why should I become a Christian? It sure didn't stop Bill and Joyce from getting a divorce." Has God stopped working, or have we Christians stopped listening to God? In three decades of counseling, one thing has been made clear to me: *There is usually very little difference between Christian marriages and non-Christian marriages.*

Here's what I mean by that. As Christians, we tend to have higher moral and spiritual standards for our prospective partners. But once those criteria are met, we tend to go right back to the same system for marriage that the world uses.

Recently, I met a young man who said he would not date anyone who did not adhere to the following criteria: she had to be a Christian, regularly involved in a church, learning the Scriptures through Bible study, and also regularly demonstrating a personal ministry. Very commendable, I thought. Yet, these important issues can lead to a false sense of security if one is not careful. Why? If these important criteria are not followed with clear understanding of God's plan for marital success, that couple may still end up similar to most American marriages.

Obviously, selecting a mate with a proven track record of spiritual faithfulness is a vital first step. But the second step is to realize

God has given us some very specific guidelines that must be applied daily before couples can experience a blessing in marriage. In other words, a successful marriage is not guaranteed by a good beginning; it must be lived out by *two people who daily apply God's Word to their marriage.* Marital oneness requires two people who individually possess a supernatural mindset from God. As these two people obey the Lord and His Word, their faith will be rewarded with blessing and oneness.

Marital oneness requires first *knowing* something, then *acting* on what one knows, and then *persevering* through faith. Part II of this book tells us what God wants us to *know* concerning marriage as well as how to live it out. Part III tells us how to *apply* what we know to the various practical areas of marriage.

WHY GOD MADE US

Why did God make man in the first place? Why is God's creation of man and woman important to your marriage? If God created humanity and marriage, it certainly makes sense to consult God's instructions concerning how to make marriage work. God's purpose for man and for marriage is stated in the first two chapters of the Bible, Genesis 1 and 2.

First, it is important to realize that these two chapters (along with Revelation 21 and 22) are different from every other chapter in Scripture. These two chapters refer to a time when sin and self-centeredness did not exist. Both Adam and Eve were perfect, without sin, when God spoke these first words. Therefore, we can conclude that God's purpose for man as stated in Genesis 1 and 2 was His perfect intent for man and marriage.

Second, according to Scripture (see Isaiah 14:12-17 and Ezekiel 28:2-5; 12-19), God's authority had been challenged by a fallen angel named Lucifer (or Satan), who planned to make himself "like" God. In other words, Lucifer, in those verses, states that he does not need God to experience life. He set himself up as God and became independent from God. This reality is important because we will see that part of God's purpose in creating mankind and marriage was to demonstrate that only *dependence on God* can bring fulfillment and success in life.

Third, realize that marriage was God's first social institution. It came long before Israel or the church. Adam and Eve were blessed with the responsibility to carry out one of God's great purposes.

Years ago, as a new Christian, I remember being amazed that Christ placed so much responsibility on His twelve disciples. Now I realize that the commissioning of the twelve was not the first time that God placed so much importance on a few people. Adam and Eve were given an awesome responsibility. If you are married, then you too are blessed with that same awesome responsibility before God.

In summary, each of us must realize that God's creation of the earth, and Adam and Eve, were not just an "afterthought" of God. God introduces marriage as His first divine institution. He created marriage as the basic foundation of all social structure on the earth. Adam and Eve, and every couple who would follow, have a tremendous stake in God's plan of the ages.

In Genesis 3, when sin entered the heart of man, it became even more vital for couples to become one together in their dependence on God. John Barnhouse best summarizes the drama that was unfolding in his book, *The Invisible War*: "We shall give this rebellion a thorough trial. We shall permit it to run full course. The universe shall see what a creature, even the greatest, can do apart from God. We shall set up an experiment, and permit the universe of creatures to watch it, during this brief interlude between eternity past and eternity future, called time. In it, the spirit of independence shall be allowed to expand to the utmost. And the wreck and ruin which shall result will demonstrate to the universe, and forever, that there is *no life, no joy, no peace* apart from a complete dependence upon the MOST HIGH GOD, possessor of heaven and earth."[1]

Adam and Eve's dependence on God, as opposed to Satan's independence, was vital! As we consider God's plan, we must recognize the important part our marriages play in that plan. Let's see what our responsibility is.

GOD'S THREE PURPOSES

With this background, let's look specifically at why God created man. Genesis chapter 1 describes all of creation. Verses 1-25 describe the creation of the heavens, the earth, vegetation, and animals. Our focus will be on verses 26-31, which describe the creation of mankind.

From these few verses, God introduces three distinct purposes for mankind and marriage. These purposes are implied by the language God uses while describing His creation of humankind.

Reflect His Image.

The first purpose for mankind in marriage is to reflect the image of God as a couple.

> *Then God said, "Let Us make man in **Our image**, according to **Our likeness**; and let them rule over the fish of the sea and over the birds of the sky and over all the earth, and over every creeping thing that creeps on the earth." And God created man in His own **image**, in the **image** of God He created him; **male and female** He created them* (Gen.1:26-27).

Three times God uses the word "image" and once "likeness." It is apparent that God wants us to realize that it was important to Him that mankind reflect His image.

In Matthew 5, believers are exhorted to be the "salt" and "light" of the earth. The concept of reflecting God's light to a lost world is a familiar thought in Scripture. That same thought is initiated in Genesis 1 as the first purpose for humanity. What a privilege it should be for us to be a reflection of God. From the plural pronouns "us" and "our" used in verse 26, it is clear that God intended mankind to reflect the wholeness of the Trinity, the Father, Son, and Holy Spirit. Each part of the Trinity is different in person and function, but one in nature and purpose.

A very important delineation is made in verse 27. God mentions that "He created him; *male and female* He created them." Even though God made Adam and Eve to individually reflect His image, it is also true that together, in a profound and mysterious way, they would be able to reflect the *unity* or the *oneness* of God (see John 17:20-21; Eph. 5:31-32). (So what about singles? Singles can reflect the image of God as men and women join in oneness in the "church" or the "body of Christ." Since this book is about marriage, we will not deal with singles. Yet, they, along with married couples, are to reflect the image of God in His church.)

God made you and me to reflect His image. In marriage, that is accomplished by husbands and wives *becoming one*. God created Adam and Eve as the parents of humanity and designed them to model this reflection to all who would follow.

When couples display oneness, God is truly glorified. On the other hand, when husbands or wives do not become one, their marriage misses its greatest opportunity. Nothing could be more tragic than to be married and fail to reflect the unity of God's image. Yet, most couples are not even aware of God's desire for them to do so. Equally tragic is society's reflection of maleness and femaleness. The distinction of the sexes is under attack today. Men and women desire to be like the other. Dress and roles have become blurred between the two. Each sex is in an identity crisis. The full expression of each sex has suffered. In a very real sense, so has the reflection of God's image. Did God make a mistake? Certainly not! Each sex is vital. God is pleased when one fully man and another fully woman come together in oneness to show forth His likeness and unity.

Men and women, God is instructing you from this passage that *oneness* in your marriage is *not optional*. If you hope to please God, then you must reflect His image. His reflection requires both male and female. If God has called you to marriage, as opposed to being single, then you and your mate must understand and experience God's eternal purpose.

Today many people seem to be uncertain about all of this, either trying to decide whether to marry or, if married, whether to divorce. Most are not aware of God's stake in their marriage. Since the day that I first understood God's purpose for Sally and me to reflect His image, *divorce* has not been an option. I would be incomplete without my wife. To lose her would literally limit our ability to fully reflect God's image. Since I have understood the significance of reflection, Sally's importance to me has multiplied many fold. *Oneness is not an option if we want to reflect the image of God as a couple.*

Reproduce After Our Kind.
The second purpose for mankind and marriage is revealed in the first half of verse 28: *"God blessed them (Adam and Eve); and God said to them, 'Be fruitful and multiply, and fill the earth.'*

No question here. God intended for marriage to produce children. It is important to note that God considered children to be a blessing of the highest order. This word "blessing" refutes any notion that God created marital sex in a negative light. He blessed Adam's family, and He blessed their sexual union in marriage.

> ONENESS IS NOT AN OPTION IF WE WANT TO REFLECT THE IMAGE OF GOD AS A COUPLE.

At first glance, since we have six billion people on planet Earth, it seems that this is the one purpose of God that man has completed. Yet, when one adds to this verse the rest of God's instructions concerning children from Scripture, numbers do not tell the whole story.

This purpose could be better stated, *"Reproduce a godly heritage which will also reflect God's image."* First, God told Adam and Eve to reflect His image. Next, God told them to increase that reflection through godly offspring. Adam and Eve together were to produce one small light on this huge earth. Through reproducing godly children (who love, honor and obey God), God desired that today Adam and Eve's reflection would be increased to six billion "lights." Each light would reflect that only a dependence on God would bring real life. *Coming together in oneness is not an option if we desire to raise godly children.*

A second category of reproduction is in the area of discipleship. God wants us to also reproduce people in the body of Christ. Each time a person becomes a Christian, he enters into God's eternal family. In the same way we nurture children in the home, we are to nurture and train disciples to further God's kingdom on earth. Jesus said in Matthew 28:19-20, *"Go therefore and **make disciples** of all the nations, baptizing them in the name of the Father, and the Son and the Holy Spirit, **teaching** them to observe all that I commanded you; and lo, I am with you always, even to the end of the age."*

Reign Over The Creation.

God's third purpose for mankind is stated in the second half of verse 28, "subdue it (the earth) and rule over (it)." God intended Adam and Eve to rule or have dominion over the earth. To fully understand what He meant by "rule" requires a study of the rest of Scripture. From Genesis to Revelation, God describes what He means by ruling. God wants married couples to take charge of everything that He gives them dominion over, such as, property, each mate's spiritual gifts, their children, their financial assets and income, their social and political influences, etc. They are to use those things as God's Spirit directs to bring honor to God.

> IN THE SAME WAY WE NURTURE CHILDREN IN THE HOME, WE ARE TO NURTURE AND TRAIN DISCIPLES TO FURTHER GOD'S KINGDOM ON EARTH.

Another brief, but vital thought, concerns what was included in His reference to the Earth. Certainly, God intended Adam and Eve to control and take care of the physical Earth. The Bible says, *"the earth is the Lord's and all it contains."* We have been given a "caretaker's" job over it. But, Scripture also points out that in addition to the physical earth, God wants couples to also rule in the spiritual realm. All through the Old and New Testaments, the Holy Spirit exhorts believers to *"be strong and courageous"* (Joshua 1:6, 7, 9), *"put on the full armor of God,"* and *"stand firm against the schemes of the devil"* (Ephesians 6:10-20). God's command to Adam and Eve to rule included not only the physical earth, but the spiritual realm as well. *Oneness is not an option if we want to reign on planet Earth and bring glory to God.*

LET'S REVIEW GOD'S PURPOSES.

He intended that every couple from Adam and Eve on would: (1)*Reflect God's image*; (2) *Reproduce a godly heritage*; and (3) *Reign over the earth*, both physically and spiritually.

How many couples do you know who are reflecting the image of God together? How many are raising children who are reflecting the image of God? How many are reigning together in spite of the spiritual warfare going on all about us?

Every Christian married couple should be challenged by the thought of developing their marriage in accordance with God's design and purpose.

APPLYING GOD'S PURPOSES

In summary, we see that God established a plan that was dependent on male and female joining together in oneness to reflect God's image, reproduce a godly heritage, and reign over the earth. Their faith would demonstrate to all creation that only a dependence on God would produce a fulfilling life here, and eternal life in the future.

In marriage, it is utterly impossible to accomplish these goals unless each mate has a personal relationship with the Creator, made known through acceptance of Jesus Christ as Savior. Secondly, each mate must become one with the other. Every day couples get married thinking they can reach their goals without God. The results are evident. No one can effectively reflect, reproduce, or reign apart from being one with God and one with their mate.

Stop and think for a moment. Can you really succeed in the following without being one with your mate? Can you really *reflect* God's image if you are not one in your marriage? Can non-Christians really be attracted to God through your example if you are divided as a couple? Absolutely not!

Or, do you really think you can *reproduce* healthy and successful children without being one with your mate? When questioned, children list as most important to them, the fact that mom and dad love each other. When divided moms and dads attempt discipline, without realizing it, they establish opposite poles in their child. Later, they seek counsel to find the reason why their child always seems to take the opposite position from themselves. Couples are shocked to find that their lack of oneness has "modeled" division. Apart from oneness, child rearing can be like grasping the wind.

Do you think you can really successfully *rule* the earth with conflict in your marriage? Can you handle the tremendous pressures of life without another to lean on? Maybe you can handle momentary pressure, but a lifetime of handling pressure alone takes its toll. People who venture through life without oneness in their marriage can be distorted by the pressure. Yes, they have great plans, but those plans are frustrated because of their division.

When Sally and I married, we had not discovered God's purpose for marriage. Therefore, the Holy Spirit could not call upon these Scriptures to convict us of our division. We suffered terribly at times because of it. God's image, as reflected by us, suffered as well.

Since discovering these principles many years ago, the Holy Spirit can now instantly remind us when we falter in our oneness. We realize we cannot reflect, reproduce, or reign without it. I literally shudder at the thought of not being one with Sally.

What I fear most, though, is the thought of displeasing the heart of God: the God who created me and sent Christ to die for me; the God who loves me to the end, in spite of how undeserving I am. If I am not one with Sally, I am blocking His plan and missing the opportunity to reflect Him to others.

God is unchanging: *"Jesus Christ is the same yesterday, today, yes, and forever"* (Hebrews 13:8). Therefore, His plan for marriage is unaltered. God has not changed His plan of marital oneness since He first created mankind. We are either going to believe it, or we are not. We are either going to follow His plan and experience life, or we are not. *Oneness in marriage is not an option.* It is as simple as that.

---

1. John Barnhouse, *The Invisible War*, Zondervan, p. 51.

CHAPTER SIX

HOW ONENESS HAPPENS

AS WE SAW in Genesis 1:26-28, God refers to male and female as "them": *"let them rule"* or *"God blessed them."* Clearly, God viewed them as "one" in reflecting the unity of God. In fact, their ability to reflect, reproduce, and reign was dependent on their oneness. If oneness is presuppositional to marital success, then how do we accomplish it?

To answer that question, God does something unusual in the second chapter of Genesis. He elaborates on the creation of man, except this time, He illustrates with a specific couple, Adam and Eve. Even though we know to whom God was referring in the first chapter account, Adam and Eve were not mentioned by name. In chapter one, God used generic terms that refer to mankind as a species.

In chapter two, God refers specifically to the world's first two people. Adam and Eve formed the first marriage. God demonstrated through Adam and Eve, and to every couple who would follow, how He intended two people to *become one*. Apart from coming to know Jesus Christ as Savior, this passage has had more impact on my life and marriage than any other single passage of Scripture. If you do not catch this, you will miss much of God's blessing in life. If you are not "one" with the most important person in your life, all else pales. Chapter two of Genesis is the *Magna Carta of Marriage*: it is God's blueprint for how marriage is to work. We are now going to read the directions on marriage as written by the Creator of marriage.

A significant point of Genesis 1 is that married people can best fulfill God's creation purposes (reflect, reproduce, reign) by being one with their mate. Genesis 2 describes oneness and tells us *how* to experience it.

In Genesis 2:15-17 God was talking to Adam, giving him instructions concerning the trees of the garden. Then in verse 18, God "steps back" and makes a very profound statement. I believe that in this verse, God established a *principle* for Adam and Eve, and for every couple who would follow. Our focus in this chapter will be on verses 18-25. As you read the following section, notice that there are *four* very important parts to this principle.

GOD CREATED A NEED

Then the Lord God said, "It is not good for the man to be alone; I will make him a helper suitable for him" (Genesis 2:18).

At the time of creation, Adam was different from you and me. How? First, *Adam had no sin*. He was created perfect! Second, his physical *environment was perfect*. Third, and most importantly, Adam had the most *perfect relationship* possible *with* the living *God*. Adam could actually experience God with two of his five senses. He could see the *Shekinah glory of God*, as Moses would later see, and he could actually *hear* God speak. Scripture says he walked and talked with God.

God stated in verse 18 that it was not good for Adam to be alone. Now put yourself in Adam's place for a moment. You are perfect, with a perfect environment and a perfect and satisfying relationship with the very One who created you. When God said that he was alone, Adam probably didn't have a clue what God was talking about. What did "alone" mean? Didn't he have God? And the whole earth? Wasn't that enough?

All my life I have heard a subtle teaching throughout evangelical Christendom. "Me plus God is all I need." I can remember making that statement shortly after Sally and I were married when a student asked what I would do if something happened to Sally. I said something to the effect that it would be hard, but I would go on, because, after all, "all I need is God." God nullified that concept forever in Genesis 2:18!

Every step was according to His perfect plan and timetable. Adam did not give God the thought of being alone; God gave it to Adam! It should be noted that this is the only time God used the words "not good" during His creation of the world. Everything He had created before Adam "was good." God emphasized very clearly that

> GOD CHOSE TO CREATE A NEED IN MAN FOR HUMAN RELATIONSHIPS, IN ADDITION TO HIMSELF.

man was not yet complete. He was *not* created to stand alone, then or now! God was saying, "Adam, in the way in which I have chosen to make you, I need a tool to meet your total needs." God *chose* to create a need in man for human relationships, in addition to Himself. Relationships are not an option.

This does not lessen our need for and dependence upon God in the least. All that God creates is designed to *increase* our dependence upon Him. God could have created Eve simultaneously with Adam. But to insure dependence upon Himself, God clearly showed Adam his need so he would trust God for the fulfillment of that need. Thereby Adam began a life of total trust in the perfect plan of the Most High.

The words, "suitable to," mean "to complete or to correspond to." In other words, God was saying that Adam was incomplete. In Genesis 1, God continually referred to humanity as "they" and "them": "Let Us make man in Our image... and let them..." It is clear that God saw Adam and Eve as *a single unit of two*. Well, after stating that Adam was alone, we would expect to see God create Eve. But instead, God gave Adam a project with a specific purpose in mind:

And out of the ground the Lord God formed every beast of the field and every bird of the sky, and brought them to the man to see what he would call them; and whatever the man called a living creature, that was its name. And the man gave names to all the cattle, and to the birds of the sky, and to every beast of the field, but for Adam there was not found a helper suitable for him (Genesis 2:19-20).

GOD SHOWED ADAM HIS NEED

What a shock! Instead of Eve, God brought all the animals to Adam. Why? The answer is stated in the last part of verse 20. *"...but for Adam there was not found a helper suitable for him."* God rarely gives man anything without first showing him his need. Adam had not yet understood what God meant by "aloneness," so he could not have fully appreciated Eve at this point. How did Adam discover his need through naming the animals?

> GOD RARELY GIVES MAN ANYTHING WITHOUT FIRST SHOWING HIM HIS NEED.

To begin with, animals don't talk! He named the first and went on to the next. Same response! Silence. Was he beginning to see a need? Animal after animal was named, presumably without any of them talking back in a language he understood. And he must have observed that even though there were two of every animal, they were made differently. They were paired off—animal families, if you will. Most importantly, Adam learned there was nobody suitable for (similar to, corresponding to) him. There was no one to talk to, no one to eat with, and no one to complete him as a companion. The point is, *one must see his need before he can appreciate the provision for that need.*

I remember when my son Todd was born. I was so excited, I bought him a football at birth. Todd didn't appreciate it! Why? *He had no need.*

Well, I'm a slow learner, so on Todd's fourth Christmas I decided it was time for him to ride a bicycle. I had always pictured

Todd on a bike. Christmas day found Todd excited, but it only lasted about two hours. In the months that followed, the bike sat unused in the garage. *He had no need* for a bike.

When he was six, we moved to Little Rock and Todd observed a neighbor boy with a very special bike—a black one, without training wheels, and with mud tires. Todd excitedly ran in exclaiming, "Daddy, I've got to have a bike like Brent's!" Even though I was a slow learner, I was beginning to catch on. "Todd," I said, "Daddy would love for you to have a bike like Brent's, but if you remember, you have not ridden the other one much, and bikes cost a lot of money."

So Todd rode his bike, without training wheels, for four months, all the while praying daily to the Lord for a big bike. Not one night passed in four months that Todd didn't pray for that bike! We were amazed at the fact that Todd didn't want to go to bed without praying. Before this, we had been encouraging him to pray, but he could never think of anything to say.

As we neared Christmas, we were short of money. Sally told Todd he would need to pray for our finances, even to make our house payment. Well, he prayed earnestly for money for our house *and the bike*. As parents, we learned a lot about prayer from the faith of a child.

About a week before Christmas, a large, unexpected check arrived. Todd was not at all surprised! He *expected* God to answer. On Christmas morning, under the tree, there was his big black and yellow bike with mud tires! How real God was becoming to him. His excitement did not stop in two hours or two months or even two years. Todd cleaned and polished that bike and put it in the garage every night. It was very special to him because it was *God's provision* for a need that he had.

Do you see your need for your mate? If Christ returned today and asked how He could help me in working with couples, I would ask Him for a project similar to the naming of the animals. It is so tragic when couples marry before God has prepared them. After experiencing only ten percent of what God intended for marriage, they think they have experienced all there is and want to throw it away. Couples are getting divorced today without ever realizing what they've missed. God showed Adam his need *before* giving Eve to him so that he could fully appreciate God's gift.

GOD CREATED THE PROVISION FOR ADAM'S NEED

God, having first created in Adam a need for a relationship, and then having shown him his need, now creates Eve to meet this need.

So the Lord God caused a deep sleep to fall upon the man, and he slept; then He took one of his ribs, and closed up the flesh at that place. And the Lord God fashioned into a woman the rib which He had taken from the man, and brought her to the man (Genesis 2:21-22).

God caused Adam to sleep while He created Eve—a picture of *God's part* meeting our needs, and *man's part*, resting in God's promises. Most of us are not resting in God, we are actively looking, inspecting the assembly line of "Eve's," hoping we get the perfect one!

I've heard it said that God chose a rib, as opposed to a piece of the foot or head, to signify the perfect picture of the relationship of a wife to her husband. She is under the protection of man's arm but protects the man's most vital part, his heart. She was not taken from his head to rule over him, nor from his feet to be beneath him, but is alongside to complete him, and he her. They are to be "joint heirs" in the grace of life, i.e. companions, lovers, friends, parents, etc.

The most strategic statement in the passage is one that at first seems odd. "God *brought* Eve to Adam." It seems God would have created Eve right next to Adam. Why did God bring her to Adam? God wanted Adam to know that just as it was He who had created her, it was also *He alone* who would *present* her to her husband. I believe God asks us today, "Will you trust Me to bring your mate to you?" God desires complete dependence on Him for all our needs!

ADAM RECEIVED GOD'S PROVISION

Adam responded with belief in verse 23: *"And the man said, 'This is now bone of my bones, and flesh of my flesh; she shall be called Woman, because she was taken out of Man.'"*

The English text does not fully communicate what the Hebrew words say. Adam was excited! A better translation would be, "Great! Fantastic! Thank you, Lord! I'll take her!" *Adam was 100 percent excited about her. Adam totally received Eve*!

Was it Adam's ability to inspect Eve that caused him to totally receive her? Certainly not! Don't misunderstand me. I am sure Eve was very attractive to Adam. But Adam had never seen a woman before; he had no one else to compare her with! What, then, was Adam's *basis* for receiving Eve? On what

> ADAM'S ACCEPTANCE OF EVE WAS BASED ON WHO GOD WAS TO HIM.

basis was he confident that she was "right" for him? When Adam fully received Eve, it was **based on who God was to him**, not Adam's ability to inspect Eve. *God* was the One who had created him. *God* created his need. *God* showed Adam his need. And *God* met his need with Eve. Because *Adam trusted God*, he received Eve by faith. He displayed great excitement because of *God's faithfulness*, not because of Eve's performance or lack of performance.

What is God saying? That He alone can meet your needs. He has created a need in you for relationships, which He meets primarily through a mate, but also through the church and friends. He put this need in you to teach you dependence upon Him and to equip you to reflect His image to an imperfect world. You can then reproduce a godly heritage and reign on the earth. He will meet your aloneness need through someone who is also alone and imperfect. (Beware of inspecting with your eyes, because Satan's strategy is to deceive you, as he did Adam and Eve in Genesis 3.)

We are at a key point in God's plan. God sought to protect man from Satan's sin of self-dependence by insuring that he would have to trust God to meet his "aloneness" needs. Therefore, *God requires that man receive his mate from Him.* God went out of His way to demonstrate the *pattern* of how He would work in history. Adam chose to believe God, which was demonstrated by his response in receiving Eve as a gift from God, totally perfect to meet his "aloneness" needs.

HOW TO VIEW WEAKNESSES

You are probably thinking at this point, "If God will not allow my mate's weaknesses to limit Him in meeting my aloneness needs, how then should I view his or her weaknesses?"

Years ago, when I first understood what God was saying, I was fearful of having to live with Sally's weaknesses, which, I thought, were a limitation to me and might never change. Viewing them *as no limitation* to God's ability to meet my needs seemed almost impossible. But, I realized that God would never let Sally limit *His* responsibility to meet the needs He created in me. I asked God to give me the faith to view her weaknesses as no limitation. I also realized that I needed to believe God and receive Sally as His personal provision, with all her strengths and weaknesses. I immediately began to experience a new freedom and hope in my marriage. I began to share this truth with others, and as the first faltering months passed, I realized how great our marriage had become. What had changed? Certainly, God had not changed. But, as my view of God grew deeper, my perception of my wife dramatically changed.

What began as a tough step of faith years ago has since become one of the most blessed realities in my life. Sally might as well be perfect, because God has graciously allowed me to be totally satisfied with her. These truths have released Sally and me to experience hope and enjoyment in our marriage. God is reinforcing our belief in them by continually showing us the many reasons He specifically created us for each other. The very things I would have changed in Sally in the beginning of marriage have turned out to be the very things I needed to complete me. Let me illustrate.

One of the things I observed about Sally early in marriage was that she wasn't very goal-oriented. Now, I have always had a five-year plan and a purpose to every plan. I used to say to her, "Don't you have any goals?" She would give me this puzzled look and say, "I don't know. I guess I need to think about that." But, every day she would wake up and whatever happened, happened! Well, one of my early goals was to prepare for retirement. At the time, the best way I thought I could do that was to buy and sell houses. So, during the time she had our four children in six years, I moved her into six different houses. She *never* complained. We would just pack up the boxes one more time and move.

Along about our sixth house, it dawned on me what I had done to her. The Holy Spirit immediately revealed to me that the very thing I would have changed about Sally in the early part of our marriage, was now turning out to be a blessing to me. The lights went on for me, and I began to thank God for who she was. My wife has made every move, and there have been more, fun for the whole family. The friends we have established in every city through her have been "life-long." I don't want to tamper with Sally or to change her in any way. She is God's gift to me. Each year I discover more reasons why God gave her to me. God is so gracious, if we will dare to believe Him.

This step of faith opened my eyes to five ways of viewing weaknesses in our mates:

1. Genesis 2 has assured us that God will meet our "aloneness" needs, regardless of our mate's weaknesses.
2. We must realize that God's only agent for changing our mate with promised results is agape (unconditional) love. (We will see more in Chapter 8.)
3. God actually uses our mate's weaknesses as a tool to perfect our character.
4. Our mate's weaknesses are an opportunity for us to be needed in their life.
5. Sometimes what we view as a weakness in our mate, at one point in our marriage, may turn out to be a blessing later.

Can you believe God for your mate now, or if you don't have a mate yet, can you believe Him for your future? If you don't have the faith to believe God for your mate, don't get married. If you are married and are inspecting instead of believing, then your mate is under performance. Ask God to forgive you, then receive your mate from God, and give thanks to Him for His provision for your needs!

> WHAT WE VIEW AS A WEAKNESS IN OUR MATE MAY TURN OUT TO BE A BLESSING.

We are to accept our mates from God and trust God to meet our needs, in spite of our mate's weaknesses. To reject your mate in any way after marriage is to doubt God and His ability to provide. It is failing to reflect, reproduce, and reign, and it calls into question God's motives. We must trust that God still creates Eves for Adams, and that He knew your needs when He created both you and your mate.

I believe as certainly as God gave Eve to Adam that God gave my wife to me, not because she is perfect, but *because God is*. Will you receive your mate from God right now?

FORMULA FOR MARITAL ONENESS

God concludes this passage by stating another principle for every married couple. This principle reveals the *formula* for marital oneness. For those who follow it, God promises blessing.

> *For this cause a man shall **leave** his father and his mother, and shall **cleave** to his wife; and they shall become **one flesh**. And the man and his wife were both naked and were not ashamed* (Genesis 2:24-25).

Leave

How do we know that God is now concluding with a *marital principle* after His example of Adam and Eve? The first hint comes from the statement, *"a man shall leave his father and mother."* Did Adam have a literal mother and father? Obviously, not. So we know that this is a principle for all couples who will follow. The word *"leave"* means to "abandon" or "break dependence upon." While no one should ever stop honoring their parents, if we want to be one in marriage we must stop depending on parents. In fact, this principle would include any prior dependence: being single, sports, job, finances, etc. These things can hinder oneness if you do not 100% leave your former state. It is not that these things cannot exist after marriage, but they should include one's mate.

Cleave
The second part of the principle is, *"and shall cleave to his wife."* The word *"cleave"* means, "to stick like glue." At the time Scripture was written, one usage of this word referred to metals, melting together to become a stronger alloy. Obviously, faith in God is required to cleave. Our part is to leave, God's part is to cleave us together. To the extent that both mates trust God for the outcome of their marriage, both will have the faith to "stick like glue."

Obviously, God intended this principle of leaving and cleaving to apply to all marriages, not just Adam and Eve. We know this principle was intended for future marriages by the fact that this passage becomes the *standard* for all marriages throughout the rest of Scripture. Christ Himself refers to this Genesis passage in Matthew 19:4-6.

> *Have you not read, that He who created them from the beginning made them male and female, and said, "For this cause a man shall leave his father and mother, and shall cleave to his wife; and the two shall become one flesh? Consequently they are no longer two, but **one flesh**. What **God** has joined together, let no man separate."*

Clearly, God has established this principle as the basis of marriage. *For the cause that God created mankind with a need for relationships, a man must 100% leave his former state and then 100% cleave to his mate. I have found in counseling that* every marriage problem stems from either a failure to leave or a failure to cleave. *The only way we* can 100% commit is to trust God with the outcome. Before marital oneness can occur, both mates must exhibit faith. This certainly eliminates the concept of the fifty-fifty relationship.

One Flesh
In verse 25, God reveals a wonderful *result* and blessing of oneness: *"and they shall become one flesh."* Loving one's mate by faith, instead of putting them under performance, releases amazing blessing and transparency. God says, "And the man and his wife were both naked and were not ashamed." The word "naked" implies being totally exposed without threat: physically, emotionally, spiritually, and intellectually. Total openness, transparency, with no walls or masks. Oneness (one flesh) is the result of marital faith.

> EVERY MARRIAGE PROBLEM STEMS FROM EITHER A FAILURE TO LEAVE OR A FAILURE TO CLEAVE.

With the advent of sin, natural oneness was destroyed. Today, couples can find marital oneness only through faith in God, and then in understanding His principles of marriage. Each of us desire to be loved unconditionally. However, that will not happen on this earth unless someone chooses to love you by faith.

If you were formerly divorced, or not a Christian when you married, or just cannot be sure your spouse is your Eve or Adam, the principle of oneness still works for you. Scripture tells us that God hates divorce (see Malachi 2:16), and He desires for you to stay married. Therefore, the principle of leaving and cleaving and becoming *"one flesh"* is still God's desire for your marriage. If you leave and cleave by faith, God indicates oneness will result!

We also know from Scripture that God forgives past failures when they are confessed to Him. He gives us a new beginning and tells us not to look back. No matter what our past was, God's plan for marriage works today. Do not let Satan confuse you or rob you of a wonderfully satisfying marriage. Become one and move ahead to reflect, reproduce and reign. God is honored each time a couple commits to His plan for marriage.

The couple who believes that God brought them together, and that He will meet their needs, in spite of their mate's weaknesses, will experience oneness. We must choose to follow Adam's example. The question is: Will you?

CHAPTER SEVEN

POWER IN ONENESS

APART FROM the decision to receive Jesus Christ as Savior, I know of no other more practical issue than understanding the role of the Holy Spirit in marriage. Many Christians know nothing about the Holy Spirit: who He is, what He does, or how to release His power in their lives. It is estimated that up to 95% of believers do not understand the ministry and power of the Holy Spirit, and there is much confusion today concerning His work in our lives.

Why should you be motivated about the Holy Spirit in your marriage? Is it really all that important for your mate to understand and respond to the Holy Spirit? If you are unsure of your answers to these questions, your chance for long-term blessing in marriage is limited. Why? Because only God can give you the power to overcome your self-centeredness, and therefore, allow you to humbly love your mate by faith. Power to live the Christian life comes from the Holy Spirit. *"That He would grant you, according to the riches of His glory, to be strengthened with power through His Spirit in the inner man"* (Ephesians 3:16). Nothing is more important to your marital peace than releasing God's power in your relationship. To be uninformed concerning the Holy Spirit, from a Christian perspective, is equivalent to choosing to fail. The first question you must answer is "Who is the Holy Spirit?"

WHO IS THE HOLY SPIRIT?

Above all, the Holy Spirit is God. He is part of the Trinity: the Father, the Son, and the Holy Spirit. The Scripture itself refers to the Holy Spirit as God (2 Corinthians 3:17-18). He possesses divine attributes: He is eternal, all knowing, all powerful, and is present everywhere (1 Corinthians 2:10-11; Genesis 1:2; Psalm 139:7-8). Yet the Holy Spirit is distinct from the Father and the Son. Scripture reveals that the only unpardonable sin occurs against the Holy Spirit: to reject His convictions concerning the work of Christ at the cross. Clearly, the Holy Spirit is God.

> NOTHING IS MORE IMPORTANT TO YOUR MARITAL PEACE THAN RELEASING THE HOLY SPIRIT'S POWER IN YOUR RELATIONSHIP.

In addition to His divine attributes, the Scripture tells us that the Holy Spirit possesses a personality, which includes emotions. Scripture actually portrays a vital relationship between the Holy Spirit and mankind, you and I. It is a relationship in which we can obey or disobey Him (Acts 5:3). We are warned, *"And do not grieve the Holy Spirit of God, by whom you were sealed for the day of redemption"* (Eph. 4:30), and *"Do not quench the Spirit"* (1Thess. 5:19). The Holy Spirit is One who desires an intimate relationship with each of us.

Paul, at the end of his second letter to the Corinthian church, signed off this way, *"The grace of the Lord Jesus Christ, and the love of God, and the fellowship of the Holy Spirit, be with you all"* (2 Cor. 13:14). The Holy Spirit wants to be involved in your marriage. Are you having fellowship with the Holy Spirit? Do you know for sure what that means? Why is fellowship important? This brings us to our next question.

WHAT DOES THE HOLY SPIRIT DO?

Probably one of the most significant indications of the Holy Spirit's importance in our lives and marriages is the way Christ valued the Spirit's role in God's plan. In His final discourse (John 14-16), Christ repeatedly draws attention to the Holy Spirit's vital role in living the Christian life after His departure.

> *If you love Me, you will keep my commandments. And I will ask the Father, and He will give you another Helper, that He may be with you forever; that is the **Spirit of truth**, whom the world cannot receive, because it does not behold Him or know Him, but you know Him because He abides with you, **and will be in you**. I will not leave you as orphans; I will come to you* (John 14:15-18).

> *But I tell you the truth, it is to your advantage that I go away; for if I do not go away, the **Helper** shall not come to you; but if I go, I will send Him to you… But when He, the Spirit of **truth** comes, He will **guide** you into all the truth; for He will not speak on His own initiative, but whatever he hears, he will speak; and He will disclose to you **what is to come**. He shall **glorify Me**; for he shall take of Mine, and shall disclose it to you* (John 16:7, 13-14).

These statements were made at a key transition point in God's eternal plan. Christ is preparing to momentarily finish His role as Savior. In these passages, He is obviously going out of His way to point out that, after His death, the Holy Spirit would be God's provision for mankind.

Helper

Two points stand out. First, Christ mentions that, *"The Father will give you another Helper, that He may be with you forever."* Some translations use the word "Comforter." The word means to "come alongside and strengthen." Christ was signifying that the Holy Spirit would fill His own place, doing for the disciples what He had done for them while He was on earth.

The second point is mentioned by Christ in John 16:7: *"But I tell you the truth, it is to your advantage that I go away; for if I do not go away, the Helper shall not come to you; but if I go, I will send Him to you."* Christ says that He must leave before the vital role of the Holy Spirit can begin. The coming of the Holy Spirit was second in importance only to Christ's completion of His glorious work at Calvary. Therefore, just as believers honor the work of Christ, they should also honor the work of the Holy Spirit. Because the Holy Spirit is God, He is worthy to be sought after, worshipped and praised. The Holy Spirit brings honor to God the Father, and God the Son.

If we desire to succeed in the Christian life, then Christ tells us that His Helper should become a major part of our lives. To become one in marriage both mates must understand the work of the Holy Spirit. They must become involved in His plan through daily fellowship with Him. Now, we are ready to scan Scripture to see how the Holy Spirit desires to help us.

Convicts And Pursues Us

The Holy Spirit's role in our life begins before we become Christians. While we are yet lost, the Holy Spirit convicts us of sin, *"And He, when He comes, will convict the world concerning sin, and righteousness, and judgment"* (John 16:8). He enlightens us with the story of Christ, then regenerates our soul with new life in Christ (Titus 3:4-6). Finally He seals (puts God's seal on) our new salvation for all eternity (Ephesians 4:30). Is that important to you and your marriage? Absolutely! The Holy Spirit continues to convict and enlighten us throughout our lives. Marital oneness is dependent on His continued renewal in these vital ministries.

Teacher

Another indispensable ministry of the Holy Spirit is His teaching ministry. The Holy Spirit is our teacher. Christ said it this way. *"But the Helper, the Holy Spirit, whom the Father will send in My name, He will teach you all things, and bring to your remembrance all that I said to you"* (John 14:26).

In the initial chapters of this book, we have been talking about developing a faith relationship in marriage, instead of a performance relationship. A faith relationship can be defined as one in which the participants look beyond their mate's performance to God's sovereignty and promises. In other words, instead of focusing on our mate's weakness, which is natural, we instead believe God's Word concerning our marriage. Based on His Word, we trust Him to accomplish what He says, in spite of our mate's weaknesses. That is what the Bible calls faith. Scripture tells us where faith comes from, *"So faith comes from hearing, and hearing by the Word of Christ"* (Romans 10:17). Where do we find the words of Christ? They are found in the Bible.

> FAITH IS TRUSTING GOD TO ACCOMPLISH WHAT HE SAYS, IN SPITE OF OUR MATE'S WEAKNESSES.

If you want to be one in your marriage, faith will be required. Faith requires your involvement in studying the Word of Christ. The One who illuminates the Word is the Holy Spirit. *"For to us God revealed them through the Spirit; for the Spirit searches all things, even the depths of God. For who among men knows the thoughts of a man except the spirit of the man, which is in him? Even so the thoughts of God no one knows except the Spirit of God"* (I Corinthians 2:10-11).

You might wonder why I take the time to write out Scripture verses throughout this book. The reason is obvious. Every time I read verses like Genesis 1:26-28 and 2:18-25, and a host of others, a rush of hope and conviction come over me. If your life and marriage is touched by them, it will be because the Holy Spirit taught you. Don or Sally Meredith cannot do that. The Holy Spirit is our guide, imparting spiritual knowledge and faith, using the Word of God.

Power

Christ makes another significant point concerning how the Holy Spirit ministers to us. The Holy Spirit provides us with the power to witness, overcome sin, and serve Him, as well as the power to be one in our marriage. When Christ commissioned the disciples, he said, *"But you shall receive power when the Holy Spirit has come upon you; and you shall be My witnesses both in Jerusalem and in all Judea and Samaria, and even to the remotest part of the earth"* (Acts 1:8).

If you do not experience much power in your life and marriage, faith is the missing ingredient. Why? Because Christ left this earth in order that the Holy Spirit would come to indwell believers. All we have to do is call upon His power. In my life, one of the greatest indications that I am not depending on the Holy Spirit is the absence of power in my life. I cannot overcome my critical spirit in my marriage without His power. I cannot even be a testimony to my wife, or anyone else for that matter, if I don't have His power. We cannot be a testimony to others, as a couple, without understanding and applying His power in our marriage.

> ONE OF THE GREATEST INDICATIONS THAT I AM NOT DEPENDING ON THE HOLY SPIRIT IS THE ABSENCE OF POWER IN MY LIFE.

Leading

Nearly sixty years on earth has taught Sally and me that life has many twists and turns to it. Sometimes we anguish in our desires to follow His leading. As we respond to Him, we draw tremendous comfort from yet another ministry of the Holy Spirit. The Spirit promises to lead us through life's ups and downs. Paul, the apostle, when talking about our walk with Christ, says, *"So then, brethren, we are under obligation, not to the flesh, to live according to the flesh. For if you are living according to the flesh, you must die; but if by the Spirit you are putting to death the deeds of the body, you will live. For all who are being led by the Spirit of God, these are sons of God"* (Romans 8:12-14). Clearly, Paul exhorts us to be led by the Holy Spirit.

I love the way Ezekiel describes this leading of the Holy Spirit toward the nation of Israel. *"Moreover, I will give you a new heart and put a new spirit within you; and I will remove the heart of stone from your flesh and give you a heart of flesh. And I will put My Spirit within you and cause you to walk in My statutes, and you will be careful to observe My ordinances"* (Ezekiel 36:26-27). That's what you and I need in our marriages. We need the Holy Spirit to take away our stubborn and hardened hearts and cause us to be soft and pliable in His hands. Marital oneness will never happen unless both mates earnestly beseech the Holy Spirit to lead them. "But when He, the Spirit of truth, comes, He will guide you into all the truth. . . . " (John 16:13). His will be done, not ours. We will never be one by *our* wills, but only through seeking and following His will.

Comforter
While there are still more ministries of the Holy Spirit, I'll mention just one more. After thirty years of marriage and nearly sixty years of life, one ministry of the Holy Spirit that I desperately need is His ministry as Comforter. Four times Christ refers to the Holy Spirit as "the Comforter." While mentioning suffering, Paul says this:

> *Blessed be the God and Father of our Lord Jesus Christ, the Father of mercies and God of all comfort; who comforts us in all our affliction, so that we may be able to comfort those who are in any affliction, with the comfort with which we ourselves are comforted by God* (2 Corinthians 1:3-4).

Life is full of disappointments and afflictions. Sometimes our dreams shatter, and our visions go unfulfilled. I, personally, have been burdened with deep discouragement at times. I thank God for the Holy Spirit's comfort. Many times He comforts me through my wife, and vice versa. The Holy Spirit replenishes our souls and reminds us of truth that may not be presently seen. In His divine power, He replaces fear with hope. He imparts peace instead of despair. At times, this ministry alone sustains us.

What does the Holy Spirit do? He is our sustainer in life. As we release our will to His, He gives perspective and hope. As the Psalmist said, *"Come, let us worship and bow down; let us kneel before the Lord our Maker"* (Psalm 95:6). Often, just kneeling before the Lord as husband and wife, acknowledging Him as Lord and Creator, brings hope to weary souls. God, the Holy Spirit, brings comfort in the passages of life and marriage.

HOW DO WE RELEASE THE HOLY SPIRIT'S POWER IN OUR LIVES?

Releasing the power of the Holy Spirit in our lives is not something that we necessarily do. Rather, it is something we allow the Holy Spirit to do in and through us. It is something we accept, we believe, and then release by faith. It can be measured by the fruit it produces in our lives. The Holy Spirit produces the power; we simply act on it by faith. The Scripture calls this faith interaction with the Holy Spirit *"fellowship,"* or *"walking by the Spirit"* (2 Corinthians 13:14; Galatians 5:16).

CONDITIONS FOR FELLOWSHIP

Sacrifice of Self

In order to adequately experience releasing the power of the Holy Spirit, we must acknowledge that our lives belong to Him. This includes our past, our present, and our future. All things must be given to Him, to do with as He desires.

> *I urge you therefore, brethren, by the mercies of God, to **present your bodies** a living and holy sacrifice, acceptable to God, which is your spiritual service of worship. And do not be conformed to this world, but be **transformed** by the renewing of your mind, that you may prove what the will of God is, that which is good and acceptable and perfect* (Romans 12:1-2).

If He created us, He also knows what is best for us at all times. Therefore, it is our *reasonable* service to give Him, not only our lives, but everything He entrusts to us. He then shows us that His will is good (for us), acceptable (to us), and perfect (in us). Are you willing to give up your rights, pride, and willfulness? Can you trust God and His Word? To experience His power requires our total trust in Him.

Confession

How do we "fellowship" or "walk in the Spirit?" In his first epistle of John, we are introduced to some conditions that must be met before we can fellowship with the Holy Spirit.

> *And this is the message we have heard from Him and announce to you, that God is light, and in Him there is no darkness at all. If we say that we have fellowship with Him and yet walk in the darkness, we lie and do not practice the truth; but if we walk in the light as he Himself is in the light, we have fellowship with one another, and the blood of Jesus His Son cleanses us from all sin . . . If we **confess our sins**, He is faithful and righteous to **forgive** us our sins and to **cleanse** us from all unrighteousness (I John 1:5-7,9).*

John tells us that we must submit to God's perspective, or will, if we want to walk and fellowship with Him. He uses light as a metaphor for God's holiness and purity.

Obviously, you and I are not holy or pure, apart from the cross. The only way you and I can walk in the light is through the grace shown at the cross, and by submitting our wills to His control. If you and I submit to follow Him, he graciously commits to fellowship with us, while continually cleansing us from our sin through the blood of Christ at the cross.

> HIS WILL FOR US IS GOOD, ACCEPTABLE, AND PERFECT.

Releasing the Holy Spirit's power in our lives involves turning from our selfishness. Confession of sin means agreeing with God that what we did was sin. We then turn from our sin (repent), asking for His forgiveness. His power is released as we ask Him to live His life in us, loving through us, forgiving others through us, etc. He does what is *natural* to Him—live the Christian life. But, now *He lives His life through us*. Therefore, we are not "trying" to live the Christian life, instead, we are trusting *Him* to live it through us. This process of trusting, not struggling, should be continual, and life-long. This means a sacrificial life, a cleansed life, a life filled with power. What a freeing experience!

Walking

Paul calls this leading of the Holy Spirit "walking by the Spirit." *"But I say, walk by the Spirit, and you will not carry out the desire of the flesh. For the flesh sets its desire against the Spirit, and the Spirit against the flesh; for these are in opposition to one another, so that you may not do the things that you please. But if you are led by the Spirit, you are not under the Law"* (Galatians 5:16-18).

Notice that Paul refers to a struggle that occurs in believers' lives. He says, *"For the flesh sets its desire against the Spirit, and the Spirit against the flesh: for these are in opposition to one another . . ."* The flesh refers to the natural self-centeredness present in every Christian's life. These old patterns and tendencies constantly contend with the Holy Spirit for control. When we become Christians, we don't lose our flesh with its desires. The Holy Spirit is the only One who can control the flesh: self-centeredness, insensitivity to others, pride, greed, etc. Under the control of His Spirit, Scripture tells us that the flesh is dead, or powerless.

Flesh Vs. Spirit

How do we know who is in control of our lives, the flesh or the Spirit? We know by the fruit that is evident in our lives. First, Paul mentions the fruit of the flesh by saying, *"Now the deeds of the flesh are evident, which are: immorality, impurity, sensuality, idolatry, sorcery, enmities, strife, jealousy, outbursts of anger, disputes, dissensions, factions, envying, drunkenness, carousing, and things like these . . ."* (Gal. 5:19-21).

The first thing I check when couples enter my counseling room is their fruit. If their fruit reveals arguing, jealousy, outbursts of anger, etc., I know they are not in fellowship with the Holy Spirit. Oneness in marriage is not possible in that state.

The fruit that the Holy Spirit produces contrasts with the fruit of the flesh. *"But the fruit of the Spirit is love, joy, peace, patience, kindness, goodness, faithfulness, gentleness, self-control; against such things there is no law"* (Gal. 5:22-23). Notice, this is the fruit of *His Spirit*, not something we try or struggle to gain. Christians do not possess these wonderful virtues in and of themselves. We possess them because we possess Christ. Couples controlled by the Spirit exhibit the fruit of the Spirit. Oneness is a natural by product. Peace reigns in their homes. The unity exhibited in their marriage is an example to others of their submission to God's Holy Spirit.

Paul reveals that each of us can **choose** who controls our lives. *"Now those who belong to Christ Jesus have crucified the flesh with its passions and desires. If we live by the Spirit, let us also walk by the Spirit. Let us not become boastful, challenging one another, envying one another"* (Gal. 5:24-26). Because we have become Christians, we no longer are bound by our selfish tendencies. We can choose, by faith, to let the Holy Spirit take over.

RELEASING THE HOLY SPIRIT IN OUR LIVES BY FAITH

Releasing the Holy Spirit in your life and marriage involves faith and will. The Holy Spirit describes this action: *"I have been crucified with Christ; and it is no longer I who live, but Christ lives in me; and the life which I now live in the flesh I live by faith in the Son of God, who loved me, and delivered Himself up for me"* (Gal. 2:20).

Walking in the Spirit simply means, seeking a deeper, closer walk with Him. The more He has of our lives, the more the fruit of the Spirit will be manifested in us. Walking in the Spirit starts with the belief that Christ crucified the power of sin in your life by His death on the cross.

> COUPLES CONTROLLED BY THE SPIRIT EXHIBIT THE FRUIT OF THE SPIRIT.

That takes faith. It is completed by believing that the Holy Spirit will do what He says. *"For if you are living according to the flesh, you must die; but if by the Spirit you are putting to death the deeds of the body, you will live. For all who are being led by the Spirit of God, these are sons of God"* (Romans 8:13-14).

In the same way, Christ called on His disciples to activate the Holy Spirit by faith. *"But you shall receive power when the Holy Spirit has come upon you; and you shall be My witnesses both in Jerusalem and in all Judea and Samaria, and even to the remotest part of the earth"* (Acts 1:8). He asks us to do the same.

Fellowship with God, and walking in the Spirit, involves faith more than anything else. Christ said we needed the Helper, His Holy

Spirit, in order to do that. The Bible is clear about what the Holy Spirit will do in our lives if we will let Him. The only question is, will we take Him at His Word? If we do, the power of the Holy Spirit will be released in our lives and marriages. As the Holy Spirit convicts us of any known sin, we need to agree with Him that it is wrong. We then ask His forgiveness, and seek His will. He is then free to exhibit the fruit of the Spirit through our lives.

> WHAT WE ALLOW THE HOLY SPIRIT TO DO THROUGH US WILL DETERMINE THE OUTCOME OF OUR MARRIAGES.

The Holy Spirit gives us the power to be one, to reflect God's image to a lost world, to reproduce His image through children and disciples, and to rule this world to His glory. The message is clear; the challenge precise. What we allow the Holy Spirit to do through us *will* determine the outcome of our marriages.

CHAPTER EIGHT
LOVING WHEN IT HURTS

NOT LONG AGO, I met a man who challenged the concept of viewing his mate's weaknesses as being used by God in his life. "If I don't help her change, she'll never change."

Nowhere in Scripture are we told to change people. Only God changes people. God has ordained only two forces for change in marriage: the *active force of love* (see Eph. 5) and the *reactive force of blessing* (see 1 Pet. 3:8,9).

Most counseling sessions with married couples uncover a struggle for the "rights" of each mate. They want their right to *say* what they want, *do* what they want, *think* what they want, and *be* what they want. In marriage, God says the only right one has is to *love and bless* the other. Demanding rights has no place in marriage.

> NOWHERE IN SCRIPTURE ARE WE TOLD TO CHANGE PEOPLE.

When people marry, they get the good with the not-so-good. Do not be deceived into thinking you may subtly be able to control, discipline, or manipulate change in your mate. Of course, we all feel particularly gifted as judge, jury, and executioner, but what we don't understand is that we are totally ineffective when we demand change in our mates. Trying to force change usually brings out the worst!

God created humanity. He knows what works. Don't think your plans will succeed apart from God's plan. Only *love* and *blessing*, not human ingenuity, produce rewarding results in marriage. Let's look at both of these concepts.

LOVE: THE ACTIVE FORCE

Most people are fighting to cope with the realities of life: aging, prejudice, broken relationships, physical problems, rejection, competition, fatigue, isolation, boredom, etc. The one potential blessed isle in the midst of those troubled waters is a love relationship. But when couples come into my office with problems, they are usually there because that once blessed isle has become an erupting volcano. How did it happen?

Much of the problem stems from America's definition of the word "love." In the world, combinations of circumstances totally determine love. Following are some of the reasons people get married: feelings, their need for emotional and sexual attention, social status, to escape from home, school, or social pressure, aging, or the desire for children. When the right combination of circumstances line up just right, couples say, "I think I'm in love. Let's get married." All of these circumstances are vital, but they cannot produce love. Couples considering marriage must settle in their minds what real love is before getting married.

When you stop and think about it, most examples of love today could be destroyed simply by changing the circumstances. If one changes from rich to poor, sexy to unsexy, young to old, social to antisocial, athletic to non-athletic, healthy to unhealthy, skinny to fat, faithful to unfaithful, spiritual to unspiritual, most people would lose what they define as love. With counterfeit love, circumstances and performance are very important. Feelings of love can be destroyed in a matter of minutes when one mate reveals an ugly truth to the other. Pain or disappointment can dissolve feelings in an instant. Do you want to base your marriage on a love that can be shattered so easily? Couples must ask the question, "What is true love?"

Three Levels Of Love

The Greek language used in the New Testament specifically enumerates and defines at least *three levels of love.*[1] *The first level is **eros**.* This kind of love accentuates the emotional and physical, with emphasis on the selfish desires of the one who loves. Sexual attraction and involvement are primary. Eros love is ultimately a *self-centered* or *selfish love*. It says, "Perform for me, and I will love you." Many couples today get married with eros love as their focal point, and do not even realize it! Why are so many marriages ending in divorce? It is because eros love is selfish, not sacrificial and giving. When performance lowers, and feelings subside, eros love evaporates.

*The second level of love is **philos***. This love involves *mutual*, *tender* affection between two people. It infers "brotherly love." While eros love is self-centered, philos love is mutually satisfying. It appreciates and respects the other person. It says, "Yes, I love what you do for me, but I also sincerely respect you."

> AGAPE LOVE CAN ONLY BE MEASURED BY THE SACRIFICIAL ACTION OF THE GIVER.

This level of love involves more sacrificial commitment than eros. The overwhelming majority of marriages in America are based on either eros or philos love. The problem with philos love is that when respect is lost, couples tend to revert to eros love.

*The third level of love, **agape**,* is far superior to either of the other two and is defined *as God's love*. It is best described in Scripture as the kind of love that God gave to His Son in particular, and then gave to man in general. This kind of love is the opposite of eros in that it is *totally sacrificial*. This love can only be measured by the sacrificial action of the giver. It is not primarily emotional or sexual because it is drawn out, not by the attractiveness of the object loved, but by the commitment of the giver. The lover is acting in obedience to God's commandment; therefore this level of love is *God-directed*. It is first an issue between God and man, not between two people, and it does not always run with the natural inclinations of feelings. This love is responsible and does not change as feelings change. When we say our marriage vows, this is the kind of love verbalized: a never ending commitment.

If you are a Christian considering marriage and you tell your future mate you love him or her, you had better count the cost and discern which level of love you mean. God never called anyone to marriage apart from agape love. Marital oneness is impossible without it. God teaches dependence on Himself in marriage; therefore it is absolutely necessary to trust Him and not your mate for this kind of love.

A Lifestyle Of Love

Biblical (agape) love is best described in 1Corinthians 13. I would like to mention a few of the dimensions of this love and then expand on their meaning in marriage.

Love suffers long: This is the quality of enduring offense from your mate, even though there is a tide of emotion welling up within you demanding that you retaliate. Application: (1) Have the kind of patience that waits and prays for the reformation of your mate rather than exhibiting resentment. (2) The person who loves by suffering long can handle insults and neglect from their mate until God can work through His Word.

Love is not easily provoked: Love does not become bitter or resentful as a result of continuous irritation or offenses. Agape love will not respond to these offenses with touchiness or anger. Application: A weakness or offense in your mate should not produce bitterness or anger from you.

Love bears all things: Love endures offenses from your mate and throws a cloak of silence over your suffering, so that the offenses of your mate are not divulged to the world. Application: If you have a non-Christian or non-spiritual spouse, while this may be known to godly leaders in the church, or a few close friends, this should not be exposed in casual prayer groups. Your mate needs to be able to trust you.

Love believes all things: Love chooses to believe the best about your mate and always assumes his or her motives and intentions are right. Application: Often people become what we convince them to be. If we indicate that we suspect them, they will tend to be untrustworthy. To trust in your mate gives him or her a feeling of self-worth and acceptance, a key to effecting change in your mate.

Love endures all things: Love has the power to enable one to endure any trial with confidence and peace. Trials produce perseverance and blessings from God. Application: Divorce is an indication that you don't endure all things; agape love doesn't quit when things get tough. It demonstrates permanent commitment.

A thorough study of 1 Corinthians 13 is an encouraging premarital or marital project. All the verbs in this passage are in the present tense, indicating that these characteristics of love are to be habitual. Because a person does not manifest one of these qualities in every instance, however, does not necessarily signal non-commitment. The apostle, Paul, is referring to a "lifestyle" of love.

> AGAPE LOVE DOESN'T QUIT WHEN THINGS GET TOUGH.

God's love leaves no place for the statement, "I don't love you anymore." God's love does, however, hold some absolute promises for us. Only God's love releases the power of God's Word. For example, read I John 4:18. It says, *"There is no fear in love; but perfect love casts out fear, because fear involves punishment, and the one who fears is not perfected in love."* The word used for love here is agape. The verse says two things will result from agape love. First, fear will be driven out. Second, this love perfects. Fear is the opposite of faith and hope. If you love your mate, based on performance, they will be fearful of failure. On the other hand, if you love by faith, as Christ did, and look beyond your mate's weaknesses to God, your gracious love will drive the fear from your mate because there is no punishment. Your mate's fearlessness will then provoke them to faith and hope. Usually, your mate will then return the faith love to you. In addition, God implies that agape love perfects the object of your love, your mate. How do you change your mate? You agape them, and allow God to do the changing.

Another example of the power of faith love occurs in a passage where God ties the promise of Christ's love to marriage. In Ephesians 5:25-33, a great biblical passage on marriage, the husband is charged with the same role in marriage as Christ Himself has with the church. Like Christ, the husband also inherits several promises that Christ received. In verse 25, we see God's command to husbands to love their wives as Christ loved us. In verses 26 and 27, God reveals two results of Christ's love. First, His love "sanctifies" the church. Second, because of Christ's love, the church will be presented back to Christ in a perfected state. While husbands cannot hope to fully love as Christ does, it is apparent that God also gives similar promises to husbands. If husbands will follow Christ's pattern of love, they too will benefit from some of the same effects that Christ received. They too will have the promise of participating with Christ in changing their mates. Consider these results:

First, if we love our mates as Christ loved, we will *"sanctify"* them or set them apart by our special commitment to them. In other words, a woman who is loved unconditionally, apart from her actions, is set apart from other women who are not loved in this way. A woman who is loved unconditionally is free from marital anxiety and fear, and is better able to live a godly life.

Second, like Christ, a husband who loves with agape love, will have the hope of seeing change in his mate. She will be presented back to him, "having no spot or wrinkle, or any such thing; but that she should be holy and blameless." One day, Christ will show husbands who exhibit such love to their wives how their faith was used to help accomplish these spiritual results. In my life, I have seen God do these things in Sally's life right before my eyes. I cannot wait to see the eternal perspective when I meet Christ face to face. Learning to love with God's love is very rewarding.

In all my years of counseling, I have never seen any other active approach gain these kinds of results. It is not unusual to hear complaints about having to love God's way. But, nothing else works. Neither manipulation, verbal assault, bribes, nor subtle lying will work like agape love. Don't experience a poor counterfeit of God's love. Experience agape love toward your mate, and believe God for the outcome. The fearlessness, transparency, and peace of such a relationship is what married life was meant to be. Bless your mate by giving them the assurance that he or she will never hear you say, "I don't love you anymore."

BLESSING: THE REACTIVE FORCE OF LOVE

I can still remember the anger and flashing eyes of the woman who related this story to me. "For three years, since my husband started his new business, the children and I have not had a vacation. We have done without a lot of things so Bob could succeed. Then two weeks ago his real appreciation for us came through loud and clear. First of all, I got the Master Card bill and discovered that Bob had bought a used motor boat to the tune of $5,000. When I called him at the office, he exploded, and told me that he and some of his buddies were going fishing for ten days in Mexico and needed a boat! I was so furious I hardly spoke to him for the next two weeks. The day he left, I took the Visa Card and all the children and flew home to Mom's for ten days of fun, to the tune of $5,250." She got him! One up!

And then I got them three months later! The hurt, bitterness, and ruin were still flaming! Vicki had done the human thing. She retaliated. She had "gotten Bob back." But how did it help her? Did it change Bob? Did two wrongs make a right? Was Bob more in love with her than before? Did he appreciate her more? Did it serve any useful purpose to have two people insult instead of one?

Couples today are not prepared for the potential shock that can result from the insult cycle in their marriage. Yet, many end up as victims. As time passes, these cycles become vicious whirlwinds. Scripture tells us that we can stop these insult cycles by returning a blessing when wronged or insulted. Our human nature does not want to hear that. Our instinct is to follow Vicki's example: "I'll show him. He hasn't seen anything yet! I've just begun to fight." In our "rights oriented" society, God's way seems ridiculous, and we don't think it will work. Yet, as couples continue to turn from love to hate, isn't it time to listen to God?

To better understand what God means when He says to "return a blessing when insulted," we need to define what the Scripture refers to as an insult and a blessing. There are many examples of each, we will look at a few.

INSULT DEFINED

Scripture gives many exhortations concerning insults. Five are particularly relevant to marriage:

Name-calling: God admonishes us not to belittle others. Name-calling is always a threat to marital love and causes fear in the one receiving the insult. Any consistent negative reference (dummy, stupid, bitch, moron, idiot) to someone is demoralizing and destroys self-confidence. (See Matt. 5:22.)

Sarcasm and ridicule: Implication of intellectual, social, or physical ineptness certainly hampers marital oneness. Examples: "You burned the food again!" "Why are you so quiet when we're with our friends? I wish you'd just speak up!" "You can't do anything right!" (See Prov. 18:6; Eph. 4:29.)

A nagging wife: Scripture is bold in its condemnation of a woman who doesn't trust or respect her husband enough to stop nagging on any given subject. "How many times do I have to tell you . . ." (See Prov. 21:9; 27:15,16.)

A contentious man: Scripture speaks just as forcefully of a quarrelsome man who is always picking a fight. This kind of man thinks he is always right, refuses to back down, and is unable to ask for forgiveness. (See Prov. 26:21.)

An unbridled tongue: Scripture speaks of the powerfully negative effect of the tongue when it is not controlled. Our words can poison and destroy another person. Sometimes the effects can scar our mate or child for life. (See James 3:5-10.)

Lying to Spouse: Scripture speaks of the serious consequences of not telling the full truth, "covering the truth," or using "little white lies." This results in a lack of trust and openness between spouses and causes disunity. (See Proverbs 12:22.)

Insult and abuse in general: Immorality, adultery, homosexuality, sorcery, bad language, pornography, rage, drunkenness and unrighteousness of all types are grouped in this last category. (See Galatians 5:19-21.)

BLESSING DEFINED

In this context, the opposite of an insult would be a "blessing." God says to bless a person instead of insulting him. An insult is usually the natural human response, while blessing a person requires a decision of the will, empowered by the Holy Spirit. Consider the following uses of the word, "blessing," from Scripture, and apply them to marriage.

Praise to God: What positive qualities about my mate can I verbally praise him/ her for? (See Luke1:64, 6:28, and 2 Timothy 1:3-6.)

Giving thanks to God for His gifts and favor: What qualities about my mate am I thankful for, and how can I communicate this to him or her? (See Luke 1:64, 2:28-32, and Mark 6:41.)

To call God's favor down upon: What specific areas of my mate's life should I pray that the Lord will bless? (See 1 Samuel 12:23.)

Benefits bestowed: What benefits (gifts, acts of service) could I bestow upon my mate? In what way can I be of blessing to him or her? (See Mark 6:41 and Luke 11:13.)

Seeking of counsel: In what ways can I be of help to my spouse in order to cause blessing in his/ her life? (See Proverbs 27:9.)

Encouragement and fellowship: In what areas of my spouse's life do I need to encourage him or her? Am I spending quality time, i.e. communicating deeply and often with him or her? (See Philippians 2:1-4.)

All of us know what blesses and what insults our mates. These examples from Scripture are mentioned to broaden our perspective. Be aware and anticipate your own tendencies to hurt and insult your mate. Become an expert on what causes blessing to occur. Practice giving blessings often. Remember, *"Give, and it will be given to you; good measure, pressed down, shaken together, running over, they will pour into your lap. For by your standard of measure it will be measured to you in return"* (Luke 6:38).

INSULT CYCLE

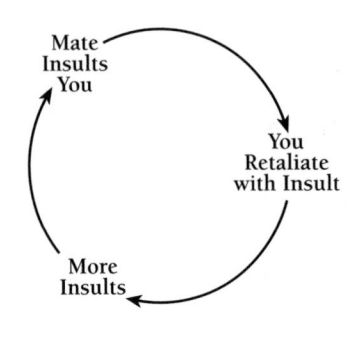

Mate Insults You → You Retaliate with Insult → More Insults →

Results in:
Failure to be one in your marriage
Failure to reflect, reproduce, and reign
Failure to receive a blessing

BLESSING CYCLE

Mate Insults You → By Faith You Return a Blessing → Mate Becomes Convicted → You Give More Blessing → Blessing from Mate Likely →

Results in:
Oneness
Ability to reflect, reproduce, and reign
Receipt of blessing

With these definitions in mind, let's think for a moment about why marriages turn into insult contests instead of blessings, as God intended. The answer takes us right back to a central theme running throughout Scripture. If you are a Christian, there are two forces operating in your life. One is your self-centered will. The other is your "new spiritual creation," given to you at the point you received Christ as Savior. These two are in conflict with one another. Your will follows natural human thought, while your "new spiritual creation" heeds God's will, as revealed by the Holy Spirit. The Spirit uses Scripture to reveal God's will. These two forces approach life from entirely different perspectives.

The following chart attempts to compare this divergent thought. As you read through the chart, you will be amazed at the difference between God's perspective and man's. God says it this way, *"For My thoughts are not your thoughts, neither are your ways My ways"* (Isa. 55:8). As husbands, we tend to develop ideas and passions that conflict with God's Word and plan for our lives. The following comparisons point out some of the conflicts between the way men and women naturally think, compared to God's perspective.

MAN'S VIEW (THE WORLD'S SYSTEM)	GOD'S WORD AND PERSPECTIVE
1. People are my problem.	For our struggle is not against flesh and blood, but a against the powers, against the spiritual forces of w wickedness in the heavenly places (Eph. 6:12).
2. Success is the first priority	Seek first His kingdom and His righteousness; and all these things shall be added to you (Matt. 6:33).
3. Hold on to what you've got at all costs or you will lose everything.	Give, and it will be given to you; good measure, pressed down, shaken together, running over, they will pour into your lap (Luke 6:38)
4. Material possessions will bring more happiness.	Blessed are those who hunger and thirst for righteousness, for they shall be satisfied (Matt. 5:6).
5. Most of my problems are caused by the one in authority.	Let every person be in subjection to the governing in authority. authorities. For there is no authority except from God, and those which exist are established by God . . . For rulers are not a cause of fear for good behavior, but for evil. Do you want to have no fear of authority? Do what is good, and you will have praise from the same (Rom. 13:1,3).
6. Love your friends, but get your enemies before they get you.	But I say to you, love your enemies, and pray for those who persecute you (Matt. 5:44).
7. If only I had married someone more gifted I would be happier.	But one and the same Spirit works all these things, I would be happier. distributing to each one individually just as He wills (1 Cor. 12:11).

(continued)

MAN'S VIEW (THE WORLD'S SYSTEM)	GOD'S WORD AND PERSPECTIVE
8. In this life, you've got to take care of Old Number One.	. . . If anyone wants to be first, he shall be last of all and servant of all (Mark 9:35).
9. My mate can't do anything. If only I had married someone God could use.	I planted, Appolos watered, but God was causing the growth. So then neither the one who plants nor the one who waters is anything, but God who causes the growth (1 Cor. 3:6,7).
10. I'll teach him or her not to cross me.	Never take your own revenge, beloved, but leave room for the wrath of God. For it is written, "Vengeance is Mine, I will repay," says the Lord (Rom. 12:19).
11. I'm going to the top and I don't care who I have to step on to get there.	Humble yourselves, therefore, under the mighty hand of God, that He may exalt you at the proper time (1 Pet. 5:6).

I don't know about you, but when I read through that chart, I feel the Holy Spirit nudge me. "Don, wake up to My ways." The term "faith relationship," demands dependence on God's perspective, not man's. Humanly speaking, it does not make sense to bless when wronged. Yet, as the Holy Spirit applies God's perspective through His Word, we begin to think, "Wait a minute, maybe God has a better way!"

The next question we must ask, "Does God ever give us the right to retaliate?" No, He does not! He does tell us to seek wise counsel. He does give us specific instruction concerning church discipline. He does tell us not to be drawn into sin. But, he never gives us the right to retaliate. The following verses are good examples of what He does say concerning retaliation.

See that no one repays another with evil for evil, but always seek after that which is good for one another and for all men (1 Thess. 5:15).

Bless those who curse you, pray for those who mistreat you (Luke 6:28).

WHY RETURN A BLESSING?

No question about it, God condemns revenge—all the time! Every time! With that established, it is opportune to look at God's better way. 1 Peter 3:1-7 instructs husbands and wives concerning marriage. Then in verses 8-12, Peter makes a summary statement. From this passage, we can observe four reasons why it is better to return a blessing when wronged than another insult.

*To sum up, let all be harmonious, sympathetic, brotherly, kind-hearted, and humble in spirit; **not** returning evil for evil, or **insult for insult**, but giving a **blessing** instead; for you were called for the very purpose that you might inherit a blessing. For, "Let him who means to love life and see good days refrain his tongue from evil and his lips from speaking guile. And let him turn away from evil and do good; let him seek peace and pursue it. For the eyes of the Lord are upon the righteous, and **His ears attend to their prayer**, but the face of the Lord is against those who do evil"* (1 Peter 3:8-12).

Peter gives us four reasons why it is better to return a blessing when wronged. First, Peter says, *". . . for you were called for this very purpose that you might inherit a blessing."* In other words, **a blessing begets a blessing**. That's what God desires for us. He doesn't want us to insult, because He knows that will result in a returned insult. Frustration ensues.

Second, God implies that blessing one another will result in **"*good days*," or a long life**. Certainly, that is true. Stress destroys, while blessing prospers and benefits.

Third, when we bless, we have the hope that we are pleasing God, and that **His ears will attend to our prayers**. That is a significant promise. When we are in God's will, *"all authority in heaven and earth"* is available. Returning a blessing allows God to bless us through answered prayer.

Last, God further releases us from the need to return an insult by saying, "If your mate is really wrong, I will take care of it." *"...but the face of the Lord is against those who do evil."* In other words, **God can better deal with your mate**, because of His great love and forgiveness. When God disciplines, He redeems. When we try to play God in our mate's life, we destroy.

> WHEN WE BLESS OTHERS, GOD ANSWERS OUR PRAYERS.

Which makes sense now, returning a blessing or an insult? The Holy Spirit speaks through His Word to our hearts. Why return a blessing? Because *it works*! It is God's will. It opens the door to blessing, life, good days, and God's favor.

The next question is, "How do we give a blessing?" To answer that question, let's look to Christ's example. In 1 Peter 2:21-25, we find an excellent example of how Christ responded to insults. The context is suffering in trials, yet a wonderful picture emerges, which shows Christ's response to insults. Think back to Vicki's response to Bob. Consider the results of her reactions as compared to our Lord's response.

HOW TO RESPOND TO INSULTS

*For you have been called for this purpose, since Christ also suffered for you, leaving you an example for you to follow in His steps, who committed no sin, nor was any deceit found in His mouth; and while being reviled, He did not revile in return; while suffering, **He uttered no threats**, but kept entrusting Himself to Him who judges righteously; and He Himself bore our sins in His body on the cross, that we might die to sin and live to righteous-*

ness; for by His wounds you were healed. For you were continually straying like sheep, but now you have returned to the Shepherd and Guardian of your souls (1 Pet. 2:21-25).

Remove Any Sin In Your Own Life.

The first thing we note about Christ's response was that He was innocent. He had committed no sin! When our mate insults us, the first thing we need to do is ask this question, "Did I do anything to provoke my mate?" Ninety percent of the time when Sally insults me, I did something to provoke her. The first step in responding to our mate's insult is to confess our sin, first to God, and then to our mate. "Sweetheart, I know I must have done something to provoke your response. Please forgive me. Can we talk about it?" Only when you confess your failure will God be able to work in your mate's life.

> WE MUST MAKE A *WILLFUL DECISION* TO RETURN A BLESSING, IN SPITE OF THE HURT EXPERIENCED.

Return A Blessing When Wronged.

The second step is to return a blessing when insulted. Christ died to heal the very people who had killed Him. The implication is clear: Christ not only refused to insult them, but blessed them. Each mate must make a *willful decision* to return a blessing, in spite of the hurt just experienced. Your will must be submitted to God's will. Look beneath the insult to the *reason* for the behavior or words. Look for ways to bless your mate. Look for ways to praise your mate. Communicate your love to them. Do something specific to build up their spirits.

Most people insult others because they are hurting inside, and have tremendous emotional needs themselves. Insulting can be a release mechanism. You can interrupt this tendency with kindness. Jesus uttered no threats when insults were thrown at Him. He had every "right" to threaten the people who were sending Him to the cross. But Jesus knew that insults and threats do not work. They only cause more hatred. By not returning an insult, we humble ourselves, therefore allowing God's principle of blessing to work.

Commit Yourself And Your Situation To The Lord.
The third step is just as important. Jesus Christ turned to His Father for hope, insight, and strength. Commit yourself and the situation to the Lord. Humanly, Christ did not want to suffer, but He kept His Father's perspective. He knew that even though it was momentarily tough, in the long run His Father's will was best. We too must yield to God's will and perspective.

As we yield to the Holy Spirit, He will change our perspective. We will begin to say, "God gave me this person, and therefore my struggle is not against my mate, but Satan, who deceives me into thinking that my mate is my problem" (see Ephesians 6:12). As we catch God's perspective, we can thank Him for the situation. As we yield the situation to the Lord, it can be used to make us more like Christ. Only the Lord can convict and adequately deal with your mate's offense.

Be Willing To Suffer In Order To Heal Your Offender.
The last step implied by this passage is that you should be prepared and willing to suffer so that God might heal your offender. In 1 Peter 2:24,25, we see that Jesus purposed to die on a cross so that you and I might be healed. God never says the momentary cost of returning a blessing will be small. In fact, God implies that at times it will be very tough. Yet, God guarantees a blessing for your efforts. It may not be just what you expect, but God will bless you in ways you never dreamed.

Determine, through the power of the Holy Spirit, to stop the insult cycle and return a blessing instead. The more you learn to bless, the more blessings you will receive in return.

How do you change your mate from God's perspective? You *apply the active force of agape love*. When wronged, you *apply the reactive force of love*, which is to *return a blessing*. Both of these go against our human nature. That is why faith is necessary. Faith occurs when we override our human instinct by acting on God's Word, through the power of the Holy Spirit.

---

1. These definitions of love are found in W. E. Vine's Expository Dictionary of New Testament Words.

CHAPTER NINE

LOVE AND SUBMISSION: FRIEND OR FOE?

YEARS AGO, a deeply agitated woman came to me with her concerns regarding her role as wife. She had always thought she knew what God intended for women, but lately she had been confused by discussions over the equality of women and men. She concluded, "I have struggled with guilt feelings lately because I've begun to question the issue of submission for a woman. I am confused about what submission means and if it applies to women anymore."

Often I find that men are equally confused in their roles. Christian couples with marital problems rarely fail to mention confusion over biblical roles. When one begins to analyze this frustration over the issue of headship and submission, several questions seem to be at the crux of the debate. "Did God create men and women equal?" We have already discussed this in Genesis 1 and 2. He created us to be equal. But He didn't create us to be the same. *God made us two parts of one entity*. We are to be companions, lovers, parents, and joint heirs of the grace of life. We are to complement one another.

> GOD MADE MEN AND WOMEN TO BE EQUAL BUT DIFFERENT IN ROLE AND FUNCTION.

The question in this chapter then, is not one of equality, but of *role or function*. "Did God intend for men and women to be different in function?" And, "Does the man have any advantage over the woman, from God's point of view?" These issues have reached great magnitude because of our cultural emphasis on the "oppressed" wife. To answer these questions we will begin with the scriptural "job descriptions" for men and women *in marriage*. The man's responsibility is stated in Ephesians 5:25-33 and I Peter 3:7, and the woman's responsibility is found in 1 Peter 3:1-6.

When we approach these Scriptures most of us think to ourselves, "Oh, not that again! If I hear these things one more time I'll scream!" Admittedly, these issues are important, yet they must be placed in the larger context of God's whole plan for marriage, or they can become legalistic. From God's perspective, love and submission should not be a source of struggle, but a hope of a loving relationship. We will define, Biblically, what these words mean.

GOD'S PERSPECTIVE OF LOVE AND SUBMISSION

	HUSBAND'S ROLE: **LOVE** (Eph. 5:25-33; 1 Peter 3:7)	**WIFE'S ROLE:** **SUBMISSION** (1 Pet. 2:13; 3:1-6)
ABSOLUTE COMMAND	LOVE without conditions	SUBMIT without a word
PROMISES	1. Sanctify her 2. Present her 3. Prayers answered	1. Silence foolishness 2. Husband won to Christ 3. No fear 4. Precious to God
PICTURE	1. Love her as your own body 2. Nourish her 3. Cherish her 4. Honor/understand her 5. Exemplify Christ	1. Gentle and quiet spirit 2. Respect husband 3. Women of God hope in God 4. Example of Sarah 5. Exemplify Christ

IS GOD PREJUDICED?

Let's review these two passages for one main purpose: to demonstrate that there is no favoritism on God's part toward either the man or the woman. In fact, the two passages are *parallel* in several important ways in their context and structure. The previous table demonstrates their parallel breakdown.

Each passage begins with an absolute command that is very strong in the original language. It leaves little doubt about the responsibilities of both the husband and wife. Each passage lists a number of exciting promises that result from following the commands. These promises motivate, soften, and become the hope of the commands. The writers of these passages include illustrations, to help seal our understanding of each role, and give a hint as to how one can apply them successfully.

We also need to consider the similar contexts in which these two passages are written. Ephesians 1-3 says that in light of what Christ has done for us, we are to walk in a manner worthy of His calling. In Ephesians 5:15-20, Paul says as we walk in the Spirit of God, four things will result:

1. You will speak to one another with psalms and hymns (understanding God's motivation).
2. You will sing and make melody with your heart to the Lord (praise Him for that motivation).
3. You will be able to give thanks for all things in His name (because you understand His will).
4. You will make yourselves subject to one another, in the fear of the Lord (you will understand God's provisions for relationships).

If a man will seek the mind of Christ, he will understand the command. Without that perspective, a man will never fulfill his role. In like manner, Peter talks about Christ's perspective just prior to instructing married women. The whole of 1 Peter deals with responding to suffering. It's an interesting fact that Peter first draws our minds back to Christ's perspective in going to the cross to win us to Himself, before getting into the importance of submission from a woman's standpoint. Peter says that Jesus Christ submitted himself to unjust suffering, *and "kept entrusting Himself to Him [God the Father] who judges righteously"* (1 Pet. 2:23). Peter is saying, "Women, before you can properly understand your responsibility to your husband, you too must have the perspective of Christ." So, the contexts of both passages are parallel, in that both ask us to keep the perspective of our Lord.

THE ABSOLUTE COMMANDS

As we compare the two passages, let's look at the absolute command to each. First, we read the command to the man: *"Husbands, love your wives, just as Christ also loved the church and gave Himself up for her."* The word for "love" used in this command is the word "agape," which you will recall is a God-given and God-directed love that does not exist humanly, apart from God. We called it commitment-love. That is why it is illustrated by Christ's love for the church.

What was the church doing when Christ came and died for her? She was nonexistent. People were moving in direct opposition to Christ, and ultimately crucified Him! By Christ's example, we learn that God's love is totally initiated by the Giver; it does not take into account the actions of the one given to. The same must be true as husbands love their wives. Like Christ, he is to love sacrificially, while setting aside his rights.

Now men, read that command again! Talk about one hundred percent responsibility! There are no exception clauses here. There are no excuses. Should God ask you one day, "How did you love your wife?" You might be tempted to say, "Well, Lord, you know I loved her in certain areas. But it was hard to love her completely. She didn't always deserve it. And remember, Lord, she had an affair, and she was untrustworthy. I just couldn't love her unconditionally." You might try to prove she didn't deserve your love. But the Lord will say, "I didn't ask you about your mate's weaknesses. I asked you, 'How did you respond to *my command to love her as I loved you*?'"

There are no exceptions! God knows your mate's weaknesses,

because He created her. He even knows her sins, because Christ died for her. He wants you to love her, no matter what she does or does not do. That is your one hundred percent responsibility! Hard? Impossible on your own! But by His Spirit working in and through you, you can love your wife as Jesus Christ loved us and gave Himself up for us.

The wife, on the other hand, is given an equally firm command. *"In the same way, you wives, be submissive to your own husbands so that even if any of them are disobedient to the word, they may be won without a word by the behavior of their wives, as they observe your chaste and respectful behavior"* (1 Peter 3:1-2). Just as Christ was submissive to the cross, wives are called upon to submit to their husbands. The word submission is a very strong word in the Greek language. It was a military term, meaning literally, "to place oneself under another." Notice, it means that *you place yourself under;* it is one hundred percent your responsibility. It is *never* the right of the husband to make his wife submit. *His only right is to love her and serve her, demonstrating Christ's attitude toward the church.* Christ placed Himself under His Father, which resulted in His death on a cross. This kind of submission is not based on emotion, but upon the very character and example of God. Submission in marriage means, *"respecting your husband enough to follow his leadership in the home."* A synonym for submission is *respect*. Ephesians 5:33 says, *"and let the wife see to it that she **respect** her husband."*

Women are to submit themselves to their husbands *as they entrust themselves to God*. Again, the wife, like the husband, will have to answer the Lord when He asks, "How did you submit yourself to your husband?" No matter how strong the proof of her husband's weaknesses, there are no exception clauses in God's command to her. Peter goes out of his way to make this clear by stating, *"even if any of them are disobedient to the word."* Then Peter seals the strength of the command by saying a wife must submit to her husband's leadership with a *respectful attitude*. Certainly it takes tremendous spiritual perspective to submit as Christ did, yet He requires it of godly wives.

I see no favoritism in these parallel commands to the husband or wife. Both are overwhelming commands that are to be willingly followed under the loving care of a mighty God! Be careful not to inject your cultural thinking at this point. God never says to do this as unto your mate, only as unto the Lord. God is not talking about winners and losers. He is talking about His will and purposes that require oneness. Trust Him that when He says love and submit, for He intends only blessing and unity.

PROMISES TO HUSBANDS ABOUT WIVES

The Lord is gracious to quickly draw our eyes from these strong commands to the associated promises. First, the man draws encouragement from the results of Christ's love.

> *That He might sanctify her, having cleansed her by the washing of water with the word, that He might present to Himself the church in all her glory, having no spot or wrinkle or any such thing; but that she should be holy and blameless* (Ephesians 5:26-27).

The promise to the husband is twofold: (1) *that he might sanctify his wife* and (2) *that he might present his wife spotless*. A husband cannot accomplish these things in the eternal sense as God does, but this kind of love on the man's part will *effect similar results to Christ's love*. And though I have commented already on this passage, let me mention a few additional truths.

To sanctify means to "set apart from the rest." We are set apart in Christ, in that we are free from death, because of His death on the cross. A wife is set apart by her husband because his love is not based on her performance, and she is therefore free to be "more than ordinary."

Just as the Spirit reminds us daily of our forgiveness by washing us with the Word of God, so a wife must be experientially able to trust her husband's commitment to love her. And men—this seemingly impossible command to love is not so hard when you realize the results will be a receptive and appreciative wife! A woman who is loved with agape love is a pleasant and beautiful woman indeed!

Next, God promises the husband that if he loves his wife sacrificially, she will be perfected by this love. When I first heard this promise I did not understand how it could happen. Now, I envision it this way: When Paul speaks of having *"no spot or wrinkle,"* the word *"spot,"* means "moral stain," and the word *"wrinkle,"* means to be "filled with inner struggles." The use of these words imply the external and internal results of Christ's work. Christ's work results in eternal perfection, but Paul implies the similar, temporal, result of the husband's sacrificial love. Christ's love is so freeing and creative in our lives that we are able to experience both external joy and inward peace. The face and countenance of a Christian should not show the signs of inward stress and pressure that an unbeliever may have.

During our married life, God has graciously demonstrated the *"no spot or wrinkle"* promise to me. Sally has always desired to please God with all her heart. But I also believe Sally has become a godly wife and mother, partially because I have dared to love her unconditionally, by faith. When I place her under performance, fear results. Yet, when I love her as Christ loved the church, hope and faith are the results. Sacrificial love produces a more beautiful wife, internally as well as externally.

Husbands, I am not saying here that God will make your wife a "beauty" right before your eyes. I am saying that my wife, Sally, does not spend even minutes a day being distressed over our relationship. My commitment-love has freed her to become characterized by an outward glow and an inner joy that makes her very attractive. I am convinced that one day God will show me that my faith was used by Him to make her more internally and externally beautiful. Added to that is a change that she has expressed to me and others. Sally has actually loved God more, and understood the unconditional love of God better, because God's love has had "arms" through me.

God promises husbands that if they can keep Christ's perspective in loving their wives, then He will actually use them as instruments of redemption in the lives of their mates. Her peace and joy will be noticeable. People will say, "What a joy it is to know your wife. Her life really motivates me." Even physically she will become more radiant.

God gives another powerful promise to husbands: *"You husbands likewise, live with your wives in an understanding way, as with a weaker vessel, since she is a woman; and grant her honor as a fellow heir of the grace of life, so that your prayers may not be hindered"* (1 Peter 3:7). If husbands will honor their wives, as "joint heirs" with them in the grace of life, God will answer their prayers. Men are so different from women. *Understanding* her will involve a great deal of time and energy. It involves *asking* her how she feels on any given subject and not always trying to solve her problems. Sometimes she doesn't need solution, just a listening ear.

> HUSBANDS ARE TO HONOR THEIR WIVES AS "JOINT HEIRS" IN THE GRACE OF LIFE.

What does it mean to honor your wife? It simply means to consider your wife's needs above your own. *Honoring* means listening to her and communicating with her. It involves giving her *quality time*, not leftover time. If you value your wife's insights concerning life, marriage, raising children, friendships, careers, church, decision making, how your gifts differ, etc., she will truly be a joint heir with you. There will be harmony, not discord. Sin will not be obstructing your relationship with God, and He promises answers to your prayers! Husbands, you cannot demand respect from your wife, you can only earn it. You do this through tenderly and patiently understanding and honoring her.

PROMISES TO WIVES ABOUT HUSBANDS

Likewise, the woman also has been given promises resulting from her submission to her husband. Respectful submission is *always voluntary on her part*. It requires faith in God's perspective and plan.

> *For such is the will of God that by doing right you may silence the ignorance of foolish men . . . And let not your adornment be*

merely external braiding the hair and wearing gold jewelry, or putting on dresses; but let it be the hidden person of the heart, with the imperishable quality of a gentle and quiet spirit, which is precious in the sight of God. For in this way in former times the holy women also, who hoped in God, used to adorn themselves, being submissive to their own husbands. Thus Sarah obeyed Abraham, calling him lord, and you have become her children if you do what is right without being frightened by any fear (1 Peter 2:15; 3:3-6).

God instructs women to submit to their husbands, not because of the husband's perfection, but because of God's faithfulness. Submission is never to be seen as unto the husband, but as unto the Lord. God's faithfulness is your hope, just as it was the hope of Christ as He went to the cross.

The first promise occurs in 1 Peter 2:15. While not yet speaking directly of marriage, Peter mentions a result of submission that occurs from a relationship other than marriage. Peter tells us that if we do what is right, we can "silence the ignorance of foolish men." That is powerful.

This is followed closely by a second promise in 1 Peter 3:1. Wives who submit themselves, as unto the Lord, may win their husbands, without words, by their behavior. Again, God is promising wives that they can be an instrument of the Lord, causing their husband to be won to Him. Notice, there is no other way to effect change in a husband. The mouth is neither a way of making peace nor of making a husband do what is right. The woman who struggles with submission has never really believed God that her respect is the key to his response. Her resistance only leads to frustration.

Notice, wives, we are *not talking about poor communication here.* Throughout Scripture we find instruction on how and when to communicate. However, this passage is dealing with weakness on the part of the husband. The wife is nearing the point of "nagging or preaching." Wives must get out of the way, so that God can work in her husband's life. This is a tough decision and requires faith and a complete dependence on God.

I have grown to so respect my wife, that when I am wrong and she is gracious toward me, I feel overwhelmed to confess my mistakes. She may say something like, "Don, I have expressed my opinion on that subject, but I want you to pray about it. Before the Lord, whatever you decide, we will do." As a man, I can bear witness to the power God releases in my life through her gracious attitude. When she does that, I want to do right! I always pray about decisions, especially when she has expressed her feelings on any given subject. I can listen to her so much more effectively, if I feel that she is not judging me or mistrusting me. I have often found that her "intuition" has kept me from making a mistake that I would have made if I hadn't consulted her. Her gracious attitude frees me to go to the Lord and seek His will. We can then pray about it together, and God always shows us what to do.

> HUSBANDS LOVE YOUR WIVES AS YOUR OWN BODIES.

Finally, God promises that the woman who keeps His perspective and trusts Him more than human devices (trickery, flattery, manipulative words, physical charms) will be very precious to God. What a promise! God places a very high value on a woman who esteems her husband. He says her trust will cause her to have a "*gentle and quiet spirit.*" Gentle means "not causing her husband to be frustrated or ruffled." Quiet means "causing her husband to be soothed when he is upset or frustrated."

To the woman who seeks God's heart, it means a great deal to be "precious" in His sight. Peter says submissive wives will be like Sarah, who had no fear. Most women are paralyzed with fears: fears of growing old, losing love, appreciation or wealth, facing death, and more. Most would love to be fearless. God chose Sarah to illustrate His promise. Abraham, her husband, was far from perfect. Yet Sarah submitted herself and was not afraid. A very wealthy man, Abraham was called by God to leave his home in search of a new place. God promised to lead him. He went by faith, taking Sarah and all their servants. During the trip, Abraham came upon a very harsh kingdom. Rather than trusting God that he wouldn't be killed, he told Sarah to pretend to be his sister, so she would find favor with the king and therefore spare Abraham's life. And Sarah remained silent!

Let me ask you: has your husband ever told you to do anything quite so ridiculous? Probably not! Abraham pulled this trick, not once, but twice! Sarah's hope was not in Abraham at this point, but in God who judges righteously. God protected her both times. And God will protect you from your husband's mistakes.

Considering both the commands and promises to the husband and wife, there is no advantage to either role. Both commands call for total faith. On the other hand, God's promises to both husbands and wives take the sting out of the commands, and give hope.

HIS TO CHERISH, HERS TO TRUST

The New Testament gives us two practical pictures of how these concepts are implemented. First, to the husband, is the picture of loving his wife.

> *So husbands ought also to love their own wives as their own bodies. He who loves his own wife loves himself; for no one ever hated his own flesh, but **nourishes and cherishes** it, just as Christ also does the church, because we are members of His body* (Eph. 5:28-30).

We are to *love our wives as our own bodies*. I am so instinctively aware of the value of my own body that I do not have to consciously think about loving it. If anyone, or anything, hurts or threatens it, I respond with corrective action. God is telling us that this is how important our wives are to be to us. I am to be so sensitive to her that if anything hurts or threatens her, I should take immediate corrective action to protect her.

I am to nourish and cherish her. These two words are beautiful ways of describing the love God is talking about. Both words are used only twice in the New Testament. The word *nourish* literally means, "to keep warm at the point of melting." It was used to describe a mother bird keeping her babies under her wing at perfect body temperature. I am to be so involved in my wife's care, that I know from moment to moment what her needs are, so I can meet them.

Even more descriptive is the word, *cherish*. This word is used one other place in Scripture in 1 Thessalonians 2:7: "But we proved to be gentle among you, as a nursing mother tenderly cares for her own children." From experience and counseling, this word picture triggered understanding for me. Have you men noticed how women are almost perfect in responding to the needs of their newborn? Even women, who normally struggle with serving others have an uncanny ability to give joyfully, without resentment, to their babies. An infant makes selfish demands with little capacity to appreciate its mother's sacrifice. Yet, a good mother will *reshape her life* for her baby with very little struggle. She does it because she feels blessed, and senses her absolute responsibility. She has an innate desire to do what has to be done.

This illustration opened my eyes to God's perspective. I realized that God was saying that if I really understood how important Sally was to my creation purpose, I would gladly treat her as a mother nursing a newborn baby would. The light went on. Now, what God said in Genesis 1 and 2 took on an even more beautiful meaning. Like naming the animals for Adam, this passage registered for me. The meaning of Sally, as a gift and provision, deepened tremendously. She became valuable and precious to me.

Men, our culture does not teach us to view marriage this way. Such care and concern for wives is not found in the average American home. This is God's pattern. Let me ask, do you love your wife as much as you do your own body? Do you know her needs? Are you sensitive to her? Have you altered your lifestyle in order that she might be set apart and glorified? Do you take this responsibility from the Lord, as completely as Christ took His responsibility for you? Regardless of performance? Are you totally committed to her?

God illustrates submission to wives by talking about their *"respectful behavior,"* their *"gentle and quiet spirit,"* and their *"hope in God."* Each of these perspectives are dependent on knowing and trusting God. First, the wife begins by exhibiting a respectful attitude toward her husband. God says, "Love him into right behavior." When your husband is wrong, your first response is usually to tell him so! God says there is a better way, a way that will win him without condemning words. The only way a woman can act respectfully when her husband falters is to view God as the guarantor of her needs. When a wife understands how God made her husband, she will discover from Scripture how to wisely influence him to submit to God.

> SUBMISSION MEANS HAVING RESPECT FOR YOUR HUSBAND.

A woman who puts her hope in God, instead of in human schemes, exhibits a gentle and quiet spirit toward her husband. Again, the picture of her outer and inner beauty is contrasted. Peter says not to ignore your physical appearance, but to concentrate on the inner qualities. Wives, you do need to look good for your husbands. But your primary efforts are to be in developing your spiritual walk with the Lord, so that "Christ-like" qualities will come through to your husband. Jesus loves your husband and died for him. Your life should exemplify that. A gentle and quiet spirit will soothe the soul of your husband like nothing else in the world. He will enjoy coming home to you.

The woman who places her hope in God will be able to call her husband "lord." This means she is able to esteem him above what he deserves, because she views him from God's perspective. Her loving spirit toward him will free him to then submit to the Lord and grow spiritually. With proper love and submission, there will be oneness in marriage. The cycle of loving and esteeming is a "blessing" cycle indeed!

LEVELS OF UNDERSTANDING

In working with Christians, I have discovered three basic levels of understanding of the husband's and wife's roles and responsibilities. These levels are as different as night and day. Evaluate them and decide where you are and where you need to be!

The Legalistic Level: Many church people are at this level of understanding. This person only understands that God commands us to be a lover or a submitter. They know these two commands but feel they are impossible to obey. After a talk on "headship and submission," these people always try to find a way out. The woman may say, "Please pray for me as I try to submit to this monster I'm married to." The husband may say, "I'm the head, but she won't do anything I tell her to do." (They've both missed the point altogether.)

Down through the centuries men have used the issue of "headship" as a "club" over their wives' heads. Completely missing their responsibility to love, they hear only the command for the wife to submit. They feel right in "lording it over" their wives. No wonder wives resent their husbands!

An equally unfortunate response can be seen by some wives who have been so offended by God's command to submit that they deny the command altogether. Their need to defend their rights reveals a basic legalistic fear that God is going to deny them something. Or they fear that they will not be fulfilled as a person. They think the word submit, means "to be walked on," or "to be a doormat." These women have missed the bigger picture of Christ's commands. The concepts of "lording it over" and "being walked on" have no basis whatsoever in Scripture. Fear and rebellion result from these misunderstandings.

There is very little hope for the legalistic man or woman. Either defensive or defeated, they run from one book to the next, trying to find the key. This week they might try a new plan. For several weeks their hopes are high. Soon, however, the newness of the project wears off. Things happen that discourage them. Once again, they begin to search for the next book or marriage seminar. Books and seminars are fine, but *rightly understanding the word of God*, mixed with faith, is what endures!

The Promise Level: The next level of understanding is significantly better. The promise level is one in which couples begin to look beyond God's command to love and submit, to His promise of blessing. Many successful marriages are at this level of understanding because they are focusing on God's promises. They live with joyful expectancy of God working in their marriages. They believe and act upon God's Word, which produces results in their lives and reinforces their efforts. They characterize their marriages with hope, based on the certainty of God's Word. In and through God's promises, they are assured of everything they need to make life successful. The potential of a marriage focused on God's promises is clear.

> *Seeing that His divine power has granted to us everything pertaining to life and godliness, through the true knowledge of Him who called us by His own glory and excellence. For by these He has granted to us His precious and magnificent promises, in order that by them you might become partakers of the divine nature* (1 Peter 1:3-4).

Beyond leaning on God's promises, what could possibly add to our understanding of love and submission? One important insight is missing. Christians need to ask, "How did we come to question God in the first place concerning roles?" If we do not answer that question, we could still be vulnerable to future confusion.

The Wisdom Level: The next level of understanding is wisdom. Wisdom involves living and seeing life from God's perspective. Only through God's wisdom, made known through the Holy Spirit, can we come to fully accept and embrace love and submission. Each of us must individually come to the point of totally rejoicing in our roles, because they are from God's loving hand. It takes wisdom to do that.

Wisdom is non-negotiable. Why? First, because you are still vulnerable if you do not have it. Second, and most importantly, the God of all creation, the great I AM, deserves it. Most of us have never stopped to realize that our questioning of love and submission, in the end, really questions the character of God. If that does not motivate you, than nothing will.

Several things are vital if Christians desire wisdom. First, each of us must ask the Holy Spirit to teach us. Second, we need to understand who caused this problem in the first place. Originally, who was the author of sin? Satan. How did he deceive Adam and Eve? He lied to them. Who do you think is the source of the world's rejection of the order in marriage? Yes, Satan. The father of lies is still at work. In the next chapter, Satan's deceit will be revealed.

After understanding Satan and how he deceives us, each of us must embrace God and His Word. When we establish our trust in Him, and bind Satan, then we can step out in faith. Wisdom will allow us to set aside our fear (of limitations) in the roles of love and submission. Rightly understanding the Word, revealed to us through the Holy Spirit, releases us from being deceived again. God's promises can be understood and enacted upon more freely. Oneness is then possible, to the praise and honor of God.

CHAPTER TEN
WISDOM OR DECEIT

WHEN A MAN becomes frustrated over God's command to love his wife even if she has disappointed and hurt him a thousand times, he may recoil with, "I don't have to put up with this. She's driving me crazy!" Or when a wife has just reviewed her responsibility in Scripture to submit to an insensitive and irresponsible man, it's not unusual for me to hear, "It's not fair! I won't submit to a man like that."

How can we handle these situations wisely? Love and submission sound great, but regrettably, they are tough issues in real life. Let's see if we can discover why we all struggle with these responsibilities.

A REVIEW OF ROLES IN MARRIAGE

Thus far, we have established that God is the author of relationships. It was God who created the need in us for relationships, and God who chose to make Adam and Eve His example for marriage on the earth. Since God is ultimately responsible to meet our needs, we know that He will not allow anything to prevent Him from meeting these responsibilities. Therefore, God guarantees the outcome of relationships that are directed by Him.

As we learned in the previous chapter, God does not consider either role in marriage as "better." God did not create the roles to be issues of performance, importance, success, or even superiority. Both are vital to marital blessing. When God tells couples to love and submit, he did not intend strife to be the result. These are simply God's order for a godly life. He created husbands and wives to accomplish His purposes by being one. Everything God has designed shows order, and marriage is no exception. In the previous chapter, we learned that oneness cannot occur without love and respect.

1 Corinthians 11:3 says, *"But I want you to understand that Christ is the head of every man, and the man is the head of a woman, and God is the head of Christ."* Obviously, God has created an order for successful relationships. The good news is that His intention for marriage is compared to His relationship with the Trinity. Clearly, God intended no less for marriage than for Himself. In fact, Christ is both lover and submitter, and saw no threat in either role. He knew that His role, compared to His Father's, had nothing to do with winning or losing. Is Christ any less God than the Father? Any less glorified? Certainly not!

When God tells us to love and submit, He intends no struggle, only order, blessing, and oneness. The problem, then, is not that God made a mistake providing roles, but rather that we have been deceived. A person who is looking at life from God's perspective, and who understands God's purpose concerning relationships, will not question His order. Husbands and wives who are controlled by self-centeredness will question any differences between the roles as being unfair.

DECEPTION IN THE GARDEN

Our problem with roles comes from the fact that Satan has deceived us. Satan wants us to see our mates as the problem rather than himself as the deceiver. *"For our struggle is not against flesh and blood, but against the rulers, against the powers, against the world forces of this darkness, against the spiritual forces of wickedness in the heavenly places"* (Eph. 6:12).

What did Jesus say about Satan?

".... he was a **murderer** from the beginning, and does not stand in the truth, because there is no truth in him. Whenever he speaks a lie, he speaks from his own nature; for he is a **liar** and the father of lies" (John 8:44).

Satan wants to destroy marriages. Why? Because oneness in marriage is a threat to his purposes. If he can destroy marriages, he can also limit God's purposes for that couple. That's his strategy. He knows that if he is successful, he will end oneness on earth. With our divorce rate at an all time high, he appears to be winning the battle. Thankfully, as Christians, we know the battle is far from over, and the ultimate victor is Christ Himself.

> OUR STRUGGLE IS NOT AGAINST PEOPLE, BUT SATAN.

Let's look at the example of Satan's deceit in the Garden of Eden in Genesis 3. God created a perfect environment; every need had been met. Adam and Eve had no desire for other things, no longings, no dreams of things being better. God desired this perfect relationship to last for eternity, therefore, He placed within the garden the "Tree of Life." If Adam and Eve had eaten of this tree first, they would have lived for all eternity in a perfect state.

The only threat to this eternal perfection was another tree, the "Tree of Good and Evil." God told Adam and Eve not to eat of that tree. He told them, *"If you eat of it, you will surely die."* Since they had no sinful nature, and since they were perfectly dependent on the Lord, they did not even consider the tree an issue of struggle. Adam and Eve trusted God. They knew that *not* eating from that tree was totally for their good!

In Genesis 3:1-7, Satan distorted the *purpose* of the tree. He disputed God's purpose by calling His Word into question. He said they would not die if they ate of the tree, and implied that the real reason God did not want them to eat of the tree was because they would become like God. "God is really trying to limit you. He is trying to keep you from being like Him." *Satan subtly changed God's purpose from one of protection, to one of limitation.* Satan appealed to their eyes, appetites, and pride in tempting them. They believed a lie, and they sinned.

TRUSTING SATAN'S LIES

Satan is still in the business of deceiving! He uses the same tactics today. When God originally instructed us to love and submit, what was His purpose? It was to allow us to experience relationships, accomplish His plan of the ages, meet man's needs, and to equip man to reflect, reproduce and reign. God knew that without love and submission, there would be no satisfying relationships and no oneness.

Satan has distorted God's purpose by suggesting that love and submission present a limitation, by telling husbands to resist being lovers, and wives to resent submitting. "Why should I love her? She doesn't deserve it." Or "Why should I submit to him? He's no better than I am. I'm smarter, more talented, and more successful." Like in the garden, Satan deceives us to see love and submission as *limits* to our rights and freedom.

GOD'S REDEMPTIVE SOLUTIONS

> After Adam and Eve had sinned, God inquired into what they had done. *"And the man said, "The woman whom Thou gavest to be with me, she gave me from the tree, and I ate." Then the Lord God said to the woman, "What is this you have done?" And the woman said, "The serpent deceived me, and I ate"* (Gen. 3:12-13).

What happened to their oneness? Adam immediately blamed Eve. He failed to take responsibility. Ultimately, Adam blamed God for giving Eve to him. *Adam believed a lie and then blamed God.*

Who had changed? Not God! Both Adam and Eve were

deceived and disobeyed God. This taste of rebellion birthed the self-centeredness of man. Oneness in marriage has suffered since that event.

God responded in love with several actions designed to rescue humankind and to defeat Satan's rebellion. First, God established a *redemptive* curse for Adam and Eve.

The woman was given the burden of bearing children and rearing them in the home: *"I will greatly multiply your pain in childbirth, in pain you shall bring forth children; yet your desire shall be for your husband, and he shall rule over you"* (Gen. 3:16).

The man was given the mandate to toil in life for sustenance by hard work: *"Cursed is the ground because of you; in toil you shall eat of it all the days of your life. Both thorns and thistles it shall grow for you; and you shall eat the plants of the field"* (Gen. 3:17,18). God greatly increased Adam and Eve's burden *to protect them from their selfishness.*

In verse 23, God demonstrated His grace even further by removing Adam and Eve from the garden so their struggle with sin and death would not be eternal, but temporary. The stage was thereby set for us to receive new bodies for all eternity at the return of Christ. His ultimate act of love was sending His only Son to die on a cross, so that we could once more be in perfect union with Him, in a perfect environment, with perfected bodies and minds. God's response in the garden was a curse compared to the perfect state of Genesis 1 and 2. At the same time, though, these were *gracious and redemptive solutions.*

In Genesis 3:16 is a statement that I believe has become the source of the current debate on love and submission. God said, *"The man shall rule over the woman."* Today, our culture rebels against this statement.

Prior to the fall, Adam and Eve's oneness with God and with each other functioned perfectly. Their submission to God was not in question. There was no mention of submission *between* Adam and Eve, because both were totally submitted to God "as one." When sin occurred, Adam and Eve lost their oneness. To protect them from their self-centeredness, God ordained an *order* of relationships. This order is necessary for oneness and blessing in marriage. Even though humankind is now confused because of Satan's deceit, God's order remains the same. It takes both love and submission to experience oneness.

DECEPTION IN RELATIONSHIPS

I believe Satan's second great lie, after the one in the garden, concerns love and submission. When God said to love and submit, he intended only good. Without love and submission, God cannot meet our "aloneness" needs. Without love and submission, oneness is impossible, and only through oneness can God's purposes be accomplished. Satan does not want that! If Christians do not *submit themselves to each other* in humility, they will become a threat, a discouragement, a source of rejection and judgment in the lives of their mates. Unless they *love and serve* unconditionally, they will never gain respect. There are no agape relationships without both love and submission.

> EACH MATE SHOULD ASK GOD'S FORGIVENESS FOR DOUBTING HIS CREATION OF ROLES IN MARRIAGE.

Satan has deceived us by appealing to our pride and self-centered nature. He convinces husbands that it is justifiable to demand their wives' obedience, while simultaneously whispering to wives that submission equals oppression. As was stated earlier, those thoughts are anti-Biblical. Each mate should ask God's forgiveness for doubting His creation of roles in marriage. By faith, accept God's forgiveness and power and live according to His Word.

In the future, share these truths with others to insure they are renewed in your own life. Only as we renew our minds with Scripture, can the Holy Spirit protect us from ignorance and Satan's deceit. Thank God for your new understanding of love and submission and encourage your mate with your new insight and commitment.

WISDOM: HAVING GOD'S VIEWPOINT

Christ's trust of God the Father allowed Him to view love and submission, not as limitations, but as the greatest blessings in all eternity. Christ both loved the church and submitted to His Father. Consider His perspective and the result of both roles from the following passage.

> *If therefore there is any encouragement in Christ, if there is any consolation of love, if there is any fellowship of the Spirit, if any affection and compassion, make my joy complete by being of the **same** mind, maintaining the **same** love, **united** in spirit, intent on **one** purpose. Do nothing from selfishness or empty conceit, but with humility of mind let each of you regard one another as more important than himself; do not merely look out for your own personal interests, but also for the interests of others. Have this attitude in yourselves which was also in Christ Jesus, who, although He existed in the form of God,* ***did not regard equality with God a thing to be grasped** . . . He humbled Himself by becoming obedient to the point of death, even death on a cross. Therefore also **God highly exalted Him**, and bestowed on Him the name which is above every name, that at the name of Jesus every knee should bow, of those who are in heaven, and on earth, and under the earth, and that every tongue should confess that Jesus Christ is Lord, to the glory of God the Father* (Phil. 2:1-11).

The apostle Paul says if anyone desires to experience encouragement in Christ, love, fellowship of the Spirit, compassion or affection in this life, they must be one with others and with God. He describes oneness as being of *the "same mind, maintaining the same love, united in spirit, and being intent on one purpose."* The goals that Paul mentions describe all of our desires. Oneness is God's goal for all relationships, be they in the Trinity, the church, or in marriage.

Paul gives us the key to finding oneness when he tells us to be intent on the purpose of having humility of mind toward others.

Obviously selfishness has no place here. Many people fear that to be humble is to be spineless. However, humility is not an emotional cowering, but a mark of one with a strong consciousness of God's sovereignty in any given situation. This perspective allows both husbands and wives to esteem each other above him/herself. Without humility of mind, there is no encouragement, love, fellowship, affection, or compassion. God's perspective allows us to serve each other freely, without being resentful or feeling limited. Christ is our perfect example.

> ONENESS IS GOD'S GOAL FOR ALL RELATIONSHIPS, BE THEY IN THE TRINITY, THE CHURCH, OR IN MARRIAGE.

*It was just before the Passover Feast. Jesus knew that the time had come for Him to leave this world and go to the Father. Having loved His own who were in the world, He now **showed them the full extent of His love** . . . He poured water into a basin and began to wash His disciples' feet, drying them with the towel that was wrapped around Him. "Do you understand what I have done for you?" He asked them. "You call Me 'Teacher and Lord, and rightly so, for that is what I am. Now that I, your Lord and Teacher, have washed your feet, you also should wash one another's feet. I have set you an example that you should do as I have done for you"* (John 13:1-2; 12-15 NIV).

Remember, God created us to be incomplete without relationships. He created us to be unable to accomplish our creation purposes of reflecting His image, reproducing a godly heritage, or reigning on earth without relationships. God cannot meet our needs without love and submission. As we keep God's perspective of relationships before us, His commands to love or submit become, not limits, *but the door to relationships and blessings.* Therefore, through humility of mind, we can actually esteem others higher than ourselves, even in tough situations. We can serve each other in love. That is how Jesus Christ Himself lived!

Husbands, can you graciously love and serve your wives, thereby allowing them to become beautiful women of God? Wives, can you graciously submit to your husbands by giving them respect, thereby encouraging them to follow Christ?

Every great marriage has two people who are free from the struggle of questioning God's Word. They are free from seeing their mate as the problem. They expect Satan to try to deceive them. But they don't succumb to his lies. They know that he has already been defeated at the cross. They are, therefore, victorious over Satan and his schemes, because Jesus clearly has already won the victory. *"Having disarmed the powers and authorities, Jesus made a public spectacle of them, triumphing over them by the cross"* (Col. 2:15). The result of a couple's faith and obedience will be oneness and blessing in their personal lives and in their marriage.

> HIS COMMANDS TO LOVE OR SUBMIT BECOME, NOT LIMITS, BUT THE DOOR TO RELATIONSHIPS AND BLESSINGS.

CONCLUSION TO PART II

This chapter concludes Part II of the book. We have just finished studying a number of insights that will allow you to experience a supernatural faith relationship in your marriage. Each of these insights require faith on the part of the couple. As you read through the following list ask yourself these questions. Do I understand what God is saying? Am I applying faith concerning this issue right now? Each of the following commitments are vital to a faith marriage.

1. Couples need to commit themselves to God's purposes of reflecting, reproducing, and reigning.
2. Couples must receive one another from God as His personal provision for their needs.
3. Couples must release God's power in their marriage by daily submitting to the Holy Spirit.
4. Couples must understand that they can only change

their mate through the active force of agape love or the reactive force of blessing.
5. Couples must seek God's wisdom concerning love and submission issues.

*These five commitments form the **core** of a faith relationship.* Nothing is more practical to married life than these. Review these commitments often.

Remember, Christ's prayer to His Father, just before He died for you and me. He prayed, *"I do not ask in behalf of these alone, but for those also who believe in Me through their word; that they may all be one; even as Thou, Father, art in Me, and I in Thee, that they also may be in Us; that the world may believe that Thou didst send me"* (John 17:20-21).

God's plan to reach a lost world is dependent on oneness. The major point of this book emphasizes that marital oneness requires faith. At this point you may be thinking, "These are great principles, but how do I apply them to the practical areas of marriage, such as: communication, money, sex, etc." Let me say that these five major commitments are the **basis or foundation** for the practical areas. If you don't understand the faith concepts just covered, you will not be able to apply faith to the practical areas of marriage. In Hebrews 11, faith is defined as follows:

Now faith is the assurance of things hoped for, the conviction of things not seen (Heb. 11:1).

Many times in marriage, your human instinct will override God's perspective. At those times, ideally, God will bring some scripture verse or passage to your mind and faith will take over. Your marriage will then be characterized as one that acts supernaturally, based on the facts of God's Word, not on human ingenuity.

Now we can move on to Part III and the everyday issues that occur in marriage such as: male and female responsibilities, romance, finances, trials, in-laws, male/female differences, personality differences, etc. As we keep God's perspective of the principles just covered, the daily areas developed in the next section will then fall into place.

CHRISTIAN FAMILY LIFE has produced a twelve week marriage study of the *Becoming One* material, which helps implement the principles you are learning in this book. Taking or leading this class once a year will not only allow you to help others, but it will ensure greater understanding of faith in your marriage.

PART III

CHAPTER ELEVEN

A MAN OF COMMITMENT

Let your fountain be blessed, and rejoice in the wife of your youth. As a loving hind and a graceful doe, let her breasts satisfy you at all times; be exhilarated always with her love
(Prov. 5:18-19).

WHAT IS THE MARK of a great husband? Is it financial responsibility, social prominence, sexual attractiveness, or being a successful father? As important as these areas are, there is a much greater issue. The mark of a great husband is an absolute, unfailing commitment to his wife. A husband cannot bless his wife more than to love her as a gift from God. Husbands who faithfully look to God for marital direction are rare indeed. As men, we often fail to recognize marriage as a covenant with our mate and with God.

THE MARRIAGE COVENANT

This commitment, this covenant, a man makes before God to his wife includes (1) overseeing his family, in order that they might reflect the image of God properly, (2) raising his children to love and follow the Lord, and (3) leading the way in reigning over what God gives him. To be God's man, the husband's goal is to be totally responsible to God for his wife and family.

Our Lord Jesus talked plainly about a man's marriage covenant: *"Consequently they are no longer two, but one flesh. What therefore God has joined together, let no man separate"* (Matt. 19:6). I feel deep fear in my heart when I think of men, especially Christian men, who break this covenant. Divorce is not God's will. It's always a poor solution with tremendous negative ramifications. Below is a vivid description of how God feels about a husband's commitment to his wife.

> *Yet you say, "For what reason?" Because the Lord has been a witness between you and the wife of your youth, against whom you have dealt treacherously, though she is your companion and your wife by **covenant**. But not one has done so who has a remnant of the Spirit. And what did that one do while he was seeking a **godly offspring**? Take heed then, to your spirit, and let no one deal treacherously against the wife of your youth. "For I hate divorce," says the Lord, the God of Israel, "and him who covers his garment with wrong," says the Lord of hosts. So take heed to your spirit, that you do not deal treacherously"* (Malachi 2:14-16).

God Himself is a witness and a participant in the covenant a husband makes with his wife. No man can break that covenant and be led by the Spirit of God. God not only hates divorce, but He will judge the one who does the wrong in the divorce. God considers a man's responsibility toward his wife as a *covenant* with Him. He gave marriage to man as a blessing; therefore, the husband is responsible to be faithful to that covenant, no matter what the cost. Divorce may not bring "godly offspring," rather, just the opposite. God not only hates divorce because "oneness" is destroyed, but because children are irreversibly hurt. Oneness is broken in divorce, and great pain is the result.

> THE HUSBAND IS RESPONSIBLE TO BE FAITHFUL TO THAT COVENANT, NO MATTER WHAT THE COST.

God takes His covenants seriously, and marriage is a covenant! If you want to be characterized as a great husband, expectantly take up your covenant and live it out in Christ. Put away, once and for all, any thoughts about quitting or changing mates. Place your faith in God's promises and commit yourself to sacrificial love that will soften even the hardest heart.

IF YOU HAVE TO "TOUGH IT OUT"

Several instructions come from James as he talks about responding to tough trials. This list is helpful to remember during trying times in marriage.

> *This you know, my beloved brethren. But let everyone be quick to hear, slow to speak and slow to anger; for the anger of man does not achieve the righteousness of God. Therefore putting aside all filthiness and all that remains of wickedness, in humility receive the word implanted, which is able to save your souls. But prove yourselves doers of the word, and not merely hearers who delude themselves* (James 1:19-22).

If there is a battle, in this case in your marriage, take note of the following:

1. Don't react, but listen to your wife.
2. Don't speak too quickly; wait for your emotions to subside.
3. Don't be angry; nothing good ever comes from anger.
4. Stop your immoral involvement: lying, cheating, bad language, pornography, etc.
5. Humbly study God's Word for the answers to your problems, seeking counsel when necessary.
6. Act on your faith, not on your feelings. Boldly believe God, regardless of your wife's response. (Remake your covenant to your mate by faith.)

James 5:16-18 sets forth our final two points of instruction:

> *Therefore, confess your sins to one another, and pray for one another, so that you may be healed. The effective prayer of a righteous man can accomplish much. Elijah was a man with a nature like ours, and he prayed earnestly that it might not rain; and it did not rain on the earth for three years and six months. And he prayed again, and the sky poured rain, and the earth produced its fruit.*

7. Confess your sins to your wife so both of you can be emotionally healed.
8. Pray earnestly. If God can make and stop rain for Elijah, God can change your life, motivate your wife and remove your fears.

FULFILLMENT OF THE COVENANT

The sovereignty of God really motivates me as a man. The thought that God is a partner with me in my marriage inspires me to serve and please Him. It gives me an awareness that my marriage is part of God's eternal plan. As we search Scripture to determine the husband's role in guiding a marriage according to God's will, here is what I have found to be two of the salient points.

Rule And Serve

In the Old Testament (Gen. 3:16) God says, *"The man shall rule over the woman."* In the New Testament, God compares a husband's responsibility to that of Christ's to the church (Eph. 5:25). These truths indicate two major principles in the practice of the husband's covenant to his wife. First, he is to rule. This word conveys the thought of authority and administration.

> YOU CANNOT DEMAND RESPECT FROM YOUR WIFE. YOU CAN ONLY EARN IT.

As was stated in the chapter on love and submission, men have, throughout the ages, used this word "rule" as a dictatorship position. Nothing is farther from the truth in Scripture. Men are to take authority with *humility* and a *servant spirit*. You cannot demand respect from your wife. You can only earn it. Demanding destroys a wife emotionally, and will eventually destroy the marriage. You are to take authority with a gracious, loving spirit toward your wife and children.

Second, the husband is to be a *priest* to his wife. The word priest means minister, emphasizing the role of *servant and counselor*. You are to be so aware of her and her needs that you go out of the way to meet them. Most men do not know the needs of their wives without asking them. Don't assume you know until she tells you. Serve her, be her loving administrator, and take authority for her life and needs. Do this in a way that supports and encourages her.

There must be careful balance in both of these responsibilities to rule and to be priest. If the husband overemphasizes his authority, his wife will lose respect and trust. If the husband is only a servant, she will be insecure and lack direction. In searching, both Scripture and common sense, for what it means to rule (lead) and to be a servant in marriage, I have discovered several specific areas of responsibility for a man:

- Protect
- Provide
- Initiate love
- Pray
- Take authority in conflict
- Meet physical needs
- Support relationship development
- Share time struggles
- Help with children: discipline and instruction
- Emphasize future hope

There are three major commands given to husbands in the New Testament telling us how to fulfill those responsibilities.

Understand Your Wife

You husbands likewise, live with your wives in an understanding way, as with a weaker vessel, since she is a woman; and grant her honor as a fellow heir of the grace of life, so that your prayers may not be hindered (1 Pet. 3:7).

Peter says that husbands ought to understand, or know, their wives. Sometimes after two counseling sessions, I get the feeling that I know a man's wife better than he does after ten years of marriage. Peter is commanding us to be experts about our wives.

Most *successful husbands* I know make it a point to *ask* their wives about their emotional, spiritual, physical, and intellectual needs. Seek your wife's opinion regularly. Knowing her is not an automatic thing. If you don't work at hearing from her, you won't know when she is under stress, when she just needs some physical exercise, when she needs a day off, or a night out with you. To understand her means also to honor her, to lift her up, to treat her with utmost respect.

Do you know what a perfect day is for your wife? A perfect date? What she really likes to do on vacations? If not, you'd better find out. *Is there good communication between the two of you on a daily basis?* Peter commands us to know our wives and to allow them access to us, or he warns that sin and struggle will prevail, and our prayers will not be answered. How can we be out of fellowship with our wives and expect God to answer when we call? "Fellow heirs" means that all of life and all God's blessings are to be shared by the two of you. Decisions you make, raising the children, moving, changing jobs, church, trials, joys and frustrations, etc. are all to be shared.

> HOW CAN WE BE OUT OF FELLOWSHIP WITH OUR WIVES AND EXPECT GOD TO ANSWER WHEN WE CALL?

Be Responsible For Your Wife

We must know our wives so completely that we can uniquely apply our responsibilities to fit their specific needs. Paul gives husbands a command from Ephesians 5:25: *"Husbands, love your wives, just as Christ also loved the church and gave Himself up for her."*

God's command to love includes the idea of giving up your life for her, in the same way Christ gave Himself up for the church. While I do not expect God will require me literally to die, I am willing. God expects me to sensitively get involved in all issues which cause her fear, physically or emotionally. Physical protection, financial protection, emotional protection, fear of failure, fear of aging, and meeting the spiritual and physical needs of children are good examples of issues where a sacrificial husband might give himself up for his wife. You must learn to be a buffer for your wife. The husband shields her from the fear of facing issues alone, that may cause her fear or frustration. So husbands, as you prepare to meet your wife's needs, first know her and sacrificially take responsibility for her fears.

Love Your Wife As You Love Yourself

> *So husbands ought also to love their own wives as their own bodies. He who loves his own wife loves himself; for no one ever hated his own flesh, but nourishes and cherishes it, just as Christ also does the church* (Eph. 5:28-29).

Paul commands husbands to love their wives as their own bodies: to *nourish* and *cherish* them. Because we have already defined these words, we won't need more details here. But these words connote comfort. Paul is saying to *sensitively and selflessly* attend to your wife's needs, as a mother would a nursing child. Keep her warm by your momentary monitoring of her intimate emotional and physical needs, just as you care daily for your own needs. Practically speaking, God is commanding you, in your covenant with Him, to give up your own selfishness, by putting her first in priority after Him.

PRACTICAL APPLICATION OF THE COVENANT

Husbands, develop a strategy for your wife and family. Determine the areas of importance in light of your wife's needs, then establish several objectives in each area. Develop a plan for each objective, set priorities, and then schedule their application. A little planning will improve your success significantly. The following are some ideas from counseling. Let the Holy Spirit show you which of the following you need to apply to your wife and family.

Leadership

God's man thrives on being a "shock absorber" for his wife. He anticipates his wife's needs and fears. He is in the unique position to encourage her positive self-worth.

Encourage Self-worth: All of us realize the things that affect feelings of self-worth: intellect, appearance, productivity, success in relationships and financial freedom, among others. Discover mutual areas of interest with your wife and work at communication in that area.

Seek out her intellectual interests and find one where she can teach you. Show interest in her appearance, and support her desire to have a sufficient wardrobe for career and social events. Become an expert on her abilities. If she has a hobby, encourage her. If she does something well in private, sensitively make her friends aware of those skills or qualities. Look for ways to involve her talents publicly. Help her develop part-time, in-home income, if she desires it. Monitor her relationships and assist her in developing friends. Help her organize her schedule. There are many different ways you can encourage her self-worth.

> ROMANCE WILL DIE WITHOUT COMMUNICATION.

Comfort: Never allow your wife to experience pain without sharing it with her. A death in the family, a difficult child, frustration in her career, or a disappointment in relationships, may require your help. Comfort her and take responsibility for helping her find a solution.

Facilitate Spiritual maturity: Your hope for mutual faith in your marriage is related to your wife's maturity as well as yours. Do everything possible to assist her spiritual interest. Encourage her efforts to minister to others or attend church functions. Plan to be involved, as a couple, in leading small groups, teaching Sunday School, etc. Plan activities with your children to free your wife. One of her greatest joys, however, will be watching you take spiritual leadership in your home and church. I cannot ever emphasize how many wives have expressed this to me.

Financial Security
Work at giving your wife financial hope for the future. A personal savings account for her is important, if at all possible. Special needs like lingerie, hair-styling, exercise classes, and hobbies are not all that costly, and they mean a lot to her. Take finances seriously. Study chapter 14, apply it to your own situation, and make a personal commitment to adjust according to God's will. *"But if anyone does not provide for his own, and especially for those of his household, he has denied the faith, and is worse than an unbeliever"* (1 Tim. 5:8).

Romance
Romance in marriage is a man's shared responsibility; romantic moments are extremely important to women. Be a romantic lover to your mate. Women love small, inexpensive surprises, not just on birthdays or holidays. Uniqueness is great, too. An occasional love letter catches her off guard. Quantity is not as important as quality and consistency. (Chapter 13 will be very helpful.)

Communication
Your wife must *communicate with you to maintain her confidence and emotional stability. She cannot respond adequately without a total relationship. Romance will die without communication. If your wife often says that you do not communicate with her, seek counsel to help define and correct the problem.*

Husbands, never give your wives the silent treatment. Love requires regular communication. Do not withhold yourself but open your life to her. Give her words of encouragement. Don't withhold positive words that have the power to heal.

Each of us, as human beings, get angry. Deal with anger quickly. Eph. 4:26 says, *"Do not let the sun go down on your anger."* Why? Because God knew that when we accumulate anger and hurt, it keeps us from putting the past behind us. Only forgiveness heals the past while renewing our hope.

"Do not let any unwholesome talk come out of your mouths, but only what is helpful for building others up according to their needs, that it may benefit those who listen . . . Be kind and compassionate to one

another, forgiving each other, just as in Christ God forgave you" (Eph. 4:29, 32 NIV). Be very careful about accumulating unresolved conflict in your marriage. Hurtful words tend to stay around a long time. Sometimes, after little "shots" we take at our mate, we spend a lot of time trying to undo them. Be *quick* to ask for forgiveness when hurtful things are said. Remember, *"It is to a man's honor to avoid strife, but every fool is quick to quarrel"* (Prov. 20:3 NIV).

Make *daily communication* with your spouse a priority. Ask her *often* how you are doing in this important area of marriage. And be prepared to work a lifetime improving on this skill. Don't ever take for granted that you are communicating enough.

Prayer

Pray for your wife daily. Ask God to give you love for her, and ask Him to help you be so sensitive to her needs that she will become an even more beautiful person to you. It's also important to pray for your children on a daily basis. *Ask* your wife and children what you can pray about for them. As the years pass, the children will come to you or call you with their prayer requests, even when they leave home. Prayer demonstrates to your family that you really care. God is so good in demonstrating Himself through answers to prayer. Talk about continued belief! This one aspect, more than any other, demonstrates your love to them and ultimately shows them God's love.

Authority In Conflict

Decisions and conflicts are constantly developing in the home. Men, do not be passive in these issues. Take responsibility. Get involved. If a decision is not obvious between you and your spouse, take responsibility to insure that the decision is made. If there is conflict between your children, help them resolve it. Husbands and wives need to set *examples* for their children in *conflict resolution*. A passive uninvolved father is especially frustrating to children.

Time Management

A major problem for most wives is time. A husband is in the best position to assist his wife in working out her schedule and priorities. Work out a priority list with your wife. These are some general categories that need to be considered: personal time with the Lord, marriage relationship, relationships with children, career, friendships, church ministry, recreation and work.

Set a brief planning meeting, perhaps fifteen minutes each Sunday night, to agree on a week's schedule. Help her eliminate activities that may over-commit her. After understanding her schedule, take responsibility for her creativity and diversity of activities. Arrange for her to be out of the home regularly, if you have small children. When possible, commit to staying home to give her that freedom. Taking care of your children when your wife is away is not "baby sitting." It is your responsibility as a "joint heir" in the grace of life.

A "date" once a week will do wonders for both of you, and will strengthen your communication. Take charge Friday night and let her sleep in on Saturday morning. If she has preschoolers, relieve her from the five-o'clock "horror show" at dinner and the bedtime scene.

Putting the kids to bed, disciplining them, or washing dishes is like an early Christmas for a mother. If your wife works outside the home, make sure that you *share the chores* and the responsibilities of the home with her.

Child Rearing

In the area of protecting your wife, take your share of the pressure in dealing with and caring for the children. Their academics, emotional needs, their physical and spiritual development are vital to her feeling of well being. Aggressively seek to understand these pressures as they occur, and share them with her. Children *long* for an intimate relationship with their fathers. When that occurs, you will have respect from them *and* your wife for the rest of your life. Husbands, take first responsibility for the children in two areas: discipline and instruction. *"Fathers, do not provoke your children to anger; but bring them up in the discipline and instruction of the Lord"* (Eph. 6:4).

Discipline: Discipline affects a child's character development. Stay involved in discipline and do not leave it primarily to your wife.

Watch for power struggles between your wife and your children. Monitor your wife's emotional tiredness. When it rises, check her struggle with the children. Take responsibility for special problems like tantrums or hyperactivity. Personally, take care of discipline problems at school. Do not provoke your child to anger because of your lack of discipline. Establish a relationship with each individual child. Take each child out alone at least once a month.

Spanking should be done only in the early years, and it will not be needed often if used correctly. Always explain why you are spanking, and love them tenderly afterward. As the child grows, there should be more talking and less spanking. Dr. James Dobson has written several books on the parent-child relationship. We recommend those for more study.

Instruction: Husbands, you are ultimately responsible for the spiritual development of your children. Biblical mandates are given to teach children and instruct them in the Lord:

> *These commandments that I give you today are to be upon your hearts. Impress them on your children. Talk about them when you sit at home and when you walk along the road, when you lie down and when you get up. . . In the future, when you son asks you, "What is the meaning of the stipulations, decrees and laws the Lord our God has commanded you?" Then you shall say to your son. . . .* (Deut. 6:6-7, 20 NIV).

> *He commanded our forefathers to teach their children, so the next generation would know them, even the children yet to be born, and they in turn would tell their children. Then they would put their trust in God and would not forget his deeds but would keep his commands. They would not be like their forefathers—a stubborn and rebellious generation, whose hearts were not loyal to God, whose spirits were not faithful to him* (Psalm 78:5-8 NIV).

Spending even an hour a week putting your children to bed would be a good start. Spending personal time with them on the weekends is invaluable. Communicate with your child to find out where he is spiritually. Help your children solve problems. You, as dad, take the lead in establishing rules concerning dating and sex. Work with your wife, but keep the responsibility on your shoulders. When possible, involve your children in establishing the rules. Make sure to set the rules *before* a problem develops. Anticipation is everything in child rearing. (Example: Don't wait till the child is 15 to tell them they cannot date until 16. That's too late. Stay ahead of the game. You need to tell them at age 11 or 12, before the need arises. They won't question the rule at that age, and will have plenty of time to tell their friends and to think and talk about it.) There should be regular, quality communication with each child in the family. Establish good communication early in their lives, and it will continue, even after they leave home.

Family Identity
Help your wife and children understand that they are part of a uniquely developed family by God's choice. Develop this identity with activities that promote family togetherness: vacations, sports, church activities, youth activities, family camps, etc.

Physical Activity
Take an active interest in your wife's health. Exercise with her and make sure she has physical checkups. Convince her that her body is attractive. Do not let her set unrealistic weight goals. Realistic weight goals, and a husband who sensitively cares, will result in successful weight control. Allow her to share her concerns about your physical situation, also. Don't reject her input. Exercise together if possible. Take walks together frequently. If possible, establish a mutually enjoyable sport: tennis, golf, fishing, bicycling, running, etc.

Future Hope
Always communicate your future vision and plans with your wife. *Get her full input.* Nothing affects a woman more than low expec-

tations for your future, and that of your children. Don't expect your wife to understand your future vision without explaining it to her and making sure she comprehends it.

Mutual Interests: Too many couples lose their desire to be together because they have lost their mutual interests. If you try, you can develop some mutual interests. Travel is a good possibility. Fun, sports, hobbies, and intellectual stimulation are all vital.

Aging: Without spiritual interest, productivity, relationships, and responsibilities, people really suffer as they age. Protect yourselves from slow depression. Develop spiritual interests and activities that can continue until death.

Men, your wife will begin to dream about her future goals at approximately age 40-50. The "empty nest" is right around the corner, and she will want to know that the rest of her life will be productive. Wives tend to focus on the now. Therefore, her early dreams are usually wrapped up in marriage and raising children. But, along about early mid-life, she begins to ask questions about what she wants to accomplish as she ages. Men, help your wife fulfill her dreams.

Allow your grandchildren to become part of your lives, even if they scramble your schedule and exhaust you. They can help you stay active and make you feel important. Continue to work as long as possible before retiring. Then use your talents part time. Your earlier sacrifices to make time for ministry will pay off in your later years. As your work-related activities decrease, your service to the Lord and His people can continually increase. Most of all, maintain your commitment to your wife intellectually, emotionally, spiritually, and sexually.

A MAN'S COVENANT WITH HIMSELF

Proverbs 29:18 (KJV) says, *"Where there is no vision, the people perish."* Most men, unfortunately, do not have much vision for their lives. Yet, a man who plans his life will experience fullness and joy. He and his wife will be uplifted. Consider these areas of planning for your future.

Spiritual Responsibility

Paul wrote to Timothy, *"It is a trustworthy statement: if any man aspires to the office of overseer, it is a fine work he desires to do"* (1 Tim. 3:1). In working and counseling with men, I have seen tremendous need in their lives for authority and respect. In addition, it is very important to their growth in Christ that a large part of their responsibility be associated with spiritual issues. There is tremendous joy for men in church leadership, especially in a church that views elders or other lay leaders' roles as a real ministry. If your church does not encourage personal ministry, volunteer to begin a lay program to develop spiritual responsibility. Lead a men's group, or as a couple, lead a marriage class. Become an elder or deacon, if asked. God desires that you would find His perspective on life, and spiritual leadership is vital to doing so. No matter what your gifts or abilities, seek counsel on a plan that helps you develop spiritual responsibilities in the home, in your church, or in Christian organizations. Men, are you being mentored by someone, and are you in the process of mentoring another man? *"And the things which you have heard from me in the presence of many witnesses, these entrust to faithful men, who will be able to teach others also"* (2 Tim. 2:2). Remember the axiom, "We only keep what we give away."

Accountability

As much as men like to be self-confident and independent, they have deep needs in the area of counsel. I have observed a strong need in men's lives for protection from wrong decisions, for wisdom in their marriage and in child-rearing, for encouragement in their jobs and other important issues.

Several times in my life, I have had to make a significant ministry-oriented decision that was difficult for me and somewhat threatening for my family. Finding myself suddenly under considerable emotional and professional pressure, and knowing I needed to provide firm, directional family leadership, I quickly realized I could become vulnerable to Satan's inevitable attack.

To protect myself and my family, I have always had an advisory group surrounding me to give wise counsel. I usually describe my situation to them and give a historical evaluation of Sally and myself. These men have stood with me and always give honest feedback. More importantly, they rally to my support by helping me develop an aggressive plan for the future. I usually am totally re-motivated, my wife trusts and respects my openness, and I have deepened my relationship with these men. The body of Christ demands our accountability to mature brothers. God says, *"Without consultation, plans are frustrated, but with many counselors they succeed"* (Prov. 15:22).

Work

In Genesis 3, God instructed Adam to toil and sweat. Many men never face this issue of work. Instead, they devise all kinds of ways to get out of work: changing jobs, get-rich-quick schemes, and looking for "greener grass." The times when I was unsure of my vocation were among the most frustrating and depressing periods of my life. They were also times that drove me to my knees before God.

Statistics have shown that most men change jobs several times before they discover what they really enjoy doing. About ten percent of the male population change jobs easily, while an even larger percent tend to stay in their present job, whether or not they like it. Most research indicates that the men who usually win in the long run are the men who demonstrate perseverance in their chosen field. If you notice frustration and inconsistencies in your working experience, seek counsel. Make yourself accountable to a wiser older brother. Develop a plan to gradually refocus your job. Pursue what you enjoy and do well.

CHAPTER TWELVE
A WOMAN OF WISDOM

The wise woman builds her house, but the foolish tears it down with her own hands (Prov. 14:1).

He who finds a wife finds a good thing, and obtains favor from the Lord (Prov. 18:22).

An excellent wife is the crown of her husband (Prov.12:4).

Her children rise up and bless her; her husband also, and he praises her, saying: "Many daughters have done nobly, but you excel them all" (Prov. 31:28-29).

EVERY WOMAN, deep in her heart, would like to be characterized as wise. To hear a husband say, *"You excel them all"* would bring joy to any wife. Do you consider yourself a gift from the Lord to your husband? Would you be identified as a wise woman who is skillful at living? I hope this chapter will help solidify some foundational issues and allow you to increase in wisdom.(This chapter is written from Sally's viewpoint.)

Over the years, we have counseled and worked with many wives. We've experienced joy as we've seen their faith mature, but we've also cried as some have shared their failures. Out of respect for those women and the Lord, we want to share the following insights.

There are four foundational questions every woman must answer before she can be released to enjoy life in the home.

1. Am I limited by my role as a wife?
2. What are the limits to submission?
3. Is the home the key to my success as a wife?
4. How can a wife understand and help her husband?

If you can get clear direction on these four issues, I know you'll be able to have vision and wisdom in your marriage. Ask God, even as you read, to give you understanding into His perspective of how a woman can be fulfilled in marriage.

AM I LIMITED BY MY ROLE AS A WIFE?

Earlier we tried to open your mind to God's perspective concerning the man's responsibility to love and the woman's responsibility to submit. By comparing Ephesians 5 and 1 Peter 3, we tried to demonstrate that there is no special advantage to either role.

Chapters 9 and 10 revealed God's perspective on love and submission by showing God's purpose for giving men and women different responsibilities. Love and submission make oneness in marriage possible. Oneness then allows couples to accomplish God's and man's goals of reflecting His image, reproducing a godly heritage, and reigning in life. Jesus experienced this same oneness through love and submission with God the Father and God the Holy Spirit in the Trinity.

God's perfect plan for love and submission was distorted by Satan when Adam and Eve sinned, giving birth to the self-centered nature of man. In the past few decades, our society has caused women to question and even doubt their need for God's order of relationships.

Women fight an unbelievable battle to maintain God's perspective in light of the world's programming. This battle must be taken seriously and approached aggressively. These truths, taken from the Word of God, are vital to experiencing real joy in the Christian life.

Wives, God did not stack the cards against you. On the contrary, God places special significance on wives and mothers in the home. As bad as society can be, without the woman maintaining order, demonstrating love within the home, and acknowledging God's rightful place in the home, I'm not sure society would be as peaceful as it is. The issues may be tough and sometimes confusing, but God will not fail you. Your struggle is not against flesh and blood (your husband), but it is against Satan who wants you to see your husband (or others in society) as your problem.

Equality

Many women today are asking, "Why must I be under a man's leadership? I deserve to be equal with a man. I am not less qualified, motivated, or capable. Yes, God, I do question your role for me." Women are equal to men in every respect, with the single exception of physical strength. While women function differently in some ways, they too need equal expression of intellect, emotions, and physical attributes. Women should have equal opportunities publicly, as well as privately. God did not intend for women to lack expression in any way. The problem is not one of equality, but determining *how* God intended for most women to find expression.

> THE PROBLEM IS NOT ONE OF EQUALITY, BUT DETERMINING *HOW* GOD INTENDED FOR MOST WOMEN TO FIND EXPRESSION.

God's plan has never been for men and women to become more alike. God does not want them to become more competitive and "rights-oriented." Our hope lies in stepping out in faith to find fulfillment where God places us. His placement may be different, at different stages of life.

Marriage Relationship

Let me say here that we are not talking about men and women in general. Women are not commanded to be under *any* man's leadership. She is perfectly capable to be in leadership in the work place or in government. There are a few examples of these positions in the Bible.

What we *are* addressing in this book is the *marriage relationship*. In marriage, God has placed the man in the position of servant leader, not because he is better or more qualified, but because we work better when we have structure. God knew that this was the very best structure to cause husbands and wives to function, with as little discord as possible. He also knew it was the best method for raising children. *God in no way is limiting either the man or the woman. Rather, He is giving them a method of fulfillment and oneness.*

Women, can you trust God, knowing fully who He is? Is His plan for your life best, regardless of any momentary suffering? Admittedly, submission is contrary to your human nature, and it is impossible to endure without faith. You cannot stand still in your understanding. You are either gaining or losing ground constantly.

In 1 Peter 1:12-21, Peter exhorts us to holiness and growth. He basically says, "Won't you realize that you are not serving yourselves, but God?" These precious biblical promises are given to you by God's Holy Spirit. They are so great that they intrigue even angels! Remember, submission means: *"to respect your husband enough to allow him leadership in your home."* It is not just a trial or something you suffer. As you grow in your understanding of it through God's Word, it becomes a real blessing. You will never be more loved, appreciated, and cherished. Your needs will never be more fulfilled. You see, these are the precious promises of God Himself. Women long to be loved the way God says a husband should love.

Peter goes on to say in verse 13,*"Therefore, gird your minds for action, keep sober in spirit, fix your hope completely on the grace to be brought to you of the revelation of Jesus Christ."* Your struggle is one of the mind. Do not allow Satan to deceive you into thinking you have a better plan than God. Decide that God can sufficiently carry you through tough situations. Often we have to put away our self-centered rights.

Verse 18 teaches don't trade your hope in God for a hope in temporary or perishable things, like silver and gold. These come from your futile way of life inherited from your forefathers. Place your real hope in life in the precious blood of Jesus Christ.

You will occasionally suffer in your role as a wife, but Jesus called us to follow Him, and He was perfectly submitted to His Father. Was Jesus limited in the long run by His submission? No, and neither will you be as a wife.

WHAT ARE THE LIMITS TO SUBMISSION?

I think the question of limits is a valid one. Scripture clearly communicates that submission by both men and women will be tested by suffering. While I believe that God's Word absolutely assures the greatest blessing to the one who submits, God will not absolve you from responsibility for sin just because someone told you to do it. In other words, submission cannot be used as an excuse for sin.

On the other hand, a wise woman will use this as an opportunity to be creative in understanding her husband's real need. You must ask yourself, "What is the need in my husband's life *behind* the request he is making?" Next, try to meet that need *without* contradicting Scripture.

An example of submitting to the point of sin is the story of Ananias and Sapphira in Acts 5. Sapphira agreed to sin with her husband and, as a result, God took both of their lives. I encourage you to seek counsel if your husband has asked you to do something you think is sin. For most, it will never go that far. As your husband sees your respectful attitude toward him, he will more than likely be more concerned with how you think and feel.

Another limit of submission in your role as a wife is not to submit to any physical or emotional abuse. God never intended that a husband be cruel to his wife. On the contrary, a husband is to love and serve her. If there is either physical or emotional abuse (consistently putting you down, calling you names, etc.), then counsel should be sought quickly. Many good counselors are available to deal with this devastating issue.

Before leaving this question, perhaps a word about *what submission is not* is in order. Submission is not simply "keeping quiet and doing whatever your husband says." That is *lack of communication*. Throughout Scripture, God tells us that He is more interested in our heart than our actions. Let's talk about our attitude in communication.

Communication

In an effort to help our understanding of this important area, let's begin by looking at the example God set for our communication with Him.

> *Be anxious for nothing, but in everything by prayer and supplication with thanksgiving let your requests be made known to God. And the peace of God, which surpasses all comprehension, shall guard your hearts and your minds in Christ Jesus*
> (Phil. 4:6-7).

God desires that we express to Him not only our needs, but our very wants. He doesn't promise to give us our wants, although many times, in His grace, He does, but He does promise peace beyond our understanding. The key thought is that He wants us to tell Him our wants, to talk to Him. What is prayer but simply talking to God? Now if God wants us talk with Him, would He ask that wives not talk to their husbands? Absolutely not! That would be a violation of Scripture.

What God is saying in this passage is, "Women, if your husband has an attitude of being disobedient to God's Word, then do not provoke him further by nagging or hitting him with Bible verses again and again." Instead, inwardly make a faith decision to trust God at that moment, so you can outwardly win your husband with your positive actions. As women, we must place our hope in God, not our husbands. You must allow your husband to be wrong, even fail, so that the Lord can convict him. You simply love him, and encourage him, by how you treat him. Colossians 4:6 says, *"Let your speech always be with grace, seasoned, as it were, with salt, so that you may know how you should respond to each person."*

Women, once you have told your husband you think he is wrong in some way, do not continue to harp on that issue. Turn it over to God and let Him deal with it. A wife should be able to express her opinions freely and lovingly; in fact, her husband will want her to do so. However, your hope should never be in your husband's ability or willingness to change, but in the Lord, who does the changing. You want him to know how you feel about the matter. But you must, at this time, assure him that you love him, no matter what, and that you are behind him, praying for him. Then wait for God to work in his life.

The balance to this freedom to communicate feelings is the

strong warning God gives us about the poison of our mouths. Paul, in Romans 3, tells us that the mouth is an open grave, capable of unbelievable destruction. James tells us that we should be slow to anger and slow to speak, or we will lose God's blessing. A good thermometer of a respectful wife is how she uses her mouth. Proverbs 15:1 says, *"A gentle answer turns away wrath."* Proverbs 15:23 adds, *"How delightful is a timely word!"* (15:23). If a woman has God's perspective, she will:

1. Wait for the proper time to tell her husband her negative thoughts.
2. Talk to the Lord about it in the meantime.
3. Speak peaceably when the time comes, without anger, bitterness, resentment, or belittling.
4. Trust the Lord for the outcome, even when no change is seen.

IS THE HOME THE KEY TO MY SUCCESS AS A WIFE?

To work or not to work

With all the negative publicity the homemaker has been getting in recent years, along with the glamour attributed to the working woman, it's no surprise that wives question their vocation in the home. I am constantly running into young wives who plan to have children at a late age or do not intend to have children at all. They say they cannot fully express themselves in the home. More and more wives are attributing their struggles in life to being captive to the house and the children. Again, the question must be asked, "Did God make a mistake by placing wives and mothers in the home?"

There is so much confusion and frustration in marriage today. Because of the importance and diligence necessary in a homemaker's responsibilities, she cannot afford to be without direction and vision. She will certainly struggle, and perhaps fail. Close on the heels of Satan's deceit concerning submission is his deceit concerning the value of the home. With the help of our culture, Satan has convinced women that their existence in the home is a barrier to fulfillment. Once a woman's eyes focus on herself, instead of on God, she begins a lonely uphill battle. With weak vision and lack of determination, the many struggles of the home quickly wear her down and defeat her spirit of hope. She sees her situation as offering no hope, and where there is no hope, fear abides. Fear is the enemy of faith.

Note the consistent pattern of Satan. He first catches a woman in a struggle (and a homemaker has plenty of them). At that point of conflict, the woman's consciousness of God's presence is low. The deceit does not directly doubt God; instead, it places the blame on a person or situation. The moment a woman sees a person or responsibility in the home as the problem, her commitment is broken. She then begins to subconsciously resent and rebel against her husband, the one she blames. Once she has begun to resent or rebel, her whole relationship with God and her family is affected.

Years ago the feminist movement rose to power by exhibiting "proof" of the plight of the average woman. My disagreement with the movement is on two major issues: the *cause* of the homemaker's problems and the *solutions* offered. These women were, in essence, saying that it is a mistake to have defined roles, either in or out of the home. While our country has tried to give freedom of expression to women in the workplace, and that is good, it has done a poor job of communicating the importance of being a wife and a mother. I am not downplaying the fact that many women work outside the home, some because of desire, others because of economic necessity, and others because there are no children in the home. But far too often, women work because they have been sold a bill of goods that this is where their fulfillment lies. Nothing could be farther from the truth. The majority of women work because *they want to*, not because they have to for financial reasons. There are exceptions. Many women who *have* to work wish they could stay home with their children.

Let me address an issue that I feel should be strongly emphasized and discussed. While we feel it is okay for women to have a career, we believe it is best for mothers to stay at home with children once they arrive. Children are given to us to raise and nurture for only eighteen years. This is a very short, but important time in our lives and theirs. During the formative years, it is vital that mom remain in the home for many reasons: security, faith training, time spent with children, early education, love and physical attention. There usually are some "creative alternatives" to working full time: part-time work maybe three days a week, or getting home by three o'clock, computer work in the home, etc. If you pray about juggling work and motherhood, God will give you wisdom.

Many women make the mistake of thinking that when the child enters school they are no longer needed in the home and therefore, re-enter the work place. Children still need mom at home, if at all possible, at *every* age. We feel it is particularly important for mothers to stay at home during the *teen* years. There are so many temptations that occur naturally for teens when mom is not at home: sex, crime, drugs, etc. Add to this the fact that most other moms in the neighborhood work. Therefore, you may be one of the few moms to whom kids will come and talk after school. This certainly was true for all four of our children in their teen years. I was there for them, to answer not only their questions, but those of their friends. I found it a privilege to spend time with them. We opened our home for ministries such as Young Life and FCA, so that kids were welcome in our home, day or night. Our challenge is to be a parent that influences your children and their friends with religious and moral values.

This may mean putting work, outside the home, on hold. Women who don't work —outside the home— also seem to concentrate on making the home a haven for their husbands and children. This may also warrant an adjustment in the finances, since there will only be one paycheck. But, God will honor what steps you take in order to be there for your family. When they leave home for college, you will then be free to pursue a career, more education, a ministry to other women, or even to travel with your husband. You will feel good about the time you spent with your children, and will not wish you could "do it over."

The biblical woman, the woman of wisdom, finds God's perspective and then seeks God's personal will for her life, using Scripture as the primary standard. *This in no way limits her in the home or in the workplace. It is a matter of God's calling and timing in her life.*

Godly Perspective

Proverbs 31 gives us a wonderful example of a woman who is creative in and out of her home. I believe this woman has "no name," because no woman could ever accomplish all that she did. This example is written for women of all eras to show the *unlimited possibilities* of a godly woman. Her mind was set on a different perspective than we see the world teaching us today. Her mental freedom allowed her creativity to flow. Listen to God's description of her life, mentioned in the last two verses of Proverbs.

> *Charm is deceitful and beauty is vain, but a woman who fears the Lord, she shall be praised. Give her the product of her hands, and let her works praise her in the gates*
> (Prov. 31: 30-31).

The word *"charm"* means superficial graciousness, and the word used for *"beauty"* means vaporous. God is saying that the woman who places her hope in her superficiality or temporary youthful attractiveness is headed for disaster. But the woman who fears the Lord shall find total expression and praise.

> GOD GAVE GODLY WOMEN UNLIMITED POSSIBILITIES.

The term *"fear"* is defined as reverential awe. In other words, she doesn't question God's plan for her as a woman. She doesn't place her hope in the ideologies of the world, but instead commits her hope to the Lord and His view of life.

This woman is promised praise, and God gives it to her! The *"product of her hands"* is her home and all that it contains. The *"gates"* are the public places. She will be known by what her home (her husband and each child) turns out to be. Can this example of a fulfilled wife be trusted? God may call some women out of the home, but I believe that the home is potentially the greatest place for most wives to be fulfilled.

Characterized By Hope

Strength and dignity are her clothing, and she smiles at the future. She opens her mouth in wisdom, and the teaching of kindness is on her tongue. She looks well to the ways of her household, and does not eat the bread of idleness (vv. 25-27).

Here is a woman of stature! She is not a "trampled-down" woman with a "woe-is-me" attitude. "Strength and dignity"' are best translated "a confident woman whose compassion and love free her of future worry." Her faith brings her success, and hope fills her heart.

This woman is able to *smile at the future*. She does not fear the future because she has prepared her household for it *physically, emotionally, and spiritually*. She is able to meet her husband's and children's needs, and in the process, hers are met. She *teaches wisdom and skill* in the art of living. In other words, she teaches Biblical truths to her children, so that they too, learn to follow the Lord. She leads them to salvation and instructs them in their walk with the Him. Here is a woman who can truly lead others to an understanding of God's principles. In order to do this, she spends personal time with the Lord. She views her work in the home very positively. Her role is so fulfilling and far-reaching that she thanks the Lord for the privilege of being a wife and mother.

Characterized By Work

The Proverbs 31 woman is able, emotionally and physically, to work hard and sacrificially. Work is not popular in our culture, but God commands us to work to spare us from our self-centeredness. Idleness is destructive to our self-image and our spiritual walk. This woman doesn't resent being needed, and is therefore available to meet the needs of her household.

It is important to note that this woman has a great deal of diversity in her work. It takes her in and out of the home. Women who suffer anxiety over their role in the home, suffer not so much from overwork, as from lack of diversity. Women need authority-oriented, people-oriented, and intellectually-oriented tasks. Work is vital to life. It takes a great deal of hard work to raise children properly, and to run a household well. We cannot minimize or trivialize these tasks.

> THE HOME IS POTENTIALLY THE GREATEST PLACE FOR MOST WIVES TO BE FULFILLED.

Creative With Her Abilities

If this woman had heard the feminist appeal to work only outside the home, she would have laughed and said, "What foolishness!" Just look at the creativity of this woman. Neither fighting nor questioning God, she believes and becomes creative. Men are motivated by this type of woman and her positive attitude toward her role. The following are some of the examples from this woman operating within the bounds of her own home:

> Looks for wool and flax (v. 13)
> Shops in far places for the needs of her home (v. 14)
> Cooks (v. 15)
> Buys and sells property (v. 16)
> Plants a vineyard (v. 16)
> Is strong physically (v. 17)
> Sews (v. 19)
> Works in community affairs with the poor and needy (v. 20)
> Makes and sells clothes (v. 24)
> Teaches in the community (v. 26)

Any way you look at her, she was not limited privately or publicly. Few men have the freedom to be as far-reaching and diversified as this woman. Many women have been deceived into thinking God has limited her fulfillment in the home. This woman was wise enough to believe God, and trust Him for creativity. As always, God was faithful.

Characterized By Energy

It is not a small thing that God includes verse 17. *"She girds herself with strength and makes her arms strong."* A lot of women say they want opportunities to do more things. Obviously, if you are going to be active, you need physical stamina.

In counseling, I have been amazed at the number of women who are physically tired. If a woman says she is tired, it is hard to ask her to do more. Many women believe the way to restore lost energy is to rest more. That may be true in momentary cases of exhaustion, but with any long-term problem, the opposite is probably true. You need exercise to increase your normal level of energy reserve. Our friend in Proverbs 31 kept herself strong and her energy level high. If you are overly exhausted, see a doctor. Otherwise, staying active is good for your mental attitude.

Husband And Children Glorify Her

Due to Satan's deceit, and our false world programming, husbands, children, and home responsibilities are considered to be limitations to wives. But if you assume God's perspective, you see that God has blessed the wife and mother most of all. God structured the emotions of children and the desires of husbands to *naturally seek her*. Because self-worth and self-expression can only be measured by relating to people and to God, this was a gracious act of God. In our case, five people naturally run to me, Don and my four kids! Have you ever noticed that when big football players say "Hi" on TV, they usually say "Hi Mom!" Very few say, "Hi Dad!" or anyone else! Mothers are so loved and revered. What a fantastic honor to be a wife and mother! God outdoes Himself when it comes to moms!

In Proverbs 31:10, the value of a wise woman is stated: *"An excellent wife who can find? For her worth is far above jewels."* Verse 11 indicates that her husband trusts her so explicitly that money loses its importance in comparison. Verses 28 and 29 tell how her family responds to her. Her children will grow up and praise her. They will give her the highest expression a woman could desire, and her husband will say she is the very best woman in the world! Do you know of any other role in life that guarantees this result?

What an awesome privilege God gave women in bearing and raising children. She is the one who gets to spend the most time reproducing a godly heritage. She is the one who understands each child and their emotional makeup. She gets to answer the majority of their questions. She gets to guide them into most of the spiritual truth they learn. It's her heart they hear the most. What a great and awesome responsibility. As children grow, it is to Mom they run when hurt, or when trouble confronts them. She is usually the first one who hears about who they love and want to marry. She gets to help plan their future weddings. It is her skirts that cradle the new grandchildren. I can't think of a better and more rewarding job! This is a role that has generational effects. Let's not sell our children and grandchildren short, by not spending needed time with them.

Biblical mandates are given to parents to teach children and instruct them in the Lord. Such scriptures as Deut. 6:6-7, 20; and Psalm 78:5-8:

> *These commandments that I give you today are to be upon your hearts. Impress them on your children. Talk about them when you sit at home and when you walk along the road, when you lie down and when you get up . . . In the future, when you son asks you, "What is the meaning of the stipulations, decrees and laws the Lord our God has commanded you?" Then you shall say to your son . . .* (Deut. 6:6-7, 20 NIV).

> *He commanded our forefathers to teach their children, so the next generation would know them, even the children yet to be born, and they in turn would tell their children. Then they would put their trust in God and would not forget his deeds but would keep his commands. They would not be like their forefathers, a stubborn and rebellious generation, whose hearts were not loyal to God, whose spirits were not faithful to him* (Psalm 78:5-8 NIV).

So what is the key to success for a married woman? First, it is constantly seeking God's perspective on life. Second, it is modeling a personal plan for utilizing herself, by serving her husband and children. Third, it is allowing God to meet her needs through her husband, children, and opportunities found through the home. Fourth, outside activities, including career, can be fulfilling, if the needs of the home have been met.

HOW CAN A WIFE UNDERSTAND AND HELP HER HUSBAND?

At a time in our history when women are shouting "I am not going to take this oppression anymore," men are suffering unbearably themselves. The women are shouting about oppression, but the men are closer to defeat. Consider for a moment the following statistics from the 1996 World Almanac and Book of Facts:

- There are over *six million* more women than men in America today.
- Men move toward death faster than women after age forty.
- After age twenty-four, 20% more men commit suicide than women.
- After age sixty-five, 80% more men than women commit suicide.
- Far more drug addicts and home deserters are men.
- Men alcoholics outnumber women alcoholics five to one.
- Estimation of male homosexuality in America is as high as three percent.

Lack Of Male Role Modeling

Probably the single greatest problem in America, as well as in Christendom, is the lack of male leadership. Women may feel put upon in our society, but men, according to medical records, show the greatest emotional stress.

What is happening to our men? It is not a simple question.

Our culture seems to strike hardest at the role of men. Try to understand some of their struggles.

Few men own a home without debt, and fewer own land. Almost all men work for someone else. Because their lives are monitored by loan institutions or bosses, men do not feel control or dominion over their lives. They feel that "Big Brother" is constantly watching them, and "Big Brother" can be a lot of different things to different men.

Furthermore, men are frustrated because they no longer experience natural authority over those in their care. The authoritarian influence of the past has turned into the democratic home of the 20th century. The father is often just another vote in the family. Men experience anxiety and loss of personal dignity in their families. All of this has resulted in an identity crisis for many, which tends to promote hostility or withdrawal.

Today, there is a lack of effective male role models for young men. With over one third of our children coming from broken homes and with the community-oriented society of today, young men move through their developmental years without identifying with assertive, confident, and sensitive men of direction. Many young men have no concept of what a father is, does, and should be. Girls also lack the father-love so necessary to a healthy maturing process.

Comparison

Just like women, men are affected deeply by the tremendous pressure of comparison with other fantasy supermen images. Mass media and electronic marvels daily program us with the president, the senator, the executive, the stylish athlete, the many-faceted TV celebrity. There seems to be less emphasis placed on the inner qualities of a man, such as faithfulness and consistency, and more emphasis placed on outer qualities like athletic ability, wealth, appearance, and personality. A slight self-image problem in a man can quickly become a serious issue under this barrage of comparison and competition.

The godly woman must be realistic about who her husband is

and also be able to envision what he can become. Without a plan or direction from God, the natural tendency would be to ignore these things. But a woman who desires to be God's wife to her husband, will look beyond his weaknesses, releasing him to total fulfillment. What a privilege it is to understand, love, and help your husband to be a fulfilled, motivated, and responsible man.

Compassion

As much as Christ must hate my failure and sinfulness, He always maintains compassion for me that is stronger than His hatred of my sin. He knows what I am missing and desires that I experience the best. In the same way, a wife should not allow her dissatisfaction with her husband to overshadow her compassion for him. Compassion is a "deep, unselfish concern for another that demands action."

Historically, women have had problems losing perspective concerning their husband's differences. A wife can become so discouraged and distrustful of her mate that she can no longer believe God for him. Proverbs speaks of such a woman:

A constant dripping on a day of steady rain and a contentious woman are alike; he who would restrain her restrains the wind, and grasps oil with his right hand (Prov. 27:15-16).

A woman who constantly nags her husband, in a quarrelsome and strife-ridden way, will eventually be unwilling to follow his leadership at all. The writer then says that to reverse that process would be more difficult than stopping the wind or grasping oil in your hand.

Many times a wife will ask Don if he could lead her husband to Christ, or convince him of some spiritual truth. She usually has asked several women's groups to pray for him. The place we have to start is with her. Her attitude and feeling of superiority, or "spirituality," toward him have usually angered or discouraged him, subconsciously, over a period of time. This man is really rejecting his wife's attitude, not Christ. If we can get her to go home and ask her husband's forgiveness and love him for who he is, the husband is usually open to talking about a God powerful enough to get his wife to say she was wrong!

Wives also say, "If you could just get my husband to spend more time with the children, things would be fine." Unfortunately, this wife has, usually, so covered him with guilt and rejection, that every time the children enter the room, he subconsciously feels whipped. These feelings retard his natural aggressiveness, and make him want to stay away because they are a reminder of failure. Again, if a wife can see that she will never motivate him this way, she can trust God with her children, alone, if necessary. She can then ask his forgiveness for judging him, and give him the freedom to spend time with the kids as he feels he should. This man is free to be convicted by the Lord, without being sidetracked by feelings of anger and rejection.

I have seen men treat new cars better than their wives. Why? Because a car is their total, unabridged responsibility. A man senses and responds to real dependence, so he naturally feels more responsible for a wife who's there for better or worse.

A wife who is attentive to her husband is a wise woman who knows how to please him. A man cannot easily change his self-image, but a wife has the ability to do that. As she visualizes him as near perfect, he will try to be. We need to remind ourselves often that our husbands have tremendous demands placed upon their lives from all directions. Many times we cannot control those outside demands, but we can control what comes out of our homes and our mouths.

Knowing His Needs

Your husband has certain God-given needs that must be fulfilled. Needs to *protect*, to *own*, to have *authority*, to be *productive*, to *love*, and to *reproduce* his image. These are some of the major needs implied in Scripture. Consider the areas where you can specifically help him meet his needs. Some will be mentioned briefly, since they are covered in more detail elsewhere.

Need to trust: There are fragile areas of every spouses' life that he/she does not want or need the public to know. There are intimacies, intended to be shared just between the two of you, that were not meant for anyone else. Don't breach his trust in you. *"The heart of her husband trusts in her, and he will have no lack of gain. She does him good and not evil all the days of her life"* (Prov. 31:11-12).

Vocational needs: A wife who is sensitive to her husband can do more to motivate her husband vocationally than any other person. Usually a man's work sets the pattern for the other areas of his life. A man who is satisfied in his work is a man of real potential. A wife is in an excellent position to study her husband to see what he enjoys doing. Watch him play as well as work, since many times what he does with his free time is a good indicator of what he really enjoys. Encourage and uplift your mate in his work. Many men enjoy what they are doing, but secretly feel others do not adequately respect them for it. To hear that his wife is proud of him can make a tremendous difference to any man.

Be willing to adjust your spending and standard of living to allow your husband to change jobs. Anything you do to stabilize and increase his happiness helps you, too. A man has an almost constant need in life to reevaluate his vocation. He needs the freedom of knowing his wife will support him, whatever his decision may be.

Spiritual needs: Scripture places a significant importance on spiritual leadership in a man's life. Encourage any inclination your husband shows toward taking spiritual responsibility. Especially after thirty, a man's feeling of importance can be increased if he is involved in church leadership or in a discipleship process. This may require you to have a Bible study in your home or to get child care to pursue this end. It might even require you to make friends with one of your husband's friend's wife. Whatever it takes, help all you can. If your husband is not gifted in public ministry, encourage him to *facilitate small groups* in your church. That is the best way of developing his leadership skills. All men and women have leadership skills that need to be developed. However, never feel that you have to push him in this direction. Pressuring them to lead groups is not beneficial if their spiritual gifts may lie in other areas such as service, craftsmanship, etc. Remember, God does the motivating.

Sexual needs: This area is very important to most men. Unless you are naturally motivated sexually, do not get under the pile by trying to keep up with mythical "national averages." (Detailed information is contained in the next chapter.)

Need for space: Women need to recognize that often men think and solve problems in their minds before they speak and talk about them. This is often not true of women. He needs a refuge in his home, away from the business of his work day. Men usually bury themselves in the newspaper, or TV, or the home office or bedroom, to acquire needed solace. A wise wife gives him his "down time" before engaging in conversation or having him play with the children too soon.

Relationship needs: Many husbands are loners. If you add to those the large number of couples who do not develop mutual friends, the problem becomes staggering. Relationships are very important in a man's life. A wife benefits from her husband's relationships. Communication, diversity of interest, and increased hope in life, are just a few of the possible benefits. Observe people your husband naturally likes and create social settings where he feels comfortable. When possible, pursue his interests in friends. The more you do sacrificially for him, the more he will become responsible and be encouraged to return the blessing.

Intellectual needs: Do what you can to recognize your husband's intellectual interests. Everyone is interested in something. If you can start a mutual discussion on any issue, your husband will begin to look forward to sharing his thoughts with you. A husband who feels his wife cares about his intellectual interests feels a special closeness with her. She's a real friend. In addition, if she listens to him in even one area, he can then listen to her in other areas without feeling she is "preaching."

Authoritative needs: A wife who encourages her husband's leadership in her life is a protected woman. This sounds good, but how do you do it? The following ideas illustrate some ways to give your husband authority and revive his natural desire to protect you.

Verbal Praise

The wise wife knows that God provided her mate for her and therefore understands God's perspective of marriage. This woman can honestly love her husband so completely that he does not lack self-confidence.

The mother is a model to the children. If she doesn't respect him, neither will they. Give your children a blessing, let them respect their father. Children can also have a powerful influence on the dad. If the wife is lifting him up when not in his presence, the children will compliment him to his face.

> A WISE WOMAN RELEASES HER HUSBAND TO TAKE LEADERSHIP IN HER LIFE AS SHE PLACES HER HOPE IN GOD.

Verbal praise is extremely vital to a man. When a wife praises her husband when he is not present, it demonstrates her love for him. When she is critical, it shows she does not understand the faith perspective of marriage. *"An anxious heart weighs a man down, but a kind word cheers him up"* (Proverbs 12:25).

A wise woman releases her husband to take leadership in her life as she places her hope in God. She will allow him to be fully expressed, because she views him as a gift from God, with no limitation to her fulfillment. The Holy Spirit is then free to help her understand her husband in particular and the differences in men and women in general.

Let's become women whose *"pleasant words are a honeycomb, sweet to the soul and healing to the bones"* (Proverbs 16:24).

CHAPTER THIRTEEN
NAKED AND UNASHAMED

WHAT A POWERFUL drive God created in men and women! Anyone considering marriage, and those already married, should plan to fully pursue God's sexual creation within marriage. You might say, "What an unnecessary statement! Sure, I plan to do just that." Yet marriage counselors all over America report that up to eighty percent of couples seeking counsel mention the sexual relationship as one of their most difficult areas of struggle.

In Scripture, God has a lot to say about sex. He leaves no doubt concerning its importance to marital love. God created sexual love to require faith. It should be no surprise that He wants us to depend on Him in this area. Once again, knowing Scripture will allow the Holy Spirit to both teach and convict you. Open your spiritual mind and heart to the Holy Spirit as we read God's directions. Our biblical discussions of the sexual relationship will include six major areas. They are:

1. Why problems develop
2. Biblical absolutes and guidelines concerning the sexual relationship
3. Cultural and religious myths concerning sex
4. Sexual differences in men and women

5. Wisdom from counseling
6. Premarital sex

The most important thing to realize, relative to a successful sexual relationship, is that God created it. He fully intended pleasure and blessing in its creation. Israel's king Solomon and his young wife from Shulim stated it best in the Song of Solomon 1:15-16:

"How beautiful you are, my darling, how beautiful you are!"

"How handsome you are, my beloved, and so pleasant! Indeed, our couch is luxuriant!"

This is only one of many references in God's Word to the excitement and happiness He intended for marital love. Ask for discernment in discovering how God intended the physical relationship to be a blessing.

WHY PROBLEMS DEVELOP

"I am angry and bitterly disappointed about my sexual experience," a woman told me recently. "I was so expectant and excited when I got married, only to find shock, and mediocrity. It is not at all what I had thought it would be. What surprises me most, is that I realize I am probably more of a problem than my husband."

I never cease to be amazed at the number of men and women who say similar things three or four years into marriage. It is not necessary for this to happen.

There are three basic reasons why couples experience frustration in this most intimate of relationships. The primary cause of frustration is the *cultural programming* they have received. The film and television industries create false sexual images. The media subtly implies that only the physically "attractive" really succeed sexually. Movies seldom depict sexual failure or growth! Reality is ignored and replaced with an image that is fantasy. Advertising bombards us daily with "super" bodies in exotic situations, while the fantasy escapes us in the reality of the bedroom at home. This wholesale merchandising of sex has contributed significantly to the growth of pornography. False comparison, false images, guilt, and disappointment reign in our culture as a result of these influences. We all have been brainwashed, to varying degrees. These factors confuse us, while making us unsure what God really desires for us sexually.

The second major cause of sexual frustration today is the *nature of man himself*. As we have mentioned numerous times, men and women are self-centered beings. Problems in the sexual relationship are a prime example. Self-centeredness can devastate a marriage. Each partner brings to the bedroom different standards, desires, inhibitions, and hang-ups about sex. Each may carry a certain amount of "scar tissue" from the past. Pride is also involved; we want to be self-sufficient and, therefore, we don't want to admit we don't know it all. We have difficulty asking for help. We tend to blame our spouse when sex isn't as exciting as we dreamed it would be, or as Hollywood portrays it to be.

> A SUCCESSFUL SEXUAL RELATIONSHIP IS CREATED BY GOD. HE FULLY INTENDED PLEASURE AND BLESSING IN ITS CREATION.

The third major cause of sexual problems is caused by the lack of quality Christian teaching on sex. For the most part, Christian leadership has not responded well to peoples' needs in this area, and has not taught *positive truths* concerning sex from God's Word. When there were attempts in the past, the teaching was often legalistic: a bunch of "no's," without explanations of why not.

Most couples we have worked with through counseling and seminars tell us they never received specific instructions on sex from anyone with authority in their lives. Our culture, man's nature, and ineffective teaching have resulted in a sexually frustrated society.

BIBLICAL ABSOLUTES ON THE SEXUAL RELATIONSHIP

In Scripture, God has spoken boldly concerning sexual matters. To understand His perspective, the starting point is to learn the

Biblical absolutes concerning sexual love. The following eleven points are of vital importance to a successful and healthy sexual relationship. These points establish the guideposts for spiritual counsel on sexual matters.

1. Sexuality is God's creation.
It is important that every man and woman realize that their sexuality was unquestionably created by God. Any uncertainty about that fact affects sexual perspective and freedom. Genesis 1:27 says, *"And God created man in His own image, in the image of God He created him; male and female He created them."* What is the most significant differences between male and female? Certainly, it is their physical and sexual anatomies.

God clearly created man and woman as different sexual entities who have the opportunity to become *"one flesh."* The creation of sexuality was no accident, but a deliberate part of God's unique plan. To accept one's sexuality and to seek positive fulfillment in marriage is not only good, but designed to be this way by God. Hollywood did not create sex, God did! Therefore, we are free to seek its fullness.

2. Physical love is for procreation.
The second major reality from Scripture is that God intended sex and marriage to produce children. Certainly there are exceptions, but the emphasis is clear. God created both sex and children to be a blessing. Therefore, sex and marriage give us a wonderful picture of God's love for us. The love we experience for our children gives us a small glimpse as to how much love God has for us.

Children give couples the opportunity to reproduce not only God's image, but their images as well. *"This is the book of the generations of Adam. In the day when God created man, He made him in the likeness of God. He created them male and female, and He blessed them and named them Man in the day when they were created. When Adam had lived one hundred and thirty years, he became the father of a son in his own likeness, according to his image, and named him Seth"* (Genesis 3:1-3). God commanded Adam and Eve to be fruitful and multiply and fill the earth. God further states in Psalm 127:3-5: *"Behold, children are a gift of the Lord; the fruit of the womb is a reward. Like arrows in the hand of a warrior, so are the children of one's youth. How blessed is the man whose quiver is full of them."* Sex was created by God for procreation.

Of all God's creatures, only man procreates "face to face." The world promotes the concept that sex is a natural instinct. But, God designed that sex was to be the result of the total expression of the relationship between husbands and wives. Sex was never meant to be participated in apart from communing with one another in marriage. Children were to be a result of the unique and permanent relationship between the husband and wife.

3. Physical love is for pleasure.

From His first statements in Genesis, God refers to sexual relations in the context of blessing. Blessing is a word that refers to a high state of joy and pleasure. God devotes a whole book of the Bible to describe His blessing to humankind. Song of Solomon 8:6 says of love, *"Its flashes are flashes of fire, the very flame of the Lord."* Without a doubt, God associates pleasure and excitement with the sexual relationship.

> *May your fountain be blessed, and may you rejoice in the wife of your youth. As a loving doe, a graceful deer, may her breasts satisfy you always, may you ever be captivated by her love* (Prov. 5:18-19).

4. Physical love demands a time priority.

In 1 Corinthians 7 and in the Song of Solomon, God insinuates that successful lovemaking requires a time priority. Solomon created a special bedroom and took his bride away from the activities of life. The preparation and time taken imply that God ordained special emphasis in sexual matters.

In Deuteronomy 24:5, the young men were instructed: *"When a man takes a new wife, he shall not go out with the army, nor be charged with any duty; he shall be free at home one year and shall give happiness to his wife whom he has taken."*

The words "give happiness," refer to sexual pleasure. Older men of God knew how vital the sexual relationship was to marriage, so they placed sex above other very important matters to allow the couple to initially establish their sexual relationship. Any couple who expects to be sexually satisfied must spend time developing their relationship. Not only is the honeymoon important, the years that follow require time and effort to establish mutual satisfaction.

5. Physical love requires a transfer of body ownership.

Sexual love is so important to Christian marriage that God suggests to couples that they exchange rights to their own bodies for the sake of their sexual oneness. *"Let the husband fulfill his duty to his wife, and likewise also the wife to her husband. The wife does not have authority over her own body, but the husband does; and likewise also the husband does not have authority over his own body, but the wife does"* (1 Cor. 7:3-4).

God's suggestion clearly establishes His commitment to sexual oneness in marriage. Gracious sacrifice is part of every sexual union from God's perspective. My body is not mine, but my mate's. God wants us to trust Him and give our bodies for our mate's pleasure. God intends this to be for mutual pleasure and not for selfish purposes. God makes sex a *sacrificial act* that is redemptive, in that it gets my eyes off my needs and onto the needs of my mate.

6. Physical love is passionate and creative.

The Song of Solomon describes in creative and passionate terms the verbalization of Solomon and his wife pertaining to their sexual union. In the Song, God implies that mutual sexual communication is needed. The wife as well as the husband must creatively communicate their sexual thoughts and desires. Several places in the Song, Solomon excitedly describes his wife's body. The Shulamite responds with an equally passionate description of Solomon's body (4:1-7; 5:10-16; 7:1-5; 6-9). Let's look at two passages. (By the way, feel free to smile at the language used.)

How beautiful are your feet in sandals, O prince's daughter! The curves of your hips are like jewels, the work of the hands of an artist. Your navel is like a round goblet which never lacks mixed wine; your belly is like a heap of wheat fenced about with lilies. Your two breasts are like two fawns, twins of a gazelle. Your neck is like a tower of ivory, your eyes like the pools in Heshbon by the gate of Bath-rabbim; your nose is like the tower of Lebanon, which faces toward Damascus. Your head crowns you like Carmel, and the flowing locks of your head are like purple threads; the king is captivated by your tresses (Song 7:1-5).

Notice that he starts at her feet, progresses to the mid-section, on to her head, then back to the mid-section. His primary interest is her mid-section. In contrast, the wife's interest is different.

My beloved is dazzling and ruddy, outstanding among ten thousand. His head is like gold, pure gold; his locks are like clusters of dates, and black as a raven. His eyes are like doves beside streams of water, bathed in milk, and reposed in their setting. His cheeks are like a bed of balsam, banks of sweet-scented herbs; his lips are lilies, dripping with liquid myrrh. His hands are rods of gold set with beryl; his abdomen is carved ivory inlaid with sapphires. His legs are pillars of alabaster set on pedestals of pure gold; his appearance is like Lebanon, choice as the cedars. His mouth is full of sweetness. And he is wholly desirable. This is my beloved and this is my friend, O daughters of Jerusalem (Song 5:10-16).

She starts with his head, proceeds to his abdomen, legs, and then back to his head. Clearly, the Shulamite is primarily interested in Solomon's face. His face reflects the person. His wife is motivated by her relationship with his person. In chapter 7, Solomon describes a dance the Shulamite does to excite him sexually. Mutual pleasure can be explored, with God's blessing. Creative and passionate marital love is good in the sight of God. Hebrews 13:4 says *"Let marriage be held in honor among all, and let the marriage bed be undefiled."*

7. Scripture illustrates verbal sexual communication.
In Song of Solomon 2:6, the Shulamite gives specific instructions during the act of making love.

> *"Let his left hand be under my head, and his right hand embrace me."*

She adds in 4:16,

> *"Awake . . . make my garden breathe out fragranc . . . May my beloved come into his garden and eat its choice fruits."*

God demonstrates how significant verbalization is to sexual love. For most of us, when we first get married, sexual communication is difficult. Learning to verbalize in marriage becomes more comfortable as time passes. Expressing your thoughts and feelings concerning sexuality pays great dividends as you age together.

8. Physical love should be participated in regularly.

> *Stop depriving one another, except by agreement for a time that you may devote yourselves to prayer, and come together again lest Satan tempt you because of your lack of self-control* (1 Cor. 7:5).

God specifically instructs married couples to have regular sexual relations. He warns that to disobey this command would leave the partners open to lust problems. The issue here is not to establish a standard for the number of times per week. The focus is to have *regular, mutually satisfying* sexual contact. Notice that there is no age limit mentioned. The Bible gives accounts of sexual love for the elderly. Abraham and Sarah were in their nineties, and still gained pleasure, as recorded in her statement to the Lord about her conception of Isaac. Regularity may change, but there are biblical, medical, and psychological reasons why the sexual relationship is as important at sixty as it is at twenty-five.

Song of Solomon 5:1 (NIV) says *"Eat O friends, and drink your fill, O lovers."* *"Your fill"* may be different from that of other couples. God wants you as a couple to determine what is mutually satisfying for the both of you, both in regularity and in creativity.

9. *Physical love is more than physical.*
Anytime one focuses on physical love, there is a tendency to separate the physical from the emotional, spiritual, and intellectual needs. Scripture never makes this mistake. When God said Adam and Eve were "naked and unashamed," He was plainly speaking of more than physical transparency. When studying the Song, one observes this couple's communication incorporating the total person's needs. The Shulamite rejects Solomon momentarily (5:2-8). He responds to her with love and blessing (Song 6:4-10). The importance of the total person in lovemaking is evident. God compares the union of husband and wife with the union of Christ and His church (Eph. 5:32).

I highly recommend chapters 2 and 3 of Tim LaHaye's book, *The Act of Marriage.* These chapters communicate the "wholeness" of the individual man and woman.

10. *Physical love gives comfort and healing.*
After the death of David and Bathsheba's baby, they were very distraught. *"Then David comforted his wife Bathsheba, and he went to her and lay with her. She gave birth to a son, and they named him Solomon"* (2 Samuel 12:24). Often when one or both partners have experienced a loss of some kind, the sexual union presents an opportunity to comfort and relax one another. It is a time for the couple to pull together and experience the unity that they so desperately need. Losing a job, difficulty at work, moving, problems with children, losing a loved one, etc. are examples of times when comfort is desperately needed. A wise couple will come together in physical and emotional unity during times of trial.

11. *Sexual attitudes of parents are transferred to children.*
Children need to learn that sex was created for the marriage relationship alone. It was created as a gift from God to allow two people

to come together in unity. It is no accident that in the Word of God a whole book is devoted to the sexual and romantic life of a married couple. The very last chapter of the Song of Solomon ends with an admonition concerning sex and children. The Shulamite's brothers greet her and Solomon as they come home for a visit. They ask about their younger sister, who has reached pre-puberty. They talk about watching her character development in the area of sexual values. *"If she is a **wall**, we shall build on her a battlement of silver; but if she is a **door**, we shall barricade her with planks of cedar."* The "wall" means "strong convictions in the area of abstinence." The "door" means "easily swung open, or promiscuous." If you observe your child to be a wall, you can reward them with more freedom. However, if he/she appears to be a door, we are to lovingly put more fences around them, to insure their protection from early experimentation. It is important that the older children assist the parents by being examples in the protection of the siblings. Some children need more boundaries than others. We are to be observant parents who communicate readily with each child concerning sex.

Throughout the Song the phrase appears, *"Do not awaken love until it so desires"* (Song 2:7; 3:5; 8:4). According to Scripture, we are not to open ourselves to arousal before the time of marriage fulfillment. We need to teach our children the importance of avoiding tempting situations that can lead to such arousal. Constant communication as they grow to adulthood is not optional, but crucial. We should continually pray for the Lord's protection for each child.

To a large degree, children learn from the attitudes of their parents. Deuteronomy 6 tells us that parents teach by what they do, as well as by what they say. Our convictions and actions play a major role in their development. What we as a couple model to them becomes their strongest impression of sexual love.

Attitudes are also communicated by our behavior. Children learn from *only 7% of what we say* and *93% of what we do*. If Mom and Dad are not excited about each other, the children will miss the most important picture of what love and marriage are all about. Couples may think they can subtly hide their attitudes (sexual, caring, loving, relating) from their children. Not so.

If a father doesn't have a loving relationship with her mother, it will affect his daughter's concepts of femininity, and her future role as wife, in marriage. If the father doesn't have a good relationship with his daughter, it could affect her relationship with her future husband. This is also true of the father-son relationship, and the son's concepts of being a godly father and husband.

In summary, all these absolutes from God's Word teach one thing: sexual relations were created by God and He wants His children to get with the program!

CULTURAL AND RELIGIOUS MYTHS CONCERNING SEX

Over the centuries, the depravity of humankind and its culture have produced certain sexual hang-ups for couples. Those patterns need to be identified before couples can escape its entrapment. Usually, just identifying them will help couples begin the process of overriding their effects. Occasionally, it may be necessary to seek counsel.

Male Sexual Image

Culturally, we have been educated to see the virile male as "Ready Freddie"—always ready to perform sexually. The man who is not instantaneously ready at all times is subtly suspected of being less of a man. Men, as well as women, subject themselves to this thinking. The result is that men may try to prove themselves on the one hand, or they may develop an insecurity about their manhood. Either of these can add real pressure to the sexual experience.

All things considered, a man's sexual motivation and function are not all that different from a woman's. He, too, experiences times of low interest, and needs sensitivity and motivation.

Early Female Conditioning

Every couple needs to consider the fact that women who exercise modest restraint for twenty years or more need an adjustment period before becoming an aggressive lover. It is important to note that if a woman has a *healthy relationship with her father* and a *healthy fear of the Lord*, she will have *fewer* problems adjusting to the sexual relationship. Early experimentation with sex or having multiple sex partners before marriage may produce guilt and/or problems with desire on the part of the female. The same scenario may make the male overly aggressive, sexually, toward his wife. Wise counsel may be needed to overcome past programming. While the woman needs to seek God's perspective, the husband needs to exhibit tremendous sensitivity, patience, and acceptance. His goal should be to motivate her by loving her unconditionally.

Romance And Feeling
The media has created a false image that couples need to recognize. The lie is, "If you really love me, you would be romantic and want to have sex." Certainly any *agape* marriage will experience romance and sexual desire, but feelings and romance usually are the *result* of a relationship, not its *cause*. Couples should expect to dialogue often in early marriage to discover new ways and paths to sexual and romantic excitement. Romance is not "automatic." Time, effort, and creativity need to be put into the relationship before romance can occur. Understanding God's Word, seeking counsel, and having open communication will cause the sexual union to succeed over time.

SEXUAL DIFFERENCES IN MEN AND WOMEN

God purposefully made women's sexual needs different from men's. Over a period of time, these differences reveal a great deal about the total relationship of the couple. The couple who is experiencing an *agape* marriage relationship will begin to see these differences as opportunities to serve and broaden the sexual experience.

Women
Women are motivated greatly by the *emotional dimensions* of their sexual relationship. Romantic love and feminine needs cannot be

separated. Tender moments all evening that demonstrate admiration and respect for her, prepare her for an exciting sexual experience. In fact, in the absence of romantic tenderness and emotional appreciation, she sometimes enters the sexual union with feelings of "being used."

Many women tend to be *cyclical* in their sexual desire. That is, their desire tends to rise, then drop for several days after a sexual experience, only to rise again later. Women tend to be excited more slowly and respond to tender touch and caresses. Privacy, no distractions, warmth, and darkness are usually important to helping her release her emotions. Sensitive verbalization can soothe and motivate her. She enjoys tenderness *before, during, and after* the sexual experience. To hold her afterward is probably the most vital gift a man can give to his wife, sexually speaking.

> FEELINGS AND ROMANCE USUALLY ARE THE RESULT OF A RELATIONSHIP, NOT ITS CAUSE.

Men

Men are much more *physical*. Normally, men can be struggling with a problem all evening and still be tremendously attracted by his wife's body. His sex drive is not cyclical, but continual. Tim LaHaye mentions several related issues in his book, *The Act of Marriage*. A man's sex drive is connected to his ability "to be the aggressor, provider, and leader of his family. The woman who resents her husband's sex drive while enjoying his aggressive leadership had better face the fact that she cannot have one without the other."[1]

Men usually respond *spontaneously* and *instantaneously* to physical stimuli. They are as likely to be stimulated through the eye, as much as the touch. A man normally likes to caress his wife in the light, so he can see her clearly. Men are excited much more quickly than women, and distractions usually don't bother them. They experience immediate release in their sexual orgasm. They can fall asleep immediately. With a little effort on their part, however, they too can greatly enjoy those moments after intercourse, which are extremely important to their wives.

Couples should never allow resentment to build toward the other in regard to these differences. Understand them, anticipate them, and work with them. A creative plan can turn these differences into real enjoyment. The woman who understands a man's natural, God-given, sexual drive is overwhelmed when he tenderly meets her needs in spite of his own natural desires.

There are comparatively few things in life that give men more sense of having finished a task well, than to satisfy their wife sexually. To him, it is like wrapping up a package and tying a ribbon around it. The sexual dimension of marriage is so exhilarating. The spiritual and emotional commitments between two people are sometimes best expressed in sexual oneness. You will spend hours over the next thirty or forty years discussing, reading, preparing for, and being involved in *God's adventure* of sexual love.

Be prepared for the fact that sexual love takes time. It *changes constantly* all through marriage. Early marriage experimentation, hormonal and physical changes during pregnancy and nursing, years with small children and little time for privacy, the middle years, and finally the older years all present different phases. Yet, lovemaking during all of these seasons can be extremely satisfying. All the changes that take place can be beautiful tests of your mutual and enduring love.

WISDOM FROM COUNSELING

Most sexual problems develop because of ignorance in the early years of marriage. Couples will ask advice on buying a house or car, or even about discipline of their children, but only a few will seek help sexually. I encourage couples to read several Christian books on sex together and to seek counsel when problems persist over several months.

To Husbands

Men, your responsibility is to love your wife sacrificially as your own body. If you relate to her in a godly manner, you will enjoy a rewarding sexual relationship. Sacrificial love will pay great dividends for the rest of your life. Here are some simple guidelines.

Belief: In the Scriptures, God tells men to be excited and satisfied with the bodies of their wives. Regularly communicate your acceptance of your wife's body to her. Fall in love with her so completely that you will not be affected by the inevitable changes produced by having children and aging. Sell your wife on your love of her body.

A man who is not excitedly communicating his acceptance of his wife's body will eventually discover that she begins to hide her body from him. The result will be devastating. A husband has the power to "make or break" his wife's self-image concerning her body. Your wife's mirror, and the young bodies pictured in advertisements, all tell her that her looks are fading. Only *you* can convince her otherwise!

Acceptance and communication: God says in 1 Peter 3:7 that husbands are to dwell with their wives in an *understanding* way. A husband must take responsibility for helping his wife understand her sexual frustrations. Wives who develop sexual anxiety usually may not be initially aware of it. Insecurities about her appearance, the size of her breasts, her thighs, her stomach, or whatever, can cause a wife to lose her desire for sexual intimacy. Your communication, and reassurance, are vital if you hope to keep your wife from labeling herself as unattractive.

Sacrificial love: Since so much of a woman's sexual enjoyment is tied to her emotional preparation, the husband must be prepared to take charge of easing his wife's burdens. A messy house, unattended children, uncertainty of personal attractiveness, criticism from her husband, and social pressures are the types of problems that keep wives from releasing themselves emotionally. The effective husband gets up Saturday morning and lets his wife sleep in. He dresses and feeds the children and helps clean the house. He might also take the children for several hours that afternoon so she can have her hair done or go shopping, thus allowing his wife to relax. These actions "unburden" his wife emotionally, which in turn allows her to become more aware of his needs.

When we first married, I used to blame Sally when she was

not "up" sexually. Now I blame myself. I usually have not been romantically creative, or have not been sensitive to her needs.

Wisdom: Men, protect your wife from sexual anxiety. This may seem obvious, but never take your cleanliness for granted! Brush your teeth and take a shower. Do things that take the pressure off the sexual union. Hot baths, rubdowns, and walks together just prior to intimate involvement, foster communication and associate pleasure with the sexual experience. Candlelight and soft music reduce anxiety and help her to be uninhibited. Holding her, and talking for ten or fifteen minutes before sex, adds definite pleasurable associations with the act itself. No man can guarantee a woman's sexual response every time, but he can create a satisfying experience for both of them most of the time.

Also, never allow your wife to endure sexual pain! Occasional momentary pain on entry is not abnormal, but if pain persists, seek medical help together. Rashes, infections, or more severe problems such as endometriosis, can cause pain. If these problems persist for an extended time, in spite of proper medical help, seek counsel immediately. Believe me, there are solutions.

To Wives

When a marriage is functioning correctly, according to God's perspective, women can be as sexually responsive as men. Unfortunately, many times outside pressures cause women to be emotionally unable to respond. On the other hand, men may not be as affected sexually by outside pressures. The following are some thoughts that will help men and women balance one another's sexual needs.

Natural motivation: There is a natural, somewhat predictable, level of sexual aggressiveness in most men and women. The following line represents the total spectrum of all natural sexual drives.

Not
Naturally
Aggressive

Naturally
Aggressive

|———————————————|———————————————|

Most *women* tend to be to the *right of center* (not naturally aggressive), while most *men* tend to be *left of center* (naturally aggressive). In other words, most women initiate sexual activity infrequently. These women may not be against sex, or even uninterested. They simply *may not naturally think aggressively about sex*. However, apart from being properly approached, they may not develop an internal need but every five to fifteen days. If properly motivated and stimulated by their husbands, they would be open to more frequent sexual advances. Tragically, many couples interpret this lack of natural aggression on her part as failure, or lack of interest. Big mistake! It simply may be a symptom of needed communication and support. This natural aggressiveness is only a problem when the husband and wife do not understand that it has nothing to do with their ultimate fulfillment. The level of her natural aggressiveness should not be a measure of sexual failure or success.

Men must realize that God created their natural aggressiveness for obvious creation purposes. It's okay for you to be the aggressor most of the time. It doesn't mean there is anything wrong with your wife. However, if a husband is constantly desiring sex, far too often for the wife, there may be a problem with communication, or feelings of rejection. These feelings can stem from his past. If a wife's sexual aggressiveness is lower than desired, the couple simply needs a mutually satisfying plan to change the balance. Counsel and openness can accomplish the solution to either of these problems.

Today, in our culture, it is not unusual to find men who are less aggressive than their wives. Do not attach one another with labels that destroy emotional security. This will only worsen the problem. The solution is the same: seek godly counsel.

Enjoy sex: When I first married, I thought if I could just have my sexual needs met I would be happy. It was not long before I realized that the greatest need I had was not my own enjoyment, but my wife's. Sexually speaking, the greatest gift a woman can give her husband is to *enjoy her own sexual experience*. This is very motivating to a husband.

Too many wives look at sex merely as their duty to satisfy their husband's needs. Every woman should know that God wants her to feel good and to enjoy sex. If a wife has the freedom to look at her physical union as an enjoyable experience, her attitude will change tremendously. In order to enjoy the sexual union and to reach orgasm, most women need to *concentrate* on their own body, while the man enjoys concentrating and thinking about her. She must realize that one of the greatest gifts she can give God and her husband is to enjoy the experience. Wives need to sense personal freedom in these areas:

- An understanding of the Scriptures concerning sex and marriage
- Good communication with mate
- Satisfaction with her mate
- Respect from and for her husband
- Relaxation of daily responsibilities
- Security in her sexual setting
- Cleanliness of her mate and self
- Security that her body is attractive to her mate
- Freedom to discover what feels good
- Freedom to verbalize enjoyment, feelings, instructions
- Assurance that her husband will sensitively approach her, with her needs being his first priority

Femininity: God has given men a tremendous desire to pursue and serve his wife. In the natural sense, this drive manifests itself through sexual attraction. Wives should take advantage of this God-created desire instead of resenting it. Before the Lord, use your husband's desire to motivate him, instead of condemning him. Learn to utilize and enjoy his instinctive desire. How you dress is very important to him. Most men like their wives to wear feminine clothing as much as possible. Feminine undergarments are extremely motivating to husbands. Makeup and perfume can also effect his natural desire. Ask your husband what he enjoys about your clothing, and what he would like you to change.

To Husbands And Wives

Naked and unashamed: Each couple should place the focus of their sexual relationship on being "naked and unashamed" instead of just having an orgasm in intercourse. While orgasm is a very important icing on the "sexual cake," it is not the cake. No couple can be assured of a successful orgasm experience every time, but every couple can be assured of a successful intimate experience. Do not limit your sexual experiences to just intercourse. Characterize your physical lovemaking by focusing on each mate's total person.

In our culture, many couples limit their sexual expression to fifteen quick minutes of intercourse. Couples who allow their sexual experience to dwindle to this point have, many times, guaranteed that the wife will have lower enjoyment for several reasons. Research shows that there is a large possibility that intercourse alone will not produce an orgasm for the wife. Secondly, fifteen minute "quickies" foster servitude feelings in wives, not encouragement. They are very likely to feel "used." Thirdly, fifteen minutes does not allow wives to experience a "total person" encounter. A "naked and unashamed" total person experience should take up to an hour. She needs time to be reassured, to be listened to, to have her hurts mended, as well as to give her body time to be prepare for intercourse.

> THE FOCUS OF THE SEXUAL RELATIONSHIP SHOULD BE ON BEING "NAKED AND UNASHAMED"

What are we saying? Husbands, you need to level the playing field! You can normally have an orgasm over ninety percent of the time. But quick lovemaking may limit her to orgasm to, at best, thirty to forty percent of the time. You may be angry with God for not giving you a more sexually aggressive wife, but you may have failed repeatedly in the "sensitivity and creativity department." By the way, if the above applies to you, do not expect a four or five day recovery.

Guys, wake up! If you take time to deeply engage your wife's emotions, she will enjoy the sexual encounter eighty percent of the time, even if she cannot have an orgasm. Cake is good, even without the icing. Do not allow your wife just to serve your needs. If she is at all frustrated, both of you should seek counsel.

Body freedom: Since the sexual relationship is primarily a physical act, it is very important for partners to be excited about their mate's body as well as their own. Research indicates that sexual feelings intensify when couples are open and creative with each other's bodies. The woman who can uninhibitedly open her mind, body, and body movements to her husband's rhythm and motion will certainly experience increased enjoyment and success.

Today, it is common for men to be attracted to their wife's body, and to even express that verbally, but it is not as common for wives to express their appreciation for the husband's body. It is helpful for wives to reprogram their minds through Scripture by reading the Song of Solomon. The Shulamite comments, *"He is wholly desirable. This is my beloved and this is my friend."*

It is generally much easier for a husband to develop freedom with his body and with his mate's body. Generally, women are not as free. They tend to compare themselves with the youthful, unblemished bodies of models on TV, which can result in insecurity. Christian teaching has not helped women to be free with their husbands. Some women believe that the lower parts of their bodies are extremely unattractive and even unsanitary. This sets them up for sexual anxiety. Yet men, when polled on what part of their wife's body is most attractive, overwhelmingly said the lower parts. This is a shocking revelation to wives!

Because of these natural differences, husbands need to slow down and allow their wives time to adjust. With patience and sensitivity, after several months, the couple can learn to be open and free with each others' bodies. Once a wife is motivated by her husband's tenderness and patience, sex will become a more enjoyable experience for her.

Sexual verbalization: Sexual communication is a non-negotiable in marriage. Talking about sexual excitement, instructions, hurts, fears, disappointments, joys, and anticipation are very important. The couple's ability to verbalize these to each other is imperative.

Several problems occur in sexual verbalization. It is not natural for men or women to verbalize during lovemaking. Fear of losing their focus is prevalent. It is more natural to communicate criticism than encouragement. "Don't do that," or "I don't like that," are said all too often instead of encouraging things like, "That feels good," or "One thing I love for you to do is . . . "

Because of the personal aspect of the sexual relationship, egos are easily injured. A mate who tries hard to please his partner, only to be criticized for his effort, may never fully recover. Hurt can turn a beautiful sexual experience into a bitter exchange of insults. Don't criticize *during* the physical act of lovemaking. If you have concerns, *wait* till the following day to discuss those issues. Approach the subject with humility and sensitivity. Pray first.

Learning to verbalize can involve creating a sexual vocabulary. Sally and I conscripted terms from the Song of Solomon and developed words that we personally felt comfortable with. We laughed a lot and had a good time developing our sexual vocabulary. After years of marriage, it is amazing how comfortable we are with our terminology. Read the Song of Solomon out loud to each other. Have the wife take the part of the Shulamite and the husband, Solomon. You will laugh at some of the terminology but you will begin to feel natural using sexual terms from this book. It is a beautiful book and needs to be read often by couples.

Time priority: The longer the marriage, the greater the sexual blessing. Couples need to moderate past disappointments with hope for the future. Consider the following fail-safe plan.

First, have one *two-hour sexual experience weekly* for the rest of your marriage. Schedule it if you have to, but make it happen. Plan an evening with no TV and without the children (or wait till they have gone to bed). You will be surprised at how creative you will become with your two-hour encounter.

The second commitment is very important as children come along. I suggest to couples that they take a *twenty-four-hour time period* alone together *once a month*. You can "switch-off" your children with another couple who are doing the same thing. It's fun to sometimes have breakfast in bed, or sleep late, or have an early morning "love-in." Be creative!

If a couple takes a night each week and a day every month to concentrate on their physical and emotional needs, there really aren't too many problems that they cannot conquer together. Obviously, to accomplish this faithfully in the real world is hard. Yet, if you only take *half* of these days during the year, you will still characterize your sex life as being very satisfying. Begin now to establish a *habit* of making time for just the two of you. Your children will grow up and characterize your marriage as great. They will sense that you enjoy spending time together and that you love each other. That is the greatest gift you can give yourself and your children.

PREMARITAL SEX

For the Engaged

Today in America, many counselors and well-meaning friends contend that premarital sex releases people from their inhibitions, strict morals, and so-called "religious hang-ups." While I would agree that certain hang-ups need emotional understanding, I do not believe that premarital sex is the answer. Premarital sex does *not* free couples, but in fact, it does just the opposite. It adds emotional pressure and puts you in bondage. It can rob you of the ability to clearly see God's will for marriage. To God, sexual love expresses the more important spiritual commitment between two married people. Sexual love, apart from marriage, reduces sex to a purely physical experience.

Some of you have had premarital sex. Some of you are now involved in premarital sex. First of all, you must recognize that it is sin. God didn't tell us not to be involved in premarital sex because he wanted to take away our fun. He told us "no," because He loves us and has a better way. (If you have had premarital sex, I strongly suggest a Christian counselor to help you seek God's forgiving perspective, and to give accountability.)

We must recognize that sin is forgivable, no matter what form it takes. You need to ask His forgiveness. If you are presently involved in premarital sex, you must now make a decision of your will to refrain. This will insure a much better transition into marriage.

Because of the nature of man and the cultural fantasy that is perpetrated on couples today, sexual involvement before marriage causes an unnatural emotional response. An air of false excitement and expectancy alters the normal marital sexual response. Therefore, a couple involved prior to marriage may have problems adjusting when this false expectancy is removed after the wedding. Stopping now will allow God to begin to give you an anticipation of a sexual relationship in marriage that is free from guilt, and open to godly expression.

Since we are all victims of our culture's permissiveness, let me give you some practical ideas that will help with this struggle. First, make a spiritual and verbal commitment together to stop your premarital sexual activities. *Men, you take the leadership in this decision.* Women are as responsible before the Lord as men, but God expects men to exhibit leadership. Your future wife will respect you even more for being strong here.

Let me give you an alternative to sexual involvement that has worked for many couples. I have found that while actual sexual involvement frustrates a relationship, the real need is not sexual contact, but sexual recognition and communication.

I suggest to couples that after making their commitment to stop all sexual involvement, they try the following: When you spend time together, just before you part, you should excuse yourselves from family or friends and privately kiss affectionately. Then both of you should express your excitement for future marital love. The statement should be brief and stated as unto the Lord. Yet it should be a complete expression of what you feel and need in general terms. The woman might say, "Darling, I want you to know that I am excited about giving myself to you after the wedding. You are so attractive to me. I am going to pray specifically tonight that God will cause me to be a great lover to you after we marry." I have found that a brief statement communicated sincerely can meet the need of being recognized and appreciated sexually. Creativity by both will aid the development of sexual verbalization.

The key to this project is to be certain to only attempt this communication just as the couple is parting. The sexual battle is usually lost, not at the point of contact, but at the point of putting yourself in a tempting situation. A couple who plans a day at the apartment watching television is in trouble from the start. Be verbally creative in meeting the other's need for physical attention.

I personally do not recommend a long engagement period for these obvious reasons. If the wedding is a year away, I recommend possibly moving the date up a few months. Usually it does not take more than four to six months to plan a wedding. This may not be possible, but it is easier to refrain sexually for six months than a year. If you still struggle with sexual involvement after these suggestions, the next step is to make yourselves accountable to someone else. Go together to a godly person in your church, whom you can trust. Communicate your frustrations and make a commitment to do what is asked of you. Usually, this type of accountability will do the job. Pre-marital counseling is a must if you desire for your marriage to have a good beginning.

Most importantly, remember that God created sex to be a very vital, fulfilling aspect of married life. Trust Him that He wants you to be more fulfilled than you even desire for yourself.

1. Tim and Beverly LaHaye. The Act of Marriage (Grand Rapids, Mich.: Zondervan, 1976), p. 22.

Suggested Christian books on sex: *Intended for Pleasure*, by Ed Wheat; *The Act of Marriage*, by Tim LaHaye; *Solomon on Sex*, by Joseph Dillow; *Physical Unity*, by Shirley Rice; and *The Gift of Sex*, by Clifford Penner.

CHAPTER FOURTEEN
FINANCIAL FREEDOM

MANY YEARS AGO the importance of financial planning in marriage was permanently imprinted upon my mind. It started when a surprise call came from a woman who was a spiritual leader in our community. I would have never suspected this couple to have financial problems.

When she first contacted me I had not met her husband. She loved him, but revealed with disappointment that over the years she had accumulated a great deal of resentment toward her husband's financial habits. She had prayed and prayed, but she could not resist being critical of him.

It seemed that her husband was always late paying the bills. She would receive the bills in the mail and give them to him. Months later he would pay them. All of this came to a head one day when, at the time, she unfortunately had three friends with her. She attempted to charge a dress and was refused because of their payment record. She was extremely embarrassed. The problem had become so bad that she resented her husband and felt the need for counsel.

Financial stress is a major problem in most marriages.[1] Every couple spends restless nights over financial fears, but entirely too many couples actually lose their marriages over financial stress.

Fifty percent of couples who divorce cite finances as a major cause of disagreement. Few things cause bitterness and resentment more than money and how it is used.

Paul was certainly correct when he said to Timothy:

For the love of money is a root of all sorts of evil, and some by longing for it have wandered away from the faith, and pierced themselves with many a pang (1 Tim. 6:10).

The key phrase is "some by longing for it." The first financial problem to be solved in marriage is attitude. What importance do you as a couple place on money? 1 Samuel 2:7 says *"The Lord makes poor and rich; He brings low, He also exalts."*

Is your attitude such that you are willing to believe God even if you have little money? The question points to the fact that every couple needs to agree on some financial absolutes to protect them from attitude problems. The solution is a proper combination of attitude and financial discipline. Some couples become trapped, in spite of a good attitude, because they fail to anticipate, record, and control their budget.

Financial responsibility requires proper attitudes and faithful control. Problems occur when our worldly desires conflict with God's perspective. Our culture subtly says one thing about financial responsibility, while God's Word says another. The following chart (top of next page) gives examples of some of these conflicting concepts.

You might tend to read quickly over these conflicting statements without a lot of personal conviction, but don't! Any person who has grown up in America cannot help but be influenced by our culture's thought patterns. The resultant pressures and conflicts are painful. The more couples adhere to God's thought pattern, the more freedom and blessing will result.

Financial Faithfulness

As you try to develop God's perspective on finances, look first at the example of Christ Himself. Jesus mentions that financial faithfulness is a thermometer of our relationship with God.

OUR CULTURE'S VIEW	GOD'S PERSPECTIVE
1. Fix your attention on money and possessions.	*But seek first His kingdom and His righteousness; and all these things shall be added to you* (Matt. 6:33).
2. Wealth and possessions determine happiness in life.	*Beware, and be on your guard against every form of greed; for not even when one has an abundance does his life consist of his possessions* (Luke 12:15).
3. I'll be satisfied when I have more ____.	*He who loves money will not be satisfied with he who loves abundance with its income. This too is vanity* (Ecc. 5:10).
4. A man's wealth is his security.	*God is our refuge and strength, a very present help in trouble. Therefore we will not fear, though the earth should change, and though the mountains slip into the heart of the sea; though its waters roar and foam, though the mountains quake at its swelling pride* (Ps. 46:1-3).
5. Financial success is the first priority.	Matthew 6:33 (quoted above) and *. . . not addicted to wine or pugnacious, but gentle, uncontentious, free from the love of money* (1 Tim. 3:3).

He who is faithful in a very little thing is faithful also in much; and he who is unrighteous in a very little thing is unrighteous also in much. If therefore you have not been faithful in the use of unrighteous mammon, who will entrust the true riches to you? And if you have not been faithful in the use of that which is another's, who will give you that which is your own? No servant can serve two masters; for either he will hate the one, and love the other, or else he will hold to one, and despise the other. You cannot serve God and mammon (Luke 16:10-13).

The first thing Jesus does here is compare money to a "little thing." He makes it clear in His analogy that in comparison to the important things in life, money is a small item. But this "little thing" is a big indicator of a man's faithfulness in serving God. The way a man handles his finances is a strong indication of his trustworthiness as a person. In verse 11, Jesus says that if you cannot be trusted financially, how can He give you "true riches?" This refers to the "grace, hope, and peace" that God gives to a person or couple who adheres to God's perspective. Today, men acquire money to find peace, but God says money does not bring peace or contentment.

Jesus says that every person is either serving God or trusting in the security of money. What is your choice as a person or couple? Couples who apply faith in finances experience blessing and peace. Couples who put their hope in money and possessions, however slightly, struggle greatly. Often the struggle results in questioning God or feeling depressed. There is seldom any middle ground. *I am convinced that God uses finances as few other things to teach dependence upon Him.*

To find God's perspective financially, you should consider the following issues. These four insights will do more to insure financial peace of mind than anything the world can provide.

FOUR PILLARS OF FINANCIAL MATURITY

Ownership

The minute I bought my first car, I began to feel compulsion to own things. This compulsion forced me to compare myself with others who owned more. Then came resentment and discontentment. We must remember that the advertising industry attempts to accomplish one thing: to make you *dissatisfied* with what you have. These ads tell us that *their* product will make us happier, be that a house, car, stereo, or simply their toothpaste. If that was true, we would have a lot of satisfied people in this country, but just the opposite is true. We always seem to want more, and our advertising industry plays a big role in that. God challenges this thought.

*Thine, O Lord, is the greatness and the power and the glory and the victory and the majesty, indeed **everything** that is in the heavens and the earth; Thine is the dominion, O Lord, and Thou dost exalt Thyself as head over all. **Both riches and honor come from Thee**, and Thou dost rule over all, and in Thy hand is power and might; and it lies in Thy hand to make great, and to strengthen everyone. Now therefore, our God, we thank Thee, and praise Thy glorious name. But who am I and who are my people that we should be able to offer as generously as this? For **all things come from Thee**, and from Thy hand we have given Thee. For we are sojourners before Thee, and tenants, as all our fathers were; our days on the earth are like a shadow, and there is no hope. O Lord our God, all this abundance that we have provided to build Thee a house for Thy holy name, it is from Thy hand, and **all is Thine*** (1 Chronicles 29:11-16).

God says *He* is head over all; that *all* things come from Him. We are simply tenants of God's possessions for a short time. We are to worship and glorify God with what He has given us. When others have need of what we are *tenants* over, we should be free to give. Sally and I often discuss how God uses the possessions He has given us. Often He tests us shortly after He has given us something. He wants to know if we have taken ownership because He desires us to be only *stewards* of His possessions.

Our first test came early in our marriage. We bought our first brand new washing machine. At the time, we were close friends with a couple in seminary who didn't have any money, and we told them they could wash their clothes in our machine. Every Saturday they came over to do laundry. Sally began to feel uneasy about this, thinking that the machine might break because of overuse. Then we would be stuck with the bill. We reminded ourselves that the machine was not ours, but the Lord's. We had given all our possessions to Him to be used by Him in any way He chose. We needed to change our attitude from one of possessiveness to gratefulness that the Lord had blessed us with a machine that could be used by others. That machine lasted well over ten years. It was never repaired, and we later sold it in a garage sale. God takes care of His possessions.

We don't struggle very long with possessiveness, because it seems the Lord always reminds us *who* gave it, *who* is going to use it, *who* is going to pay the bills, and *who* may even take it away! We continually give Him our lives, our possessions, our money, our children and families, etc. He has repeatedly tested our hearts in giving. However, in return, He has given us *peace and contentment*. At the same time, He has given us more material blessings than we could have ever dreamt. Being a tenant is very freeing indeed. However, when we occasionally take ownership back, our struggle returns, and God graciously reminds us once again, who owns it all.

> *Remember how the Lord your God led you all the way . . . to **humble you and to test you** in order to know what was in your heart, whether or not you would keep his commands* (Deut. 8:2 NIV).

God's Providence

Another constant struggle for Christians is that of comparing their financial situation to others. Feeling superior over those with less, or hating and resenting those with more, can destroy God's perspective in our lives. Today there is a great tendency by some to feel proud about their "simple" life-styles. God clearly speaks about differences in financial situations.

> *But you, why do you judge your brother? Or you again, why do you regard your brother with contempt? For we shall all stand before the judgment seat of God. For it is written, "As I live," says the Lord, "Every knee shall bow to Me, and every tongue shall give praise to God." So then each one of us shall give account of himself to God. Therefore let us not judge one another anymore, but rather determine this, not to put an obstacle or a stumbling block in a brother's way* (Rom. 14:10-13).

*The **Lord makes poor and rich;** He brings low, He also exalts. He raises the poor from the dust, He lifts the needy from the ash heap to make them sit with nobles, and inherit a seat of honor; for the pillars of the earth are the Lords, and He set the world on them* (1 Sam. 2:7).

God leaves no doubt on this issue: *He* makes both rich and poor. There are no accidents in business. Whatever your state, it was not the "breaks" that put you there; it was God. We have all seen "sure deals" fall unrewarded, and totally "hopeless deals" pay tremendous financial dividends. Don't waste your time blaming or watching others, because the One to look to is Christ Himself. It is not man, but God who causes all things to happen. The issue is not what you have or don't have, but what you do with what you have. *You are accountable to God for what He has given you.* God's ultimate purpose is to conform us to the image of His Son, Jesus Christ. He may use finances to do part of that shaping. Can you thank Him at all times for what you have or don't have? *Everything* we have is a gift from Him, and is a part of His plan for our lives.

Contentment

So, if we do not really own anything, and God is the One who makes rich or poor, what should be our attitude?

For we have brought nothing into the world, so we cannot take anything out of it either. And if we have food and covering, with these we shall be content. But those who want to get rich fall into temptation and a snare and many foolish and harmful desires which plunge men into ruin and destruction (1 Tim. 6:7-9).

Let your character be free from the love of money, being content with what you have; for He Himself has said, "I will never desert you, nor will I ever forsake you," so that we confidently say, "the Lord is my helper, I will not be afraid. What shall man do to me?" (Heb. 13:5-6).

Apart from basic food and clothing, there is no real hope in "things;" there is only the appearance of hope. So be content with food and clothing, if that's all you have. If you have wealth, or desire to seek it, then you need to be very cautious. Remember that God is still responsible for meeting your needs. *"He Himself has said 'I will never desert you nor will I forsake you'"* (Hebrews 13:5). Trust Him to meet your needs. He has promised to do so and in many cases has given us many of our wants as well. And consider this insight:

> *Give me neither poverty nor riches; feed me with the food that is my portion, lest I be full and deny Thee and say, "Who is the Lord?" or lest I be in want and steal, and profane the name of my God* (Prov. 30:8-9).

Our human nature always wants more than we have. God is the only one who can make us satisfied with what we have. As hard as it is to grasp, we must realize the difference between needs and wants, and claim God's promises to meet our needs. The ability to be content in these promises is a major ingredient in God's recipe for financial maturity. Throughout our married life, there have been times of real financial need. Those times have provided wonderful opportunities to acknowledge our needs to God, ask Him to meet those needs, and then watch Him answer. There is such contentment and joy in answered prayer!

> GOD IS THE ONLY ONE WHO CAN MAKE US SATISFIED WITH WHAT WE HAVE.

> *Not that I speak from want; for I have learned to be **content** in whatever circumstances I am. I know how to get along with humble means, and I also know how to live in prosperity; in any and every circumstance I have learned the secret of being filled and going hungry, both of having abundance and suffering need. I can do all things through Him who strengthens me* (Phil. 4:11-13).

> *Be anxious for nothing, but in everything by prayer and supplication, with thanksgiving, let your **requests** be known to God; and the peace of God, which passes all understanding, will guard your hearts and minds through Christ Jesus* (Phil. 4:6-7).

This verse indicates that we can let God know our *wants*, as well as our needs. It doesn't mean that God will give us our wants, but if He doesn't, He will give us His *peace*. And what more could we want than the peace of God which passes our understanding?

Security

> *Instruct those who are rich in this present world not to be conceited or to fix their hope on the certainty of riches, but on God, who richly supplies us with all things to enjoy. Instruct them to do good, to be rich in good works, to be generous and ready to share, storing up for themselves the treasure of a good foundation for the future, so that they may take hold of that which is life indeed* (1 Tim. 6:17-19).

The last pillar of God's perspective on finances is security. What is real security? It is not found in the uncertainty of riches. Security is found by fixing our hope on God, who gives us everything we need. Scripture is awash with this concept, both in finances and in human relationships. If a person will place his hope or security in God, to the point that he can release riches and actually share with others, then God promises "life indeed." Faith is acting on a statement from God, even when it goes against human thought. Financial freedom and security are in God, not in earthly possessions.

These four pillars of financial freedom (Ownership, God's Providence, Contentment, and Security) give us the foundation for applying the use of money to our lives. When we understand that all we have has been given by His gracious hand, we will be more careful how we give, save, invest, and spend. Prayerfully, we will become faithful stewards of *God's* money and possessions.

UNDERSTANDING AND APPLYING: GIVING, SAVING, INVESTING, AND SPENDING

The four financial pillars are tested and proved in the practical financial activities of giving, saving, and spending. Scripture instructs us in all three of these important activities. Develop a careful strategy for each one.

Giving

The importance of giving financially to the church and to others is a theme throughout Scripture. The Old and New Testaments give very specific direction on amounts to give, when to give, and to whom to give.

> *Now concerning the collection for the saints, as I directed the churches of Galatia, so do you also. On the first day of every week let each one of you put aside and save, as he may prosper, that no collections be made when I come* (1 Cor. 16:1-2).

Paul instructs each believer to "put aside," so that you can give regularly, and according to how much God has given you. You do this *before you spend*, or you won't have it to give. In the Old Testament, men gave twenty percent as required by the law. If you lived in Israel, the twenty percent was divided between the government (under the rule of God) and the Temple (also under the rule of God). In other words, ten percent went to the Lord's work and ten percent went to the government to keep it running. That's a far cry from our government taxes today.

In the New Testament, we are to ask the Spirit of God to direct our giving. For some, it will be ten percent, some twenty, and some more. We are to give with a gracious spirit, not one of compulsion. *"Let each one do just as he has purposed in his heart; not grudgingly or under compulsion; for God loves a cheerful giver"* (2 Cor. 9:7). Sometimes the less a couple earns, the more possessive and materialistic they become. Each couple should take seriously God's command to give liberally.

Giving is a redemptive act. There is nothing quite like giving, in that God graciously and tenderly lets us help meet the needs of others. It forces our eyes off ourselves and our needs. It allows us to keep the right perspective on *who really owns my money, and who gives it to me*. Believers will receive a blessing from God if they give sacrificially to others. I challenge you to let the Holy Spirit tell you what to give and to whom.

Paul gives additional instruction in Galatians 6:6: *"And let the one who is taught the word share all good things with him who teaches."* We are taught to *give to those who minister to us*. The ability of God's full-time servants to be available depends on your faithfulness to support them financially, be that in *your local church, Christian organizations*, or *missionaries*. Above all, *be visionary* in your giving. Trust the One who has given so much to you. God wants to use you as a reservoir to meet needs! Allow God to use you greatly so He can enlist you as a supplier for His work. What joy there is in giving to others. Giving is like the "blessing cycle." The more you give, the more God gives. Someone has correctly said, "You can't out-give God."

Give, and it will be given to you; good measure, pressed down, shaken together, running over, they will pour into your lap. For by your standard of measure it will be measured to you in return (Luke 6:38).

Even when you *loan* money to others, you should consider "giving" the money to them instead. Giving releases you from always wondering if they are going to pay the loan back. Loaning money can cause you to become resentful and bitter toward that person. We are not saying here that a loan should not be repaid, but God says your contentment should not depend on another person's lack of responsibility. Always keep an open and giving spirit toward others. God does amazing work in our lives when we give unselfishly.

You shall generously give to him, and your heart shall not be grieved when you give to him, because for this thing the Lord your God will bless you in all your work and in all your undertakings. For the poor will never cease to be in the land; therefore I command you, saying "You shall freely open your hand to your brother, to your needy and poor in your land" (Deut. 15:10-11).

There are many other ways to give to people out of our abundance. Food—when someone is out of a job, the birth of a baby, a death in the family, etc. Clothing—to others less fortunate and to mission organizations. Furniture—to church people or young couples who have need. Cars—to a missionary or pastor who is in need. Rather than selling your items, ask God who He would have you give it to. Your part is to give and God's part is to bless.

Saving

Saving is vital to financial peace and joy. I am constantly dealing with the struggles of couples who are in debt, or who have no money at the end of the month. A poor person with a little money in savings is much freer financially than a rich man who is overextended. Scripture speaks of the wisdom of saving. Proverbs 21:20 tells us that the man who keeps a little treasure and oil stored up is a wise man in comparison to the foolish man who swallows (spends) up his excess. Proverbs 13:22 says that a good man leaves an inheritance to his grandchildren.

No matter how small the amount, even $50 a month, begin immediately to save. If you run out of money at the end of the month, the pressure is much less if you have an additional $500 in savings. A good rule of thumb is to save 10% of your salary each month. Saving, like giving, needs to come first, not after spending. If you begin saving when first married, you will be amazed how much you will accumulate for houses, college education, etc. If you have money in savings, it can "tide you over" if a job is lost. Most Americans are one paycheck away from bankruptcy.

Investing

God has a lot to say about making wise investments. God graciously gives us some guidelines concerning saving and investing. First, avoid "get-rich-quick" schemes. Build security slowly. Putting a little aside weekly, following a hard week's work, is your best strategy.

The plans of the diligent lead surely to advantage, but everyone who is hasty comes surely to poverty (Prov. 21:5).

A man with an evil eye hastens after wealth, and does not know that want will come upon him (Prov. 28:22).

But those who want to get rich fall into temptation and a snare and many foolish and harmful desires which plunge men into ruin and destruction (1 Tim. 6:9).

Wealth obtained by fraud dwindles, but the one who gathers by labor increases it (Prov. 13:11).

Prepare plans by consultation, and make war by wise guidance (Prov. 20:18).

The best advice is to always seek counsel from someone who has invested wisely. Seek out several people who are experienced in investing. Those who are older and more mature will often have more wisdom. Don't be afraid to ask questions. Find someone who will take the time to listen and help you model a plan. Be very cautious about borrowing against "projected future income" to make investments, or to cover expenditures in the present. Also, be careful about seeking counsel from someone who is selling an investment product or service. Their advice might be biased toward the sale.

Come now, you who say, "Today or tomorrow, we shall go to such and such a city, and spend a year there and engage in business and make a profit." Yet you do not know what your life will be like tomorrow. You are just a vapor that appears for a little while and then vanishes away. Instead, you ought to say, "If the Lord wills, we shall live and also do this or that." But as it is, you boast in your arrogance; all such boasting is evil. Therefore, to one who knows the right thing to do, and does not do it, to him it is sin (James 4:13-17).

Debt (Uncontrolled Spending)
Debt has literally destroyed many marriages and may eventually ruin our country. The national debt is staggering and continues to climb, no matter what our politicians do. Personal debt is at all time high and continues to rise rapidly. Debt is considered "normal" today. But it should not be normal, either personally or nationally. "During 1990-91 a startling one household in 20 filed for bankruptcy. In the past, bankruptcies increased in a bad economy, not a good one . . . Driving these millions of bankruptcies is an increase in credit card debt. Every household is offered 25 new credit cards every year . . . 75 percent of users don't pay off their balances every month."[1]

Credit card debt is extremely stressful in marriage. Begin getting out of credit card debt by paying off high interest cards first, and then getting to the point where you pay for everything at the time of purchase with cash. If you have credit cards, pay the balance each month so you don't accumulate debt. Limit yourself to two or three credit cards at the most.

Most financial problems occur in the spending area. "Americans spend on average $1.10 for every $1.00 they earn and the average consumer owes about seventeen percent of after-tax income to creditors."[2]

You should know at all times, what you owe, so that you are not spending what you don't have. Paul exhorts the Romans to *"owe nothing to anyone except to love one another."* Although he was not speaking directly of finances, the application is valid.

Establish a set of standards to govern your purchases. If you don't do this, you will have problems in your marriage. Often two people come together in marriage with totally different ways of looking at spending. Pay off high monthly payments (car and house) as quickly as possible. When your car is paid off, rather than buy a new car, put the same money in the bank for the purchase of a newer car when needed. Buying a new car with limited mileage may be a better investment than a brand new car. If you have a thirty year loan on your house, begin paying an extra $100-150 a month toward the principle. You will be amazed at how fast the house gets paid off. Taking out a 15 year loan is better than a 30 year loan because of the interest saved.

The following chart is an example of the type of questions you might ask yourself to determine if your expenditures are in line with God's perspective. You may want to study this together.

Question	Scripture
1. Is my spending motivated by the love of things?	1 Timothy 6:9 1 John 2:15
2. Has God already led me to meet a need with this money?	2 Corinthians 8:14
3. Do I have a doubt about it?	Romans 14:23
4. Have I given God an opportunity to supply it?	Psalm 37:5 Proverbs 10:3
5. Will it be disadvantageous for my spiritual growth?	1 Corinthians 6:12 Hebrews 12:1 2 Corinthians 11:3
6. Is it a good investment?	Proverbs 20:14
7. Does it put me in debt?	Proverbs 22:7
8. Will it be meaningful to my family?	1 Timothy 5:8 1 Timothy 3:4

Each of these factors should be balanced against all others when making a decision. Wise counsel from another person helps. Couples who keep tight control over their purchases will have little trouble keeping God's perspective. Peace and contentment will be their reward.

BUDGET

Any family that desires to get control of their finances should start by setting up a monthly budget. A budget is simply a projection of future income and expenses. A simple budget really does not take much time, but over a period of five to six months, can help a couple get on top of their finances. It is not important that the budget be absolutely accurate at first, but it should be reviewed and adjusted faithfully each month. The couple can then evaluate any problem areas together, find solutions, and adjust their financial plans. Several good financial management books and software are usually available. Consult one of these for more specifics on budgeting.

It is very important to compare your actual expenses each month with your budget. Then you can see exactly what you are spending, and where you tend to spend too much. A budget's value is realized as you continuously review and update them. Couples who plan usually tend to "make do," and their money goes further.

SPIRITUAL ISSUES

Couples are never more aware of their lack of oneness than when they are dealing with finances.

Attitudes carry over into marriage. Therefore, you and your spouse must discuss how the two of you are going to approach financial problems. Each of you will have different ways of handling money. You must agree on your priorities for purchasing and establish your financial values. Apply the faith commitments of Genesis 1 and 2 to your finances. Agree together to transfer to the Lord all of "your" possessions. *Conflict results when there is not mutual commitment, or when one spouse acts independently from the other.*

INDIVIDUAL RESPONSIBILITIES

Men, you have *primary* responsibility for the financial integrity of your home. God has instructed husbands to provide for their families. He has never changed that mandate. Men are responsible to provide income, control the expenditures, pay the bills, initiate giving, and save for a rainy day. That does not mean they are smarter, more gifted, or even more successful at these things, but they are primarily responsible. With humility, take your leadership very seriously. If your wife is more gifted than you are in the area of finances, not only seek her wisdom, but give her major responsibility. As long as husband takes responsibility financially, the wife can do the work. But if the husband begins to hedge on his responsibility, or if the wife is struggling, she should give the finances back to him.

Wives, you must be careful when you take responsibility not to "put your husbands down" in his areas of weakness. Neither of you should belittle the other when it comes to money. Remember, you are "joint heirs" of the grace of life. If a couple communicates well in the area of finances, their marriage will exhibit peace.

The husband should take responsibility for the family's needs. Yet, he should always seek his wife's input and advice, and include her in financial decisions. He might also consider setting up an operating account for her so her freedom and responsibilities increase. If possible, when the wife works outside the home, do not become dependent on her income. It would be wise to invest her salary, so that you maintain living expenses on the husband's salary alone. This will allow you to set money aside for the future, and it will also give your wife the ability to shop for necessities. It is important for mothers to be in a position to respond to the needs of the children. Becoming too dependent on her salary will eventually affect how you care for your children. Protect yourself from allowing your desire for material things to compete with the needs of your children.

> COUPLES ARE NEVER MORE AWARE OF THEIR LACK OF ONENESS THAN WHEN THEY ARE DEALING WITH FINANCES.

Both the husband and wife should maintain a spirit of joy, freedom, and creativity in the household. Some people become extremely creative when they are low on money. They have joy in giving and yet have a tight budget. Refinishing furniture, crafts, garage sales, and do-it-yourself, is the name of the game for low-budget families. When their circumstances are approached by faith, low-budget families can many times be happier than couples who have more financial resources.

Every couple will struggle financially. It seems that God uses money more than anything else to teach dependence on Him.

When you struggle, reread this chapter to review God's perspective. If you do, the Holy Spirit will encourage and direct you. We also highly recommend a 12-week course on finances by Crown Ministries.[3]

1. I want to acknowledge James Squires (deceased), John Maisel, and Jody Dillow for their financial insights offered in 1972.
2. Larry Burkett, *Christian Financial Concepts, Inc.* April 1997 Newsletter.
3. Crown Ministries, Longwood, Fl.

CHAPTER FIFTEEN
LOVING THOSE IN-LAWS!

ALTHOUGH ALL of us have heard the standard jokes concerning in-laws, this is a "joke" a lot of couples must deal with in reality. I'm not sure that couples fully realize the potential stress, anxiety, and hurt that can come if they are unprepared for potential in-law problems. To be forewarned is to be forearmed!

About the time invitations are being sent, wedding showers begin, and planning for details of the ceremony are all underway, couples begin to realize that opinions are surfacing about their potential union. By the time the week of the wedding arrives, simple parent-child relationships have turned into complex anxiety struggles. The bride is crying, "Oh, why can't Mom understand?" and the groom is asking, "What did I do that upset them so much?" Caught off guard, the couple has unintentionally become a party to conflict that cuts deeply into the emotional needs of both the couple and their parents. Before they realize it, their in-laws have already developed opinions about their future son or daughter-in-law.

The toughest thing about preparing for a positive in-law relationship is you don't get a practice run! Your introduction to them can be tremendously personal and meaningful. The future of their son or daughter is at stake. Only after having children of my own have I understood this pressure. I remember when my oldest daughter was only eight, I could already imagine how suspect and observant I would be that day in the future when some "hot-dog" would tell me he deserves my little girl! And sure enough, eighteen years later, it happened! Fortunately, God was gracious in giving us a fine son-in-law. I know parents desire close relationships with their future sons or daughters-in-law, but their initial introduction can sometimes be emotionally hard on them.

> THE TOUGHEST THING ABOUT PREPARING FOR A POSITIVE IN-LAW RELATIONSHIP IS YOU DON'T GET A PRACTICE RUN!

Sometimes, these initial introductions take place while planning the wedding. Other couples have known each other a long time. In our transient society, it is common for a son or daughter to bring his or her future mate home just weeks before the wedding. To force two different families, often complete strangers to each other, to come together amiably, is not a natural thing. In fact, it is a miracle if it goes well.

Our In-law Beginning

I can still remember my initial introduction to Sally's parents. Because we met, dated, and were engaged within a three month period, I didn't have the opportunity to meet her family until one week before the wedding. (As I tell this story, remember that Mom and Pop Hill are extremely likable people. The slight problems encountered were not related to the people, but to the awkward situation.)

When I arrived in Boulder, Colorado, it was about two in the afternoon. I had stopped earlier to clean up and put a suit on before going to meet Sally's family. They lived in the mountains above Boulder, so I decided to drop in on Sally's dad at work to get directions to their house. Pop was a well known auto mechanic in Boulder. When I entered his shop, the supervisor told me Mr. Hill was working under a car, several cars down the line.

I was spotlessly dressed, overly aggressive, and somewhat nervous. I walked up to the car and said to his feet, which were sticking out, "Mr. Hill, I am Don Meredith." Stunned, Mr. Hill got about halfway out from under the car before I grabbed his greasy hand and said "Hello!" He was embarrassed about the grease, and we both felt rather awkward. He gave me directions to their house, and I left with my clean suit and greasy hand.

That night the pressure mounted quickly. All my life I've been a very modest person. I quickly discovered that the house they lived in at the time had only one bathroom, and you had to go *through* her parents bedroom to get there! After going to bed, my worst fears came true. I had to use the bathroom! I waited as long as I could, and then walked through their bedroom. I turned the water on in the basin and it sounded like Niagara Falls. I was so embarrassed! I felt emotional pressure from that point forward.

The first problems surfaced later in the week over the phone expenses. Sally and I had made some long-distance calls during the month before that were necessary to make our wedding plans. However, we didn't communicate to the Hills our intention of paying for the calls. All the calls were long, full of questions, congratulations, and general catch-up, and they were all expensive. Finally, Sally mentioned to me her parents' concern over all the calls. This was perfectly understandable, but in light of the tension, I reacted strongly against Sally. I took pride in my financial responsibility and felt my integrity being questioned.

These problems sound foolish as I retell them, but at the time they were very serious. Four people, who under normal circumstances would have hit it off perfectly, started out on a slightly wrong foot. Since then, things have smoothed out remarkably and, by God's grace, our in-law problems have been very minor. Our family greatly enjoys our times at Sally's parent's home, and we all look forward to our visits. This is true of my family as well.

Many couples start off wrong and are then burdened with poor in-law relationships for years. Once again, it will take faith to develop positive in-law relationships. Therefore, we need to know what God says concerning in-laws. In addition, I would like to add some practical suggestions for developing successful in-law relationships.

Leaving Father And Mother

God established His foundational thoughts concerning in-laws at the time he created marriage. God reminds us of the importance of a strong marriage commitment. This commitment becomes the basis of in-law relationships. Let me repeat Genesis 2:24. God communicates the vital importance a strong faith commitment plays in a successful marriage. Even though Adam and Eve did not have parents, God makes a statement that reveals the role future parents will play in the lives of their children: *"For this cause a man shall leave his father and his mother, and shall cleave to his wife; and they shall become one flesh."*

God makes it clear that children are to leave their parents when they marry. The Hebrew word used here for "leave" means to "abandon" or break off completely. God is saying that before a significant new relationship can begin, the old parent-child relationship must cease. By this, God means that in *issues of authority* the parents no longer have responsibility; He does not mean that the parental relationship should end altogether. Obviously, children should never stop honoring their parents.

Is God against parents? Absolutely not! But without His strong command to men and women to put their full trust in their mates, no marriage would last. Total mate satisfaction and respect cannot occur if there is any question concerning where the allegiance lies.

God knew that after twenty or so years of responding to parental authority, there would be a tendency to continue, even after marriage. Therefore, God indicates that one should end so that another can begin.

Honoring Father And Mother

While the authority of the parents ends with the creation of the new relationship, the couple's responsibility to honor their parents continues. Deuteronomy 5:16 tells us that the duty of a child is to honor his parents. This word "honor" speaks primarily of "valuing at a high price; deep respect or reverential awe." In marriage, parental experience and advice are very important, but decisions must be made by the couple independent of parental control. There will be times advice is necessary from the parents. Even then, it is better for the couple to go to the parents, not vice versa.

FOUR CRUCIAL CORDS TO CUT

I have discovered in counseling with couples that there are four ways they fail to leave their parents. These examples of failure to leave can be so subtle that couples may feel frustration without even understanding why.

Parental Wealth And Social Benefits

This problem reveals a conscious or subconscious hope of future inheritance, or dependence on present parental, financial, and social benefits, to the point that the couple fails to acknowledge their own financial or social independence. A husband may allow his mother to criticize his wife so that his financial relationship with his parents will not be endangered. Other couples tend to spend too much time at the home of parents because of social or financial advantages. This dependence may hinder the development of the new relationship. Normally, this dependence will result in couples becoming dissatisfied with their own financial situation.

Parental Model

Some couples, again consciously or subconsciously, compare some area of their mate's performance with that of their parents. This comparison can ultimately cause dissatisfaction. I have seen men become completely disillusioned with their wives because they do not develop a particular housekeeping habit or cooking ability that their mothers may have had. On the other hand, I have seen women lose respect for their husbands because they did not project the same financial stability as their fathers. These expectations are especially true in early marriage. Unfair comparisons like these can destroy marital oneness and commitment.

Parental Approval

Usually as a result of an extremely strong or domineering parent, some mates remain dependent on their parents' approval after marriage. This need for parental approval may block trust in their new mate. Women have told me that they love their husbands, yet they perform to please their mothers because they need Mom's approval. These women are frustrated when their mothers disapprove of their husbands. They clean house the way mom would want, discipline the children with mom in mind, all the while hoping for her recognition or approval.

One woman told me that every time she and her husband bought a house, her mother's approval would be on her mind. Therefore, she wasn't really free to make a decision with just her husband's input. Women who need approval in this way will jeopardize their husbands' sense of security and leadership. Men who are overly dependent on their father's approval can also be hindered. A man's misdirected dependence can affect his wife's respect for her husband.

Parental Relationship Substitute
Nothing deflates husbands and wives more than for their mate to continue to look to their parents to meet their primary emotional needs. This is especially true when their own emotional needs go unmet as a result. I have counseled men and women who will continue to call or go see their parents about most key issues in their lives. They will give affection, receive most of their security, share their criticism, and even express most of their creative abilities with their parents. All of this not only excludes their mates, but deeply hurts and divides them. Mates that do this are being unfaithful to the Lord and their mate.

SUGGESTED SOLUTIONS

To fail to leave your parents hurts *them* in the long run as well as your mate and yourself. Agree together on a mutual plan to leave the authority of your parents. Consider the following suggestions.

Evaluating Everyone's Need
First of all, parents are not the enemy! Parents just do what comes naturally. Never explode or punish your parents for loving you, even

if their method is wrong. Both mates have an innate need to be at peace with their parents, so do not be in conflict with them. Instead, when frustrations occur, analyze the situation with your mate and agree together about the cause. Evaluate everyone's real need, what went wrong, and most importantly, look for a creative solution. If either mate has wronged a parent, ask forgiveness. If a decision is needed to protect the integrity of the marriage, make it together. Then look for a creative way to communicate this to the parents.

> NEVER SHARE INTIMATE NEEDS OR DECISIONS WITH EITHER SET OF PARENTS *WITHOUT YOUR MATE'S PERMISSION.*

Second, commit together never to share any intimate needs or decisions with either set of parents *without your mate's permission.* A husband may be dreaming of a new car, and his wife simply mentions it to her dad. The father then voices his disapproval to her husband, and the husband feels betrayed. Couples must build their lives together, and everything should be intimate unless agreed otherwise.

Handling Critical Statements

Third, never be critical or allow critical statements about your mate to be made to or by your parents. The cruelest thing a person can do to their parents, as well as to their mate, is share something critical about their mate. Why? Because parents never forget the problems shared, and rarely allow that son or daughter-in-law to change (in their minds). They get overly protective of their own children.

I know of a situation where a wife shared a financial irresponsibility on the part of her mate in the first year of their marriage, and her parents are still bringing it up after twenty years. Parents don't have the opportunity to see your mate change and improve as you do. They only have your comments to go on. Never be critical of your mate to your parents. This is especially true in early marriage while you both are still adjusting to each other.

Do yourself and your parents another favor. The next time they make a critical statement about your mate, respond with a strong but loving rebuff. I know of one man whose mother was just leading up to a critical remark about his wife. He interrupted with, "Mom, I love you a lot, but please don't be critical of my wife. I want you to know she is God's gift to me, and I don't want to hear those criticisms."

His mother hastily replied, "Don't be silly; I wasn't going to be critical of her."

The wise son responded with, "Forgive me, Mom. I just so want you and her to be friends, because I love you both so much." He was strong but kind to his mother.

Visiting In-laws
Fourth, before visiting parents, especially in the early years of marriage, *be in agreement about the length of time you stay*. Don't plan long days of forced communication.

If at all possible, allow your wife to go home to her parents a few days earlier than you, so she can give her parents the attention they need before you arrive. Men, occasionally go home to see your parents alone. If you live close to either parent, this will not he a problem. Sometimes parents need special times with their children after they are married. Most importantly, when visiting as a couple, let the son or daughter-in-law in the situation have the freedom to love their own parents. If you feel somewhat ignored while at your spouse's parents' home, anticipate and discuss it before your next visit.

As an example, you might want to go somewhere with your wife while at her home. She is the one who is naturally accepted in her home, so take her aside and tell her of your need. You are free to go back and visit while she, at the appropriate time, announces the need for you both to go somewhere. She takes total responsibility for the decision. You are free from the possibility of hurting her parents, and they better understand and accept the decision.

Receiving Money from Parents or In-laws
Fifth, the husband should *work out a definite plan* for receiving money offered by parents, and then communicate the plan to both sets of

parents. If a husband will communicate with his wife's father the first time he attempts to give them a gift, her father will always respect his son-in-law. Although I discourage parental loans in almost every situation, I do believe parents should have the freedom to give gifts to their children. However, a husband needs to set boundaries that will insure his authority, as well as the parents' respect.

Parents by nature are givers, and children are takers. This tendency doesn't necessarily end when the child marries. Let's take the example of going out to dinner. Parents have always bought dinners for their children. How does a child begin to be an "adult" around the parent? These are the questions that need to be addressed. Who pays? When do you pay? Who invited whom?

> ADDRESS THE ISSUES BEFORE THEY EVER COME UP.

As with most problems, communication is the key. A good rule of thumb is to address the issues before they ever come up. Every once in awhile, take your parents out to dinner. If you offer to pay, and your parents reject the offer, then you have done your part. If your parents ask you to go somewhere that is clearly beyond your means (i.e. a trip, expensive restaurant, etc.), make sure to discuss what they think is appropriate to contribute.

Because moms and dads handle money differently, they also have different expectations of their children. Make sure that you talk to both of your parents about money issues so that resentment does not develop. Resentment over money issues can result in great bitterness.

Be Considerate Toward In-laws

Ask your mother-in-law and father-in-law what they would prefer that you call them. Let them know you will be glad to call them Mom and Dad if they prefer. You may be more comfortable calling them by their first names, especially if you have known them for a long time. Just asking gives them the freedom to say "It's up to you."

Another thing that demonstrates care would be dropping your parents-in-law an occasional card, thanking them for their role in your mate's life or for allowing you to visit. Courtesy with parents not only brings joy to them and to you, but increases the possibility of an exciting grandparent-child relationship in the future.

A WORD TO PARENTS AND PARENTS-IN-LAW

Regarding her married children, one mother said "Lord, give me the wisdom to bite my tongue." My hope for you as parents is for you to trust the Lord in your children's lives. *Let* them make some "mistakes" (by your standards). Parents tend to give advice on how they would run things, how they would spend money, how they would raise kids, and so on. If your children don't do what they know you expect them to do, they may feel guilt.

> CRITICIZING YOUR CHILDREN OR THEIR SPOUSES WILL ONLY DRIVE THEM AWAY FROM YOU.

Realize that *times* have changed, not scriptural values. Your children may live in nicer housing at their age than you did at the same age. Your children may leave their children with child care far more often than you did. Don't get into the habit of being critical of things they do or have. Criticism will eat at you like a cancer and destroy your opportunity to watch them grow to maturity and to enjoy them as friends.

It would be wise to say to your children, "Listen to what I say, and then do as you please." This assures you of always having the freedom to offer advice and suggestions based on your experience, yet it assures your children that they can make their own decisions. This leaves the door of communication open for all of you. Allow them to then do as they please without further unsolicited advice or an "I-told-you-so" attitude.

A word about critical attitude. Criticizing your children or their spouses will only drive them away from you. If it goes on long enough, they will not want to see you and will dread their times with you. Think before using the statements, "You never . . ." and "You always . . ." Also, don't do something nice for your children, and then "throw it in their faces" as if they don't remember. Sometimes it is best to just drop a subject than to cause conflict.

Be sensitive to their need for privacy. If you live in close proximity, call before you visit. Don't overstay your welcome or visit too often. Talk to your child about how you can become a better parent and in-law. Never assume your children "won't mind" if we just "drop over," especially early in marriage. When both husband and wife work, their time in the evenings and on weekends may be their only time for privacy. Be as considerate of them as you would your other friends.

Make sure your daughter-in-law or son-in-law feels welcome in your home and with your family. Balance your gifts equally to your married children and their spouses. Treat them as part of the family and they will be. If you do, God will use you in their lives in ways you would never dream. This may be their first opportunity to observe mature Christian parents. Fathers, initiate time with your son-in-law so the daughter can spend time with her mom.

> DON'T PUT UNREAL EXPECTATIONS ON YOUR CHILDREN AND THEIR SPOUSES.

Don't put unreal expectations on your children and their spouses. Balancing your visits is very important. Communicate with your son or daughter and their mate. Establish a visiting pattern that fits everyone. Exchange visits at appropriate times. When grandchildren come, more communication will be required. Exchanged visits then become even more important.

One last thing, many couples today have several sets of in-laws if their parents have been divorced. This obviously can cause problems. If this is the case with you, allow your children and spouses to visit all the parents involved. If this is true in your life, expect to seek counsel.

CHAPTER SIXTEEN
GOD'S TESTING TIMES

EARLIER I MENTIONED unexpected trials and sufferings as a major cause of marriage failure. Because many of the trials encountered in marriage are universal, you would do well to identify them and then prepare to face them. Normally, the thought of trials is not a very popular subject.

As a new Christian, I remember when I first began to understand the biblical importance of trials. My immediate assumption was that the successful Christian was the one who missed the most trials, kind of like running through a mine field and dodging the mines. Years of study, counseling, and personal experience have changed my perspective. I've hit a few of those mines and so have you.

Peter introduces God's perspective concerning trials in 1 Peter 2:21: *"For you have been called for this purpose, since Christ also suffered for you, leaving you an example for you to follow in His steps."* I had never imagined that it was actually part of God's plan for me to experience trials. The more I thought about it, the more it made sense. If I had been called to salvation by Jesus Christ and given His inheritance, it only made sense that I would be called to share in His suffering too.

I have begun to see that without trials I probably would not depend on the Lord very often. My humanity is bent toward lustful desires and self-centeredness. God, in His grace, reminds us of our need for Him through trials. Trials humble us and cause us to depend on God. When we are humbled, we tend to notice others instead of ourselves. *Trials, while sometimes momentarily tough, are redemptive in our lives.* Many times the only anchor I have is the reality of Christ and His Word.

God's purpose for allowing trials to enter our lives is revealed in the following verse. *"Consider it all joy, my brethren, when you encounter various trials, knowing that the testing of your faith produces endurance. And let endurance have its perfect result, that you may be perfect and complete, lacking in nothing"* (James 1:2-4). Several things stand out in this verse. First, James says when, not if, you encounter trials. In other words, each of us will definitely encounter trials, they are not an option. Second, these trials will result from a variety of sources. The word "various" comes from a word that means multicolored. Trials come in many hues and from different sources.

> TRIALS, WHILE SOMETIMES MOMENTARILY TOUGH, ARE REDEMPTIVE IN OUR LIVES.

In a world that is falling apart emotionally, and where unfulfilled marriages are robbing people of their best hope in relationships, endurance is no small thing. God promises that the result of endurance will be that we may be "perfect, complete, lacking in nothing." Trials not only promise endurance but maturity. The phrase "lacking in nothing" means equipped with every resource. Endurance, complete maturity, and being equipped with every resource—that's quite a promise!

To keep a joyful spirit when either you or your mate is experiencing a trial is not a natural human response, but a faith-oriented response. Christ suffered because He knew that if He went to the cross, you and I would someday be with Him in eternity. *". . . for the 'joy' set before Him [He] endured the cross, despising the shame..."* (Heb. 12:2). He looked **beyond** the cross to those of us who would spend eternity with Him. When it comes to trials, you and I must do the same thing.

> *Blessed is a man who perseveres under trial: for once he has been approved, he will receive the crown of life, which the Lord has promised to those who love Him* (James 1:12).

The word "blessed" means "the very highest experience." The man who perseveres will be approved by God. "Approved" was the word stamped on cookware after it came out of the fire with no cracks. The same is true of us. God may sometimes turn up the heat to remove the cracks in our lives. After being tested, each person is promised a "stamp of approval."

With a thought of joy and expectation, let's look at some possible trials most of us will suffer in marriage. We must not be caught off guard by trials when they come. When we are shocked by trials we have a tendency to blame others. Often couples go through trials and blame their mates for what God is allowing to happen in their lives.

THORN IN THE FLESH

I have found that almost every person has one or two areas in his or her life that are just plain tough. Paul mentions one such problem in 2 Corinthians. In order to limit his pride, God gave him a "thorn in the flesh" to keep him from exalting himself. We cannot be sure what Paul's problem was, but he clearly called it a weakness.

> *Concerning this I entreated the Lord three times that it might depart from me. And He has said to me, "My grace is sufficient for you, for power is perfected in weakness." Most gladly, therefore, I will rather boast about my weaknesses, that the power of Christ may dwell in me. Therefore, I am well content with weaknesses, with insults, with distresses, with persecutions, with difficulties, for Christ's sake; for when I am weak, then I am strong* (2 Cor. 12:8-10).

I am convinced from working with people that many of us, if not all of us and our mates, have similar burdens to bear. Unfortunately, our acceptance of our thorns. or our mate's thorns, is probably not as gracious as Paul's. You can prepare yourself for the possibility that you and your mate will have at least one area that will probably never change and you will have to view it as Paul did his thorn.

For some people it might be stubbornness, a weight problem, temper, sloppiness, or low self-image. I have seen some great men with pride problems and some with insecurities. I know in my own life, my insecurity related to public speaking is definitely a thorn in my flesh. I am convinced that it is there for my good and that it will become a source of strength in my life. This is an area I have fought, questioned, and agonized with God about; it has caused my family some trauma, and me some heartache, yet it is still there.

In working through *my thorn*, I have been able to recognize *other peoples' thorns*. I know there are millions of marriages where mates are paralyzed because of some unchangeable weakness in themselves or their mates that has robbed them of all hope and joy in their marriages.

If you or your mate has a problem that seems impossible to work with, approach it as Paul did. If it never changes, then thank God for it and ask Him to use it in your life to develop endurance, patience, maturity, and compassion.

TRIALS OF OUR OWN MAKING

If you determine that you brought the trial into your life through sin, irresponsible behavior, or a bad decision, confess it to God. After confessing, begin to take the appropriate steps to resolve it. Be sure to seek forgiveness from others when appropriate. The following are examples of trials we might create: problems resulting from divorce, unresolved broken relationships with friends, family, and children, financial irresponsibility, jealousy, gossip, adultery, uncontrolled anger, etc.

If you have not brought the trial into your life, assume it is from God's loving hand for your benefit and His glory. Begin to apply the perspectives taught in Scripture concerning trials. Thank the Lord for each trial. You will be blessed for your faith.

JOB

Each of us needs to work hard and feel productive and appreciated. As career men and women move through life, they go through many cycles in their working relationships. There are a number of factors that affect a person's happiness at work, such as knowing he or she is in the right job and in the right place, being excited about going to work, enjoying their work, and being proud of the job done.

Men and women (including wives and mothers) need to prepare for trials in their work. You can be happy one day and dissatisfied the next. Wives need to trust and support their husbands during periods of dissatisfaction, which can last for extended lengths of time. Husbands, likewise, need to understand and encourage their wives who work, either in the home or in an outside job. Job frustration is a normal and consistent problem in life.

It helps most men to become accountable to several older men, preferably in their church, to help him evaluate and keep perspective during trials. Husbands and older, mature Christian women can provide this support for wives. Continually evaluate if you are doing what you enjoy and do well. If not, seek counsel to develop a conservative strategy, and slowly move toward what you enjoy and do well.

FINANCES

We have already mentioned finances, so we will not cover them again here. Just one reminder that can't be said enough. God seems to get our attention through financial trials more than any other. Expect them. Keeping a faith perspective in these trials is a must for happiness.

CHILDREN

Children, while a major blessing in life, are also a source of major trials along the way. Men, if you stand by your wife in these trials, you will make these times much easier and a greater blessing for your family. A woman's major mission field is often her children.

She will tend to evaluate her worth in life in terms of her children's success. It is not a surprise, then, that God would use children to teach women dependence. If husbands share this responsibility properly, wives will feel less stress.

The initial trial concerning children can develop during the first pregnancy. If sickness occurs during pregnancy, an understanding and patient husband will help with meals and housework. As her body begins to change, compliment her on her new beauty and your appreciation of her faithfulness.

There are many momentary trials with babies, such as sickness, sleeping problems, and scheduling. The husband must be able to help his wife during these times, and not allow her to take all of the responsibility. Husbands need to help her through sleepless nights and hectic times of the day (usually the supper hour). When your wife's schedule is hectic, give her some time away from the house and children. A little break will help her mental attitude tremendously.

When children reach school age, parents begin to observe potential emotional, intellectual, and spiritual needs. Anticipate these trials and support one another. Fathers, be very involved in your children's accomplishments and failures. Don't leave school discipline problems to your wife.

The process of disciplining children is a continual trial, especially for mothers. Mothers live with their children twenty-four hours a day. Therefore, they can lose perspective and end up in power struggles with them. Husbands can save their wives much frustration by taking responsibility for part of the discipline. If a man takes a three-day period every two months to run a discipline check and then fine-tune his children's discipline, it will encourage his wife. Children respond beautifully to fathers who take authority, while also spending quality time with them. A father who disciplines, but does not spend time loving his children, makes a serious mistake. It takes both love and discipline to develop healthy relationships. Expect trials in raising children, but they are well worth the effort.

INFERTILITY

Infertility has always been a problem for some people. However, it seems to be a growing phenomenon in our society. The jury is still out on the question of why the dramatic increase in recent years. We do know that many couples are waiting longer to begin the process of having children. Birth control, namely the pill, is used much longer than was earlier thought safe. New research seems to point to longer use of the pill, and later pregnancy dates, as the largest factors causing infertility. Past abortions may also have a negative effect. The latest statistic is that one in six couples have difficulty getting pregnant. Some can not get pregnant without medical help.

The emotional and financial toll caused by this problem can be hurtful, as wells as discouraging. A husband can expect his wife to feel like a failure. He must convince her that his love is not contingent upon her ability to conceive and bear children. Remind her from Scripture that God not only makes rich and poor, He also controls the womb. Help turn her perspective to God. Remind her that she is your provision from the Lord, with or without children. A wife needs to emotionally support her husband who may be the reason for the infertility. He too can blame himself for the inability of his wife to conceive.

There are many doctors today who specialize in fertility. There are good support groups that focus on this potentially painful situation, and they can give much guidance and comfort. For those who face this trial, it is a significant one. It is one that couples must stand together to properly address. It is important for the couple to seek God's perspective on each possible solution. Infertility will either drive you to your knees before God as a couple, or it will drive you apart. How you face this critical, and sometimes long-term, trial can make your marriage stronger.

DEATH OF A LOVED ONE

Another trial we all face is death. As Christians, our view of death is different than the worlds'. Christ removed the sting of death, yet we still suffer the loss here on earth. Death, whether that be of a parent, child or friend, can be very discouraging and depressing. Husbands and wives need to stand together in their pain, pray for one another, and seek help when necessary. Losing a child is one of the most painful and devastating trials in life. The pain often lasts years and only God can bring you through it with hope. Others who have experienced this loss will be there to help in time of need. Support groups are very important as well.

> *[God] comforts us in all our troubles, so that we can comfort those in any trouble with the comfort we ourselves have received from God. For just as the sufferings of Christ flow over into our lives, so also through Christ our comfort overflows* (2 Corinthians 1:4-5 NIV).

RELATIONSHIPS

Another reoccurring trial in life is relational problems with friends and acquaintances. Couples who do not prepare for trials in relationships are opening themselves to potential pain. If you anticipate trials in relationships, you will not only reduce your pain, but prayerfully, you will be able to control your response.

Prepare for trials in working relationships. Realize that people will fail to appreciate you, use you for selfish purposes, blame you for failure, question your abilities, even cut you out of future plans. These typical hurts can cause bitterness. Husbands and wives, gear up for these occasional shocks. Protect one another! Losing a job or missing a promotion is a small thing for the Lord to overcome. Remember: long-term bitterness is faith's enemy. I meet people regularly whose lives are distorted because they see a particular person as their problem. Draw each other's hope back to the Lord and His Word during these trials. Remember, people are not your enemies. Satan wants you to believe that they are in order to distract and discourage you.

> REMEMBER: LONG-TERM BITTERNESS IS FAITH'S ENEMY.

Church relationships, close friends, family, and neighbors are sources of potential trials. Apply aggressively the law of love, but expect occasional hurts. When it happens, renew your mind, and you pull together as a couple. Above all, don't be critical of others.

MOVING

America is such a mobile society that almost everyone moves many times in life. Yet, few things affect the emotional security of a family more. Selling your home and buying another one, followed by the move, are only the beginning. Many other things change: relationships, church and organizational ties, friends, and security. New frontiers must be forged, new relationships built, a new job begun, and a new church home established. Probably the most difficult part of a move is making new friends. It takes several years to replace good friends. Your children also experience tremendous loss, especially their close friends. Be very patient and tender with them as they go through their tears and ask "why?"

Almost everyone moves; you cannot stop that. But you can, as a couple, agree to support one another in the move. First of all, make the decision together, and include the whole family when possible. Then, work out a total plan that gives everyone hope. God doesn't often move people into a spiritual vacuum. Before you finalize your move, also try to find a church home.

Pray about everything. Years ago, before our move from Dallas to Little Rock, we prayed for specific things. Todd prayed for a creek in the back yard, Carmen prayed for a two-story house, and Sally prayed for red brick with yellow trim. We flew to Little Rock, found a realtor, and told her what we wanted. She said, "I've got just the house." And it was. We also prayed for a neighborhood with children, friends for Sally, and a church like the one in Dallas. We ended up starting a church just like the one in Dallas. God *specifically answered all* of these requests. We had not prayed specifically for our previous moves, and for the most part, those moves were more anguishing. I am convinced that if we spend time on our knees, God will know our requests! He will glorify Himself by meeting our needs as a family.

TIME

One of the biggest trials in married life is time availability: time for yourself, for romance, for the children, for ministry, for hobbies, or even just time to read a good book. I am convinced that Christians really desire to do what is right in their marriages, but they usually lose the battle with their schedules. You must *get tough with your priorities*. There is no other way. There are so many responsibilities and "good" things to distract us that only an unbending commitment to time priority will help.

Men, take responsibility here. A wife cannot do much without her husband's involvement. First, decide on your major priorities. Then list what you need to accomplish in each area. After that, you will have to eliminate almost everything else. We make a point to discuss everything we do and to get the input and suggestions of the other. Just communicating may help us eliminate unneeded or unwanted things in our schedule. We all tend to get over-committed in our lives and trials result. Husbands and wives can help each other say "No, I can't do that right now." Those are difficult words to say, but it helps if we understand our limitations.

Because of the importance of time control and schedule in relation to a man's priorities, I occasionally will ask two or three close brothers to sit down and go over my schedule. I like to bring Sally in to share her perspective. I try to schedule a meeting with them six weeks later to evaluate my accomplishments. If Sally and I make ourselves accountable like this and have other men and women agree with us on our busy schedule, then we know it is momentarily workable and our priorities are in the order the Lord would desire.

A men's accountability group is a great idea. Men usually have difficulty expressing feelings, hurt, frustration, struggles, etc. The group will hold you accountable in these areas, not just your time. For women, small prayer groups or Bible studies are invaluable for friendships, as well as accountability and encouragement. Couples would do well to learn to be leaders of small groups within their churches. These small groups could include: study of marriage, parent-child, the Christian faith, finances, etc.

LIFE'S WORK

Often, the very trial we go through may in fact be saving our life and may eventually save someone else's. Our organization, *Christian Family Life*, and the writing of this book, *Becoming One*, were the result of trials we encountered in early marriage. Many organizations and support groups such as MADD and AA started because of trials in someone's life. Almost all biblical characters have gone through various trials. So, we are not alone. The very trial that you may be experiencing now, may in fact, lead you to your life's work. Life, at best, brings uncertainty and trials. The apostle Paul says it so clearly in Phil. 4:11-13:

Not that I speak from want; for I have learned to be content in whatever circumstances I am. I know how to get along with humble means, and I also know how to live in prosperity; in any and every circumstance I have learned the secret of being filled and going hungry, both of having abundance and suffering need. I can do all things through Him who strengthens me.

The better you are at anticipating trials, the more growth you will experience in your faith. The greater your faith, the greater your spiritual maturity. There is a difference in anticipating trials and living in worry and anxiety. Look beyond the trial and ask God how He wants to use it. God is good, and He has a purpose for every trial that we encounter.

Beloved, do not be surprised at the fiery ordeal among you, which comes upon you for your testing, as though some strange thing were happening to you; but to the degree that you share the sufferings of Christ, keep on rejoicing; so that also at the revelation of His glory, you may rejoice with exultation. If you are reviled for the name of Christ, you are blessed, because the Spirit of glory and of God rests upon you. By no means let any of you suffer as a murderer, or thief, or evildoer, or troublesome meddler; but if anyone suffers as a Christian, let him not feel ashamed, but in that name let him glorify God (1 Pet. 4:12-16).

CHAPTER SEVENTEEN

WINNING, LOSING, AND OTHER STRANGE GAMES

IF YOU STOP to think about it, Americans are naturally geared to think in terms of "winners" and "losers." Almost every issue is evaluated in terms of who won or who lost. It's true in business, in elections, in sports, and in arguments. "I cannot afford for you to be right, because if you're right, it would make me wrong."

In this chapter, let's talk about winners and losers, and other practical matters. As silly as it sounds, this winner/loser syndrome can adversely affect marriage. Counselors work hard, trying to convince couples to think in terms of "creative alternatives," instead of winners or losers. If God actually controls the universe and loves us, then there never needs to be a winner or loser. Through faith, God guarantees only winners in the long run, regardless of human weaknesses. Therefore, when a couple confronts a disagreement, a frustration, a weakness, or a problem of any kind, they should look for a creative alternative rather than looking for someone to blame.

A couple came into my office recently, and typically, each mate took thirty minutes to list the areas in which the mate was a loser. The husband was a loser because he did not spend time with her and the children, he was insensitive sexually, and he was socially inept. The wife was a loser because she didn't keep the house clean, she was unresponsive sexually, and she failed to properly discipline the children. Each mate could have presented a full-scale proof of their convictions. By the end of the hour, I was a loser, too, because I was depressed! I wanted to shake them and say, "Don't you see what you're doing to each other? If God made you one, then to criticize your mate is to criticize yourself!"

In the weeks that followed, as we sought God's perspective and initiated faith in their actions, they began to see each other as a potential asset. After re-establishing hope, we were able to review their opinions of one another, but this time we listened to understand why each was not functioning well. With just a little discernment and creativity, we were able to develop a plan that synchronized their strengths and resulted in both being "winners."

I would like to give you some examples of potential problem areas that may require creative alternatives. Review these regularly in your marriage. They are: (1) male and female differences; (2) personality differences; (3) intellectual differences; (4) vocational differences; (5) spiritual differences; (6) physical differences. Last, we will talk about the importance of putting fun in your marriage.

MALE/FEMALE DIFFERENCES

We have been blessed in recent years with many books and much significant research concerning male/female differences. Why do you think this information is important? It is important because husbands and wives have been clashing over their differences since time began, and still do not get the picture. Couples never seem to learn that husbands and wives will always approach some issues in life differently. Why? Because God made them *male and female*.

Couples who desire to honor God with oneness must understand and accept these differences, and then look for creative alternatives that will allow both male and female to be expressed. Stop resenting your mate's differences, and look for ways to fulfill your mate. Have fun with it, read a good book about it together. There are many on the market.

Make a list of every area of your marriage in which you have historically conflicted. Take them one at a time. In a non-threatening environment, discuss your male and female desires, needs and dislikes. Brainstorm ways and processes that would allow those differences to be fulfilled without frustrating the other.

Faith and creativity can open doors that have been closed for years. Seemingly simple things like planning a trip together or a romantic evening can seem impossible because each one has a different need and a different goal. Yet, when planned with each mate's needs in mind, new doors can be opened and blessings experienced. Historically, men and women approach these issues very differently. Take each one separately and talk about your differences:

communication	establishing friendships
shopping	discipline of the children
social activities	spending money
solving problems	saving money
finances	giving

Remember, God had a purpose in making us different. Neither is right nor wrong. We need to learn to work with and learn from the differences. Our differences were meant to be a blessing—a gift to the other and a completion of "oneness." *God did not call us to be the same, He called us to be one.* We were meant to be different in order to reflect Him. We were created to be two different parts of one entity.

PERSONALITY DIFFERENCES

Dating relationships tend to bring out the good side of peoples' personalities, while marriage tends to bring out the bad side. Couples who are dating tend to put their best foot forward. They tend to communicate acceptance and hope to the other, which encourages each person to open up more.

After marriage, many times intolerance often replaces acceptance. Criticism quickly leads to defensiveness. As the environment changes from positive to negative, each mate's personality is significantly affected. Quiet personalities become quieter, and tend to withdraw. Aggressive personalities tend to become more dominating or angry. In a short period of time, it is not unusual to hear a newlywed say, "I feel like I am married to a completely different person."

A man in my office a few years ago characterized his wife as extremely introverted and antisocial. From his description of her I would have thought the woman could not think, feel, or even talk at times. The next hour his wife came into the office. I was quite surprised to find that she was very pleasant. After a few minutes of small talk, we found a mutual interest in the University of Arkansas football! Any woman that loves football cannot be all bad, and for the next fifteen minutes I had a vibrant conversation with a delightful person who could relate intelligently and sensitively. I thought to myself, "How could her husband have gotten his view of this delightful woman?" As I began to ask questions, the answer came quickly.

The couple had met during their senior year in college, which just happened to have been the wife's peak of social involvement. In reality, she had always been a shy person. Her husband, on the other hand, was a perfectionist. After marriage, she had to adjust simultaneously to a high-pressure job and keeping house for a perfectionist. Two years later, her first pregnancy drained her physically. Later, she suffered a normal bout of post-partum depression, at about the same time her husband began to pressure her to return to work. With communication at a standstill, because of feelings of rejection and failure, this wife could not muster up the confidence to fight back. Happily, after just two months of counseling, God was able to reveal to them what had happened and they were able to virtually begin again. This time they could love and appreciate their differences, instead of criticizing and judging one another.

The way you handle your mate's personality will impact them, maybe for the rest of their life. If you encourage and support them, oneness will result. However, if you judge and criticize, wanting them to change, conflict and frustration will result. In trying to understand your personality as well as that of your mate, consider the wide range of personality types. The following chart represents some discernible personality ranges.

GENERAL RANGE OF PERSONALITY TYPES

Fun-loving	Aggressive	Sensitive	Calm
Outgoing	Active	Introspective	Cool
Emotional	Intense	Quiet	Assured
Affectionate	Logical	Takes things personally	Unemotional

No matter where your personality fits into this chart, one is not better than another. Every personality, functioning properly, has strengths and weaknesses. For instance, an aggressive person may be a self-starter, but at the same time might tend to be critical. The quiet personality might be more sensitive and creative, but may be withdrawn or critical.

Whatever personality you or your mate have, remember it is simply a measure of social involvement, or how you encounter people. Personality is not a valid measure of such important things as intellect, feelings, love, commitment, attitude, ideas, or spiritual perspective. When people start dating, their positive projection draws out the personality of the other in areas of beliefs, opinions, intellect, and thoughts. After marriage, we often forget that the person we married is not really contrary, but rather *a totally equipped human being, with a special personality different from our own.*

> THE MOST IMPORTANT ISSUE, THEN, IS TO BECOME CREATIVE, NOT CRITICAL, IN DRAWING OUT THE BEST ASPECTS OF EACH ONE'S PERSONALITY.

Your view and reaction to your mate's personality will have great influence over its development. The most important issue, then, is to become creative, not critical, in drawing out the best aspects of each one's personality.

Begin by believing that *God knew your needs when He gave you your mate* and that He will meet your needs with their personality. Faith, again, is the foundation of creative action. Never be critical or apologetic, publicly or privately, about your mate's personality. I shudder when a wife says about her husband, "John is not upset;

he's just quiet." The poor guy is standing there not knowing how to respond. He's been labeled by his wife so often that it would be hard for him to recover if he wanted to. Instead, she might say, "John has such neat ideas! He could comment on that." He would think, "Who, me? Why sure!"

Freely merge your personality with your mate's so that you can develop a "couple" personality with both of your strengths. Do not treat your mate as a social outcast. Stick together at social events, arm in arm. Look for natural opportunities to involve each in conversation. If you know your wife is well read on child discipline and the conversation moves toward children, you might say, "Joan was telling me an interesting story on discipline. What was that story you were telling me the other day?" Joan may never have entered the conversation by herself, but if you give her a lead she will usually be delighted to enter in and feel accepted.

After social events, talk about your evening and look for ways to help one another feel more at ease socially. Again, look for creative alternatives, not for winners and losers. Develop a strategy for your *"couple" personality*. Work together, allowing each to be expressed intellectually, socially, emotionally, and spiritually, regardless of personality.

INTELLECTUAL DIFFERENCES

Another area of potential problems is intellectual differences. I remember a case where a man was told his IQ was quite a bit higher than his future wife's. That statement stuck in his mind, and it subconsciously colored his evaluation of her. Years later he was telling me that she didn't read books and he couldn't have an intellectual discussion with her. This man was convinced he was "stuck" with an intellectual weakling! This unfortunate statement had affected his respect for her in every area.

He was deceived and didn't understand the difference between being intelligent and being a disciplined student; between knowledge and wisdom; between talking a good life and actually living one; between quickness of mind and faithfulness of heart. Almost every person has adequate intelligence, more than he or she will ever use, but each person has certain strengths and weaknesses, likes and dislikes, in intellectual matters. God knew that when He brought you together, it would make you more complete.

I mentioned earlier in the book that Sally and I had to make an adjustment in this area. I was a "Cliff's notes" man in college; she was a good student. On Sunday afternoons she would curl up in a chair and read a good book while I would watch football on TV. We were also different in how we applied what we knew. She had more knowledge, but *applied* it sometimes less practically than I. We discovered that each of us was different, but that we complemented each other.

We have since looked for creative alternatives in this area. God didn't make a mistake after all. Instead of rejecting each other because of these differences, we learned to help each other. Sally will read a book, underline its key points, and give it to me. (Remember I am a Cliff's notes man—I want the "bottom line.") I then go back and read her underlinings. The value to me with our hectic schedules is unbelievable. This allows Sally an opportunity to minister to me, makes her a part of what I am doing, and also stimulates her intellect. We also discovered we like different types of books; she likes biographical and historical books as well as novels. I like novels with suspense and intrigue. Don't be critical. Be grateful for your mate's intellectual pursuits and work your strengths together.

SPIRITUAL DIFFERENCES

A very subtle form of deception can result from the way you view your mate's spiritual maturity. A poor view of their spiritual motivation can lead to belittling and judging, which may retard their spiritual growth. In all my years of counseling Christian marriages, few things can hurt a marriage more than one mate's dissatisfaction with the other mate's spiritual maturity. If you make your mate feel like a loser in this area, then for him or her to aggressively pursue spiritual things would mean subconscious agreement with your evaluation! *The mate who judges gives the other reason to reject God.*

You may think you're being "loving" in your evaluation, with spiritual-sounding rhetoric like "I am accepting you by faith today, that tomorrow you will be better." That really sounds spiritual. I'm convinced that is exactly the kind of subtle statement Satan himself would make! It sounds good, but it is still saying to your mate, "You are less than adequate today."

God hates my sin, but He does not retract any commitment to me because of it. I am perfectly acceptable to Him today because Christ has forgiven me. I am overwhelmed by God's graciousness in giving so much when I am so undeserving. I am stimulated to worship Him because of His gracious love. You don't have to like one another's sin, but God does expect you to trust Him with that sin, as with any other problem, and be gracious toward your mate.

That kind of action allows you to be concerned with *motivating* your mate instead of judging, so that your partner will not experience rejection or feelings of dissatisfaction from you. If you are not yet married and are concerned about your future mate's spiritual maturity, don't get married. If you are married and are struggling with this problem, ask your mate's forgiveness, and look for creative alternatives. Seek counsel if you are overwhelmed and don't know how to resolve this problem. For both husbands and wives it would be good to reread 1 Peter 2 and 3 on what motivates a person toward spiritual maturity.

> THE MATE WHO JUDGES GIVES THE OTHER REASON TO REJECT GOD.

VOCATIONAL STRUGGLES

A large portion of a person's life is spent working. In the very beginning, God told Adam and Eve to reflect, reproduce, and reign. He told Adam to keep and cultivate the land. God added other commands concerning our attitudes toward work later in the New Testament. All such commands imply that God equipped men and women with a need to be productive.

Since the very beginning, happiness in life has been tied to success and productivity. How motivated a person is in his work affects his productivity. His pride in his work, and his mate's respect of it, affects his sense of value. The gifts or abilities of a person also affect his or her sense of value. Being certain of being in God's will in your job is very important to self-confidence and happiness.

Men come into my office hurt because their wives are embarrassed at what they do vocationally. Other men leave jobs they like because their wife is not satisfied financially, or because she does not like his schedule or her husband's boss. And it's not always the wife. Men evaluate themselves similarly. It's not unusual to meet a highly successful man who does not like what he does, and therefore, is not happy.

And men, don't forget: in one sense, your wife's vocation is the home, whether she works outside the home or not. The husband often does not understand or respect the overwhelming tasks she faces, so he is impatient with her. Men who will not help their wives, nor give them the opportunity to establish reinforcing, encouraging relationships outside the home, contribute unknowingly to making her feel the home is a "lesser" place to be. She then feels confined. Men who are critical of the housekeeping and the children's behavior, but won't help her with any of these responsibilities, are hypocrites. Women suffer self-image problems and often seek outside employment to meet the needs the husband could have met if he had been sensitive. Wives need the same support in her vocation as a wife and mother that the husband needs in his chosen field. Women who have careers outside the home need the same care and understanding regarding their chosen field. Couples need to support each other vocationally in two ways:

First, acknowledge that your mate's gifts and talents are from God. 1 Corinthians 12:11 says, *"But one and the same Spirit works all these things, distributing [gifts] to each one individually just as He wills."* In other words, the Spirit of God distributes each person's gifts. Whatever gifts you and your mate may have, accept them from the Lord and trust God to bless you through them.

Second, do not be quick to judge your mate's gifts early in

marriage. I am amazed at how many people, judged to be "nerds" when they finished school, later became leaders of our country. Shower your mate with encouragement and support. Most young people have no idea of their potential until later in life. Wait for your mate to blossom.

Years ago a man was released from an organization, after several anguishing years of trying to utilize his talents successfully. For the next few years, he floundered. Eventually his wife sought counsel. Several years later, this man got involved in doing some fairly menial tasks with another organization. While doing his new work, he got excited as never before about an idea associated with his job. A new drive and attitude literally changed that man's life. He went back to school and began to write and teach on the subject. Now, he is nationally known in his field. His wife is elated, and grateful to God for giving her some much-needed patience.

> HUSBANDS AND WIVES WHO SYNCHRONIZE THEIR GIFTS CAN ACCOMPLISH UNBELIEVABLE THINGS.

To insure that you don't miss the "diamond in the rough" in your mate, consider the following suggestions. Always at the top of the list is: never criticize your mate's abilities, but be an encourager of them. View your mate as part of yourself, and trust God with both of your gifts. Join your gifts together and begin to think of them as "couple" gifts. Husbands and wives who synchronize their gifts can accomplish unbelievable things.

Become an expert on what you and your mate do best, and emphasize it. Protect each other from placements that do not emphasize what you enjoy and do well. If your husband is most fulfilled by washing the car, don't reject him. Stick with him! Who knows, he may end up managing a chain of car washes! Even if you don't become rich or famous, you will be married to a happy man.

Men, if your wife does something well, do everything you can to help her pursue it. Become an expert on what she does well. Encourage her by allowing her time to develop her talents.

PHYSICAL APPEARANCES

In a world that places so much emphasis on physical appearance, it is impossible to ignore its impact. Some couples tend to be unbalanced in that they spend large sums of money on clothes and cosmetics. Diet and physical fitness are emphasized to the point that all of life revolves around these activities. Other couples can be just as unbalanced in that they allow their physical appearance to become sloppy.

Early in marriage, look for balance and creativity. First of all, accept each other's body as from the Lord. Then set "reasonable" physical goals. Over time, reasonable goals are attainable. Fall in love with your mate's body as it is today. Start here, not at some fantasy point set by the world. Do a "five star" sales job of convincing your mate that his/her appearance is exciting to you.

Second, establish health goals in your marriage, not "body beautiful" goals. Do not buy into the world's fantasies. Focus on life, fun and being a good steward with the body God gave you. Look for ways to join with and encourage your mate's health, instead of reflecting disappointment or judgment.

Get involved in constructive ways to help each other buy clothes. If your husband wears white socks with dark clothes, get him some dark socks. If your wife wears her underclothes until they have holes in them, buy her some new ones. A husband can really help his wife please him in her dress if he goes with her to buy clothes. I try to shop with Sally so she will know what I like. Husbands, allow your wife to do the same for you.

MARRIAGE FUN

You would think that nothing need be said about having fun in marriage, but unfortunately it does. Many couples are so serious about life that they miss the enjoyment of having fun. Let me tell you a story that unfolded several years ago. A couple came for counsel, and before they sat down the wife started crying. She said, "Don, I don't want you to think I don't love David, because I do. But this year of marriage has just been terrible for me."

After college, where she had a delightful time, this young woman had married. They moved to another city so her husband could attend seminary. Her husband had picked out an apartment the previous spring, without her seeing it. It was old, and furnished with dull furniture. The curtains were supposed to be white, but were so old they were beige! In addition, the apartment was insect-infected and was located in a less desirable part of town. This was a far cry from the year before. She found a job that began before she was able to finish cleaning the apartment. This was her first full-time job, and it brought multiple pressures and time commitments. All of these adjustments overwhelmed her positive expectations of marriage, and brought great frustration. Her tears reflected her disappointment with married life when compared to her fun college years.

Let me pass on to you some of the suggestions I gave to this couple. First, *become an expert on what your mate enjoys.* That sounds easier than it is. I make a habit of asking people what their mates really like to do. It is amazing how few married people really know what their partner honestly thinks is fun.

When you discuss what each of you consider fun, don't judge. It may be something like watching TV. I have seen people decide that their mate's fun was not spiritual or intellectual so they refused to participate. The result is that they belittle their mate. Don't try to become the Holy Spirit in your mate's life, convicting them of sin and convincing them your way is best. Be concerned instead with having some fun in your marriage.

Also try to *have fun doing necessary things.* Don't let them become drudgery. Clean the kitchen together while you let the kids watch an acceptable TV show. Work on the lawn together. Weed the flower beds together. Wash the car, eat by candlelight, walk around the block and discuss the day's activities. Set aside some time for organizing the pictures, slides, a movie . . . and reminisce at the same time. If your wife works, help her with cleaning and other duties so she can share her world with you.

Develop hobbies. Both of you need hobbies: something you enjoy doing. If your wife paints, has musical talent, is a writer, or whatever, encourage her to continue. If she wants to pursue a higher degree of education, help and encourage her to do that. She will do the same for you.

Set some family goals. Sally and I worked on a plan to see the entire country in the first ten years of marriage so we could take the children to see it again in the next ten. We have also taken the family to amusements parks. My goal was to ride all "top ten" roller coasters before our kids graduated from high school. We succeeded, and created a family tradition the kids still talk about.

Work on your relationships with others. Even though you might not feel a need initially, relationships with others are vital to having fun. Doing certain activities with other couples is a lot more fun than doing them alone. Friendships also encourage us to share ourselves. Invite people over, have picnics, potlucks, go to the beach, have an evening of games, take a vacation with another family. We have another family with whom we share "game nights." It's great fun!

Romance: Some romantic ideas for the two of you would be to go out to lunch together or to breakfast without the children. The husband can pick up the baby sitter and occasionally surprise his wife with a pre-planned night out. Wives, return the blessing by planning your own surprises. How about a twenty-four-hour camp out or a drive in the woods? Have fun learning once again to be romantic with each other. *Never stop dating*. Ask the Holy Spirit to give you creative and fresh ideas for fun ways of spending time together. Making time for fun in marriage will pay great dividends for the rest of your life.

SUMMARY OF
THE BOOK

THINK BACK for a moment to the first chapter of this book. At the close of that chapter, we left Jim and Betty fighting to save their marriage. A Christian marriage that started with such good intentions a few short years before, had deteriorated into a bitter and hurtful counterfeit of what God originally intended. If an outstanding couple like Jim and Betty can fail, what about you and me? Their struggle provoked this question. *"If God designed marriage, can He make it work?"* Hopefully this book has begun to answer that question for you.

The central message of this book exclaims to its readers that spiritual marriages require faith. The writer of Hebrews, when speaking of Scripture's greatest examples of faith, said , *"And without faith it is impossible to please Him, for he who comes to God must believe that He is and that He is a rewarder of those who seek Him"* (Hebrews 11:6). Faith demonstrates our belief in God. Therefore, our faith pleases God. It is no surprise that God designed marriage to increase our faith in Him. We cannot please Him without faith. Faith requires two things. First, it requires that we know and trust Him as God, the Creator of heaven and earth. Second, if we truly know Him, we should then be able to trust Him to reward us according to His magnificent promises. No individual can love by faith without believing that God's Word is more powerful than their mates weaknesses.

This book has attempted to increase your potential for marital faith by helping you review God's perspective concerning marriage. If you know Him and seek Him, the Holy Spirit will enlighten you and faith will result. True faith always produces good works. As your faith produces good works toward your mate, God will astonish you by fulfilling His magnificent promises to you from His Word. Faith allows us to override our natural selfishness by choosing to act on God's Word. Faith then releases God to do what He said He would do.

Jim and Betty, Don and Sally, or any other couple, must embrace each of the commitments discussed in this book if they hope to experience a "supernatural faith marriage." Let's quickly review these commitments:

1. Each mate must openly confess their selfish tendencies. After admitting their natural tendencies, each couple should review the five reasons marriages automatically fail. Agree together concerning the possible affects these five reasons may have had on your marriage. Commit by faith to change the course of your marriage in the future by seeking a faith relationship.
2. Each mate must accept from God, their responsibility to fulfill His purposes of reflecting God's image, reproducing His image through children and disciples, and reigning on earth to His glory. These purposes require oneness. Oneness will allow God's will to flow through you as a couple. It will allow you to fully utilize your maleness and femaleness. Both mates, through oneness can find completion and maximum expression in life.
3. Each mate must accept from God that he or she was created with a relational need that can only be met by God. Then, by faith, each mate should receive their mate as God's personal provision for their aloneness need. Based on trusting God, each mate must then leave their former

dependencies (parents, being single, etc.) and cleave to their mate once and for all. God indicates He will produce oneness and unthreatened intimacy in your marriage.
4. Loving your mate by faith will require each mate to individually submit his/her will to the Holy Spirit's ministry in their lives. Each mate must allow the Holy Spirit to convict, teach, lead, and empower them. When the Holy Spirit convicts of sin, each person must agree with God and turn from his/her sin, and then ask his/her mate's forgiveness as well. The benefits of walking with the Holy Spirit are limitless. In fact, marital oneness cannot exist apart from the Holy Spirit.
5. Marital oneness requires each mate to understand God's agent for change in marriage. God condemns selfish revenge in every circumstance. Scripture endorses two forces of change. One is sacrificial love as demonstrated by Christ, and the other is returning a blessing when wronged. Each mate must trust God to change his or her mate as they faithfully love and bless them.
6. The divine order of oneness is love and submission. Not love and submission as taught by the world, but love and submission as illustrated in the Trinity of God (1 Cor. 11:3; John 17:20-21). To fully experience marriage, as designed by God, mutual love and submission are non-negotiable. It takes great faith, spiritual insight, and trust to joyfully love and submit. Satan's worldly deceit must be bound. Each mate must ask God for wisdom on a daily basis.

These six insights form the basis of a supernatural faith relationship. Good intentions or natural desires will never result in a faith relationship. A faith relationship results from knowing and applying God's Word. How do you know if you have a faith relationship? The only way to know is for both mates to commit to the above insights by faith. Jim and Betty, as good as their original intentions were, did not understand these insights. As they later understood and committed to these principles, their marriage changed dramatically.

Faith does not stop with these insights, however. A faith relationship also requires couples to apply these faith insights to the practical areas of life and marriage. As discussed in this book, God has a lot to say about sex, finances, communication, etc. Each mate must discover what God's Word says on each subject and then apply it by faith. It takes time and effort to fully discover a supernatural faith relationship.

But make no mistake, a faith relationship starts by understanding and applying the six insights just summarized. Do not put this book down until you have made these commitments by faith. Then share them with others to deepen and revitalize your understanding over time.

Sally and I pray that you too will be able to apply the following verses to your marriage at the end of your life. *"For this cause, a man shall leave his father and mother, and shall cleave to his wife; and they shall become one flesh. And the man and his wife were both naked and were not ashamed."* We wish each of you the joy of being totally exposed to each other with no fear or threat. If you miss this joy of being one, you will have missed much of God's blessing on this earth. Only faith can release God's blessing in your marriage.

EPILOGUE

WHEN WE FIRST published the book in 1979, we had been married for 12 years. Since that time, Sally and I have experienced first hand the results of God's principles of marriage in our own lives, as well as in our family. We have been more than pleased in thirty years of marriage to still experience joy in each other; to laugh and play together, to work together, to write and create together. But, what is especially rewarding is that all four of our children are walking with God. As we have tried to reflect God's image as a couple, and reign together as a couple, God has rewarded us with a godly heritage.

Our two oldest have married spouses who love and walk with God. We have been blessed also with their spouses' godly families. What rich rewards! We say all of this, not because our kids have been perfect, but because God said if we obey Him, He would bless us. And bless us He has! We say this to give the honor where honor is due: to God the Father, God the Son, and God the Holy Spirit.

We thank God for using others to mentor us early in our married life. For Campus Crusade for Christ, which gave us our start in learning how to disciple others. For those who came alongside us in starting CFL, FamilyLife Ministry of Crusade, and in church planting. The names are too numerous to mention, but you know who you are. We thank God for giving us such wonderful friends who have loved us, believed in us, and stood by us, even when we questioned ourselves. We praise God for our children who have followed us and have become our best friends in adulthood. We thank God for our extended families. To God, and Him alone, belongs our praise and thanksgiving. He truly is a good God!

APPENDIX:
SO YOU WANT TO GET MARRIED?

A CHAPTER FOR THE ENGAGED

Some of you reading this book have not yet decided to marry. You probably want to ask, "How can I be sure I should get married?" This is one of the most important decisions of your life.

I have found over the years that each couple is a little different. Premarital counseling is absolutely vital, and most churches now have pre-marriage classes. Our 12-week marriage course, called *"Becoming One,"* is of tremendous value in building a proper foundation for marriage. I highly recommend it for the engaged, newly married and older married couples.

There are three basic issues that I feel are extremely important in determining readiness for marriage. First, is the couple *mature* enough to handle marriage? Second, how clearly do they both understand the *biblical concepts* taught in the Bible concerning marriage? Third, are they willing to earnestly work through a *premarital strategy* for addressing the practical areas of marriage? Let's look at each of these areas to get a better perspective on their meaning.

SPIRITUAL MATURITY

Recently a couple asked if I could ever be sure in advance that a marriage would be successful. The only assurance I can give comes from looking at the past track records of the two people involved. How have they responded to tough situations they have encountered in their lives? Have they exhibited faith in the past?

Obviously, the longer the track record, the more evidence there will be of potential future success. Experience and faithfulness can only be measured over time. Nearly every person performs well at some level of pressure, but as pressures rise, we all break down at some point. Therefore, the maturity of a man who has finished school before he marries is more measurable than a freshman in college. And the man who has graduated from college and worked for three years is even more measurable and predictable. The woman who has been a Christian for five years is much more measurable than the woman who has been a Christian for three months. Even more measurable is the person who has been a Christian fifteen years, and has gone through more tough testing periods. They are much more predictable as a future partner.

> A SINGLE PERSON WHO HAS A HISTORY OF BEING FAITHFUL IN TOUGH SITUATIONS WILL APPLY FAITH IN MARRIAGE AS WELL.

A single person who has a history of being faithful in tough situations can be expected to continue to apply faith in tough marriage situations. An untested person, with an unmeasured track record, is almost a total gamble, a shot in the dark, spiritually speaking. That's a strong statement, but it's true!

Therefore, how can an individual considering marriage evaluate their own maturity and that of their mate before deciding to get married? The famous passage called "The Beatitudes" contains the best statement of spiritual maturity ever set forth. It is Christ Himself who describes these marks of maturity in Matthew 5:1-16.

The passage develops eight specific points of spiritual maturity and success in living life. Jesus describes a person who is "blessed," which means they have reached the ultimate in life. The word was used during the time of Christ to refer to a "blessed isle" of joy. To find this state in life was like finding an oasis in a desert. Jesus says that the person who has these qualities is one who will be able to experience joy and fulfillment in life, despite continued trials.

Poor In Spirit

Christ says that the successful and mature person is one who is poor in spirit. The literal meaning is "having no power at all." He recognizes his powerlessness over sin. Here is a person who sees himself as he really is, his poverty, apart from God. He is not hopeless in his weakness, however, because he trusts in God. This person understands that it is better to seek the Lord than to gain the world. This person is not prideful or inflated in his self-evaluation.

In marriage, he will most likely be accepting of other's weaknesses, because he knows he has been accepted by God. Why is it important to desire a mate who is humble before God? If you marry someone who is self-assured, apart from his relationship with God, you will pay a great price in marriage. Pride can cause that person to both judge and reject you.

Those Who Mourn

Christ is referring to a person who is sensitive to his own sin. When he sins, anguish visibly pierces his heart. This person is compassionate and does not hold a grudge. Here is a person who confesses his mistakes and is broken about his sin and the sin of others. This person will say, "I'm wrong. Please forgive me."

Does your future mate admit fault easily? Do they readily ask for forgiveness, from God and from others? A person who always thinks he is right is a very difficult person to live with. Be honest about bitterness, holding grudges, or inability to forgive. No matter how good the reason, grudges destroy relationships. This type of maturity is extremely important in marriage.

Gentle

Because of His trust in His Father, Christ, though mistreated, was gentle. He was kind and gracious, in spite of the cruel treatment He received. A gentle person does not provoke their mate to anger and calms them when they are upset. A gentle person is also humble in dealing with his mate.

Does your future mate walk over your feelings, with no apparent remorse? Are they callous toward others who are in pain? If so, they would not be a good candidate for a life-time marriage partner.

Hunger And Thirst After Righteousness

This is a person who has a passionate desire to seek after the things of God. He cannot stand to be out of fellowship with God. He will actively correct any problem in his relationship with others. In marriage, this factor is an indispensable part of a happy relationship.

Do you and your future mate have a track record of seeking after God? Are you both characterized by wanting to be in fellowship with God and others? This may be the difference between an insult for insult, or blessing for blessing marriage. If a person does not seek after the things of God, they will seek after something else: material possessions, the corporate ladder, fame, fortune, etc. If this is true, that person will be neglectful of you and your marriage.

It is interesting to note that the last four Beatitudes have a *cause and effect* relationship with the first four. For example, the person who has a right evaluation of himself (poor in spirit) will tend to be merciful toward others. Evaluate the implication of this cause and effect relationship on marriage.

Merciful

A study of this word reveals that it is best characterized by "outgoing kindness," kindness that acts. This is a person who demonstrates compassion. Nothing is more important at times than a compassionate mate.

Look for evidence of compassion on the part of your future mate toward others. How does he or she view the suffering of others? Are they gracious and forgiving? Do they offer a quick helping hand? If not, expect the same in your marriage.

Pure In Heart

This is a person who truly knows God and is acquainted with His ways, through His Word. His life will be characterized by loyalty, both to God and to man. This loyalty to God carries over to his or her mate. Again, because of this person's transparency before God, he or she is open about personal failure. This is also a person who is free from guilt because confession and repentance characterizes his or her life.

Observe your future mate's openness with others, especially with those in authority. Look for signs of honesty and pure motives. Do they hide

> LOOK FOR SIGNS OF HONESTY AND PURE MOTIVES.

their sin? Are they quick to confess? Do they provoke you to follow God? Do they seek answers from Scripture? Do they pray about everything, or is prayer always their last resort?

Peacemaker

One of the greatest attributes a person can bring to marriage is that of being a peacemaker. A gentle person soothes others and makes peace where there is strife. The peacemaker hates discord and will readily strive to bring solution. This peace again results from having God's perspective. Peacemakers solve problems with truth and love. They are not afraid to get involved and find resolution.

To determine if your future mate has this quality, look for signs that he or she sows harmony and peace in the everyday skirmishes of life. Conversely, look for signs of sowing discord in relationships and groups.

Persecuted

This is a person who puts the opinion of God above the opinion of others. A strong identity in Christ is the result. This person is recognized publicly as being truly Christian. This person will "stay the course" in marriage because he has strong spiritual convictions.

Do they play at Christianity as if it were a Sunday hobby, or is it daily, personal, and a part of every circumstance? Does their Christian commitment fade when the going gets tough? At the time you need their spiritual conviction most, will it be there? Or do they want to be liked so much that they will compromise their convictions? How a person spends free time tells a lot about his or her convictions.

Result: Salt and Light
Jesus goes on to say that people who possess these characteristics are the salt and light of the earth. Remember that in marriage we are to reflect God's image. Only a mature person can do that.

> *You are the **salt** of the earth; but if the salt has become tasteless, how will it be made salty again? It is good for nothing anymore, except to be thrown out and trampled under the foot by men. You are the **light** of the world. A city set on a hill cannot be hidden. Nor do men light a lamp, and put it under the peck-measure, but on the lamp stand; and it gives light to all who are in the house. Let your light shine before men in such a way that they may see you good works, and glorify your Father who is in heaven (Matthew 5:13-16).*

Salt is a preservative. It enhances flavor. It is imperative for good health. God says that we can lose our saltiness, but how? In Israel, salt was mixed with gypsum, and then put on rooftops to keep the water out. When salt is mixed with another component, it loses its flavor, and "is good for nothing, except to be walked on by the foot of men." How interesting that the analogy is used here of being good for nothing. When we as Christians are mixed with the things of the world, we lose our "saltiness," our testimonies, our ability to speak out. The non-Christian world looks at our lives and they see no difference in the way we live and conduct business.[1] The divorce rate is an example. It's almost as common for Christian couples to call it quits as it is for non-Christians. We have been so tainted with the morals of our day (homosexuality, R-rated movies, pornography, abortion, etc.) that we are no longer listened to as having answers. We have lost our ability to speak: concerning the things of the family, raising children, love, and ultimately the Lord. Let's be very careful about taking on the philosophies of the world and combining them with Biblical principles. God wants us to be salt. The beatitudes listed above are not optional, they are vital to remaining salt to a thirsty world.

Light shows things as they really are. It brings things out into the open. When there is light, we do not stumble. Light repels darkness. Light shows the way. Light reflects God. Who do you and your prospective mate reflect—the god of this world or the God of creation?

There are no shortcuts to these dimensions in your life. If the qualities listed in the Beatitudes are not already present, in your life as well as your future mate's, postpone marriage until you have more evidence! Do not be deceived. It will be a difficult marriage if these qualities are not there. A healthy marriage is one where both parties seek to meet the needs of the other.

> *Do nothing from selfishness or empty conceit, but with humility of mind let each of you regard one another as more important than himself; do not merely look out for your own personal interests, but also for the interests of others* (Phil. 2:3-4).

Most people who are considering marriage are eager to get on with it. Therefore, they read through these traits and do not hear God. It is so easy to spiritualize these traits as being something only Christ could accomplish. Obviously in the perfect sense, this is correct. After years of living through the gut-wrenching pain of literally hundreds of couples, Sally and I exhort you, with all our strength, to be honest with yourself and your mate. Ask several couples whom you know to help you evaluate if and when you are ready for marriage.

No one is perfect. If you demand perfection, certainly no one would qualify, except Christ Himself. However, you should have the discernment to evaluate yourself and your future mate before God. Ask yourself if he/she is striving for perfection in these areas and if they have a teachable spirit concerning them. I always ask couples, "What really concerns you about your future mate?" It scares me if they say, "Nothing." That is either naiveté, dishonesty, or mental illusion! Be honest, but be wise!

Project Concerning The Beatitudes
Couples need to get away by themselves and go through the Beatitudes listed in Matthew 5:1-12—first alone and then with each other. Consider these character traits in relationship to behavior around parents, others in authority in your lives, fellow workers on projects or jobs, roommates, and relationships at church.

After going over the lists privately, get together and share them. The openness and thoroughness of each is probably the greatest evidence of maturity. After gaining the Lord's direction, ask a wise counselor, who is older and more spiritually experienced, to double-check the conclusions with you. If this step checks out, you can begin to consider other issues in determining God's will for marriage. Again, this is covered in depth in the *Becoming One* twelve week study in Chapter 7.

AGREEMENT ON FOUNDATIONAL FAITH CONCEPTS

After honestly evaluating your individual maturity, couples considering marriage should understand and commit themselves to the basic biblical concepts of marriage, presented in Part II of this book. A couple who desires marital unity must possess the common bond of oneness that God provides in His Son, Jesus Christ. In Genesis 1, as we have seen, God introduces His purpose for man and for marriage. That plan requires two people who become one unit to *reflect* God's image, *reproduce* a godly heritage, and *reign* spiritually in life together. Both partners must first feel a burden and commitment to God's plan for their marriage.

Each partner must understand that God specifically places people together in order for this plan to be carried out. Therefore, each should be able to *receive* the other from God as their personal provision for blessing. Each should trust God for the success of the relationship, not the performance of the mate.

Every couple who hopes to please God in their marriage must fellowship daily with the Holy Spirit. The *Holy Spirit* is our source of power, truth, conviction, leading, and spiritual communication.

There is no oneness in marriage without moment by moment confessing, and continued faith in the presence and power of God's Holy Spirit.

A successful marriage foundation requires two people who understand that there are only two avenues of effecting change in their mate: *love and blessing*. Both must confess the futility of human manipulation. Additionally, the husband and wife must understand Satan's deceit in their responsibilities to *love and submit* to one another, and be on guard against his stratagems.

> TWO PEOPLE BECOME ONE BY *REFLECTING* GOD'S IMAGE, *REPRODUCING* A GODLY HERITAGE, AND *REIGNING* SPIRITUALLY IN LIFE TOGETHER.

It is easy to read over these issues quickly. But these concepts, if understood and enacted, will bring the security and joy to your marriage that is provided only by God Himself. Marital oneness is dependent on continually overriding our natural instincts by acting on God's Word. This faith action produces a supernatural faith relationship.

AGREEMENT IN PRACTICAL AREAS

The last issue to evaluate before deciding to get married relates to your practical preparation. Have you thoroughly prepared yourself to take on the historical problem areas of marriage, such as the issues just discussed in Part III of this book? Finances, sexual relationships, in-laws, personality differences, vocational goals, children, and spiritual issues will be less of a problem if both partners agreed on a plan of action. Agreement on these issues is important in confirming that the relationship is in God's will. In my opinion, every couple should research and develop *mutual agreements* on each of these issues. This process should also help you anticipate and prepare for potential problem areas in your upcoming marriage. Write out your plans and discuss them together. It would help to evaluate these plans with a pre-marriage counselor.

There are other issues such as God's timing to get married, but the issues mentioned above, cover the basics. God bless you in your decisions!

---

1. Credit for this illustration goes to Dr. Tony Evans of Dallas, TX.